Once, Only the
Swallows Were Free

Once, Only the Swallows Were Free

A memoir

Gabrielle Gouch

HYBRID
PUBLISHERS

Published by Hybrid Publishers

Melbourne Victoria Australia

©Gabrielle Gouch 2013

PO Box 52, Ormond 3204.
www.hybridpublishers.optusnet.com.au

First published 2013

National Library of Australia Cataloguing-in-Publication entry
Gouch, Gabrielle, author.
Once, only the swallows were free : a memoir / Gabrielle Gouch.

ISBN: 9781921665998 (paperback)

Subjects: Jews–Romania–Migrations.
Jews–Romania–Social life and customs.
Jews–Persecutions–Romania.
Jewish refugees–Romania.
Jewish families–Romania.
Jewish families–Israel.
Romania–Ethnic relations.
Israel–Emigration and immigration
Israel–Social conditions–20th century.
Israel–Social life and customs.

Dewey Number: 362.87089924

Cover design: Art on Order
Printed in Australia by McPherson's Printing Group

Author's note: The names of some minor characters have been changed
to protect their privacy.

To Alex

Contents

Part I

From the howling of the wolves to the cries of the jackals

I

'It is fascinating how unpredictable life can be,' my father mused on one of our long walks. I loved those Sunday strolls in the cool of late summer afternoons, or in the winter when the snow scrunched under our shoes and snowflakes danced in the breeze and vanished. He had a warm, reassuring voice, and though I was a young adult by then, his way of thinking and the way he looked at the world and his life – detached, as a spectator – still intrigued and charmed me.

I thought of my father's words as my taxi travelled eastwards on the way to Transylvania. It was December 1990. It had not snowed that year; the fields were dark and bleak, but I still hoped for snow and a white Christmas. Having talked non-stop for an hour, the driver had fallen silent.

A few short hours away was the border of Romania and its province of Transylvania. Not the land of Dracula and vampires, but of mountains and rivers and exquisite birdsong. The land where stories and legends are born. The land of my birth.

Yes, life is unpredictable, and what could have been more unpredictable than the event which had sent me on that journey: the collapse of communism. The eternal and invincible communism. Who would have believed it? Part of me still could not.

'The ripples of History again,' my long-dead father whispered in my ear as the featureless scenery slid past the window.

Twenty-five years had passed since we left that part of the world, since our family emigrated – well, most of us did. Twenty-five years since the red and grey roofs of Romania had vanished into milky mist. Moments after, we emerged into blue sky and sunshine. Ahead of us, freedom. And there, above the clouds, I promised myself and the universe: I would never, ever, return.

By the time the plane started its descent to Vienna, I could think only of the future. The heavenly West was only minutes away. The past was irrelevant. And it remained irrelevant for years. Now and then a memory would surface like a bubble in water, but it soon vanished. There was an Iron Curtain between me and my past life.

The years passed. Sometimes at night, when the wind ruffled the leaves of the elm tree in front of our house, I remembered the leaves of the oak trees whispering in the wind in my native land and images of that other life, our life in Romania, would come flooding in. Good times and dreadful times. Etched in my memory, imprinted on my senses. The hills, the grazing sheep, the smell of the pine forest, the trill of the birds were alive again. Suddenly I missed my native land. No, not just the land – I missed much more.

And as I watched the dark fields beyond the window of my taxi, this afternoon in 1990, those memories were with me again and I was transported to the other side of the border, to Romania, and a little flat in a two-storey block in the Southern Carpathian mountains.

It is 1962. My mother Roza is standing at the window, watching the street corner. From that window she will one day spot the postman and his bag where, carefully stacked among the many letters, will be the one we have been waiting for.

Outside the fresh snow sparkles in the sun. White and shiny against the pale blue sky, the peak of Mount Paringu looks over the hills guarding the Jiu Valley. Driven by a northerly breeze, a few clouds are heading our way. A winter silence has settled on the town.

In front of our window, on the strip of land between us and the main street which hardly ever feels the wheels of a car, my eight-year-

4

old brother Yossi and his friends are playing in the snow.

I am sitting reading a book. The brown tiled stove in the corner of our bedroom has long lost the warmth of yesterday, but Roza has no time to light the fire. She is keeping watch. And as she rearranges the little rounded combs holding her wavy black hair, sunrays escape around her big frame and fall onto the page of my book.

'Maybe he's been, maybe I missed him,' she says, opening the window.

I reach for a blanket.

It is cleaning time. Roza grabs Yossi's doona, bends over the windowsill and starts flapping it out. Yossi's warmth from last night's sleep escapes into the sky. One by one, sheets and doonas wave outside the window, pushing the cold air in. On the table, the pages of Yossi's book fluff up like the feathers of an angry turkey. It is freezing, but Roza does not feel the cold. She is on the move.

I am trying to read. It is not easy, because Roza is coming and going, like a hungry sparrow looking for food. And my book, *The Magic Mountain* by Thomas Mann, is a reflective sort of book; you need silence to enjoy the main character's ruminations.

Outside, the sun has retreated behind a small grey cloud. In front of the window snowflakes swirl in the breeze. From the distance comes Yossi's happy laughter. It leaves a smile on Roza's face.

'The postman must be late,' she interrupts again as she piles bedding on the windowsill to air.

What if all those doonas and pillows would roll out onto the street? Nothing ever did, but you never know. Mr Bogdan is on his usual walk at this time of the morning. The image of Mr Bogdan – well known for his slow uptake – hit by a flying doona, trying to disentangle himself, and a panic-stricken Roza running out to save the doona, save the doona, not to calm Mr Bogdan, makes me chuckle. But this is only wishful thinking, because everything is sitting under the wide awning in perfect equilibrium while Roza dusts the room. She moves slowly, her thoughts miles away. She slides a cloth over the radio, then over Yossi's desk and books. She shifts the cloth to the

Louis XV chest of drawers and the painting hanging above it: a train approaching the viewer, its headlights piercing the dark. Behind the locomotive, the barely distinguishable contours of carriages, like an unending caterpillar, seem to go on forever into the night. Trains, nights, travels, destinations, freedom. And as if Roza can hear my thoughts, 'No, not yet,' she says.

She makes the beds, shuts the window and disappears into the kitchen.

Three more days of holiday, five more months to the baccalaureate. Unless – unless the postman delivers. Unless the passport arrives. Unless we emigrate to Israel. We could get that letter today. But will we? We have been waiting for five years. But today I feel especially hopeful, so I too go to the window to check for the postman. On the main street Mrs Luca, our upstairs neighbour, is walking towards the town centre. Behind her trails an old woman with a bag. No sign of the postman.

From the kitchen, accompanied by clashing pots and pans, comes a tune from *The Merry Widow*. Roza often sings in the background, songs from Kalman and Lehar operettas, the odd Schubert song in German, but at times she sings heart-wrenching Romanian songs of loss and heartbreak, of unfulfilled love, songs which would make most people cry. She sings from the soul, she sings as if she is singing about her own life. Sometimes I join in: 'Why did I leave you behind, why did I leave my home?' But usually she sings light-hearted, frivolous songs, like today. She is experimenting, trying to outdo herself. The high notes climb higher and higher. Suddenly the merry waltz stops. Roza is back, heading to the window. 'He just turned the corner.'

The postman, a tall man in a heavy grey coat, appears from behind the next block, across his chest a shoulder bag bursting with letters. Roza leans out of the window. I stand behind her, all eyes and ears. If our will could make things happen, we would get the letter today.

'*Buna ziua!* (Good day!)' Roza greets him, big smile on her face. The postman looks up, nods and walks past. 'Anything for Leitner?'

'Nothing,' he says, and disappears around the corner. But Roza is not convinced. Maybe he did not check the names properly. She is sure he did not – didn't he do that the other day? He gave her someone else's letter. Her hopes rekindled, she goes to meet him in the stairway, but the encounter does not prove any more fruitful than those of the last five years. There is no letter, there are no passports – not yet.

And so the wait for the postman was over for that day. It was January and no passports had been distributed since the previous August. But the day before, years after they applied, the Segals got their much-awaited letter: 'Your passports are ready to be collected …'

There were no private phones in town, but within hours the whole community knew because Mrs Cohen told Mrs Muller who told Mrs Izsak who happened to meet my mother on the street and gave her the news, who told Mrs Steinberg who met Mrs Klein on the way to her husband's office, who told her husband who told Mr Bieber, and so it went.

The speculation started. 'Who is the next lucky one?' My father, Stefan, would not speculate. He had more important preoccupations: his work, his children and what went on in the world. 'Political events control people's lives,' he used to say to us. So that evening, as he did every evening, he sat on the edge of my bed and turned the radio on.

'Good evening, dear listeners,' the Voice of America greeted him in Romanian, and a smile flashed across his face. But barely a few minutes had passed when the Romanian jamming cut in, and the battle between Stefan's resolve to find out what was going on in the world and a government which was just as determined not to let him, started. This was not a fight he could win, so after a while he stopped adjusting and readjusting the dial, moved closer to the radio, glued his ear to the speaker and tried to catch what words he could, what the latest utterances of prime ministers and presidents tens of thousands of miles away might mean for us, behind the Iron Curtain. Khrushchev, Gheorghiu Dej (the Romanian President), names and more names and snatches of speeches escaped through the noise, which dipped and climbed like a wave. Stefan's face strained with concentration. Good news?

'Nothing relevant to us,' he summarised later at the dinner table, and the conversation turned to passports.

'We're next,' Roza said, as if she had finally worked out how the authorities decided who went and who stayed, who got out and who was condemned to wait. We should be, but will we? There was no way of knowing. What was the logic behind it? I could see none.

'We must be,' she added. But I could hear the Izsaks, the Mullers, the Steinbergs saying exactly the same thing. I could see them sitting at their dinner tables, nodding in unison. Why wouldn't it be them, why would it be us? But deep inside I pleaded with the postman to ring our doorbell in the morning.

Stefan was silent or maybe he was just tired of listening to our guesses and speculations, tired of this game we had been playing for years.

'You are fifty-nine years old,' Roza said. Roza never addressed her husband as 'you'. She used the Hungarian *maga* (*vous* in French), which implies a lack of familiarity with the other person, a slightly inferior status to him. The reason for this went back a long way.

My father's hair might have been greying, but he was as energetic as ever. Roza hoped that he was old enough to be too old for the country. Useful engineers were not allowed to leave. Romania needed them. Socialism was built on heavy industry, and heavy industry needed engineers. It needed Stefan and it needed his friend Steinberg. But Steinberg was in an even worse predicament: he was only forty-eight years old.

Once a week in the evening, chess set beneath his arm, Steinberg dropped in for a game and a chat. Only a short chat; he was a man of few words. Passports or no passports? he speculated. But this was no mere guessing, it was a sharp chess player's analysis in the light of Khrushchev's latest pronouncements and the developments in Soviet-American relations. At times he dared a prediction, which his deep confident voice made seem a certainty. But we knew it wasn't –

when it came to passports nothing was predictable.

Passports always arrived in clusters … well, nearly always. Two or three passports over a couple of days.

'There was one yesterday, so there must be at least one more on the way,' Roza said and gathered the plates.

And I wondered: whose doorbell will the postman ring tomorrow?

While we fretted about the passports, the rest of the town must have been thinking: *The Jews are lucky, they are getting out.* Because only Jews were allowed to emigrate. 'So they can reunite with their families in Israel,' the Romanian government declared. Why such magnanimity by a government which had never shown generosity or compassion? No one knew.

They are escaping to the West, must have thought those who could not escape, to where there is plenty of food, where there are no queues, no ID cards, no Securitate (the secret service), where no one has to watch what they say. Where winters are warm. 'In the West there are medicines which can cure rheumatism, which can cure cerebral palsy,' someone said to me once. In the West the borders were open, people travelled, had holidays on the Riviera. The West was heaven. A real Romanian heaven.

My father did not believe in heaven. He kept warning us: 'It will be difficult, the hot climate, a new language.'

'I won't miss the hard winters,' my mother replied, 'nor these wretched stoves and the filthy coal.' The language did not worry us. It might take a few months, a year, even two, but then it would be as easy as our mother tongue.

'Within twenty years there will be an Arab-Israeli war,' my father warned. It had no effect. Wouldn't twenty years of life in the West be infinitely better than fifty in Romania?

But it did not look as though we would see the West soon. The Segals' passports proved to be the last that week. My Romanian baccalaureate seemed inevitable. But there was a small compensation …

'If we're still here,' my mother said one evening, 'you will get a present. A nice new dress made by Mrs Radulescu.'

Mrs Radulescu? The best and most expensive seamstress in town? Now that was a treat.

So one day in the dreamiest of moods I sat in Mrs Radulescu's lounge room leafing through fashion magazines, through pages and pages of slim women with floral dresses gathered at wasp waists. I too wanted to look slim and breathtakingly beautiful. There was such a woman in town and I wanted to look like her.

Afternoon sun streamed through the window, filling the room with cosy contentment. I was halfway through the third magazine when who should walk in? The very owner of the latest exit visa to Israel, Mrs Segal. She must have been approaching her late forties, but her green eyes sparkled, her skin was unblemished. She had come to try on new dresses, her outfits for Israel. Mrs Radulescu took Mrs Segal's new dress off the coathanger and, holding it with the care one would handle a rare piece of art, asked: 'Well?'

'It's beauuuutiful.'

It was made of navy georgette from an old dress which had once belonged to her mother. No such treasure was to be found in the only material shop in town. Mrs Radulescu unbuttoned the top of the dress, slipped it gingerly over Mrs Segal's head, smoothed it over and buttoned it up. Below the waist the waves of georgette flowed lightly and freely, like a field of bluebells wafting in the breeze.

'Another three weeks and I will see my sister again,' Mrs Segal said as she examined herself in the mirror, her hazel eyes shining with joy. Her head leant to one side then to the other, while the great seamstress, pins in her mouth, walked around her, pulled the waist in, re-arranged the shoulders, squatted beside her model and pinned the hem.

'It's perfect!' she said finally and pulled herself up.

The next dress was a yellow cotton with black polka dots.

Distracted by Mrs Segal's dresses, I was no closer to a decision but I was enjoying the atmosphere, the materials, the patterns, the colours and the dreams of wearing every one of those dresses in Mrs

Radulescu's magazines. But my eyes kept returning to Mrs Segal. She seemed to have fallen in love with each of her four dresses.

The sun had moved to the far end of the lounge. Mrs Segal was ready to go.

'That's half,' she said, handing over some money to Mrs Radulescu. 'The rest, as we discussed, I'll pay when I pick them up. By then we'll have finished selling our belongings. Anyway, most of them have gone already.' And she put her coat on and headed for the door.

Now I had Mrs Radulescu all to myself. Having weighed my choices, she decided that the A-line might look better on me, but said, 'Let's see the material first.' For that I needed my mother. Besides, it was getting late.

Outside, the smell of coke was blowing from the mines. On the main street, three barely lit shops. The bus, a rare occurrence in our town, was nowhere to be seen. The road was quiet. A few people were going about their business. A horse pulling a sleigh went past. It headed for the hills, the hills where our milk woman, Maria, lived and wolves howled at night.

Opposite, Mrs Muller had just turned the corner into the narrow street that led to her home. The Mullers would surely get their passports ahead of us, but what would Mr Muller do in Israel? He was a cobbler. He made saddles and mountain shoes for the peasants from all around the Jiu Valley. The shoes in the shop had soles like concrete; you wore your foot out before you broke the shoes in. So Mr Muller had no competition. But neither did he make much money. The Romanian peasant was poor, he barely had enough to eat.

The sun had retreated behind the hills. My breath was condensing. Mrs Radulescu's place had been warm and cosy. Our home was never as warm as hers – my parents were not skilled in the art of living. Mrs Radulescu was a real life-artist, she ran a sizable business. Unofficially, of course.

Not everybody was a life-artist; most people had barely enough to make ends meet. But somehow everybody seemed to manage.

11

The snow nearly melted, then it froze hard again. Bits of coal blown from the mines turned the ice grey. It matched the sky, overcast with thick clouds.

It was market day and my mother was out shopping. I was home preparing for exams. The Romanian Insurrection against the German troops in Romania was not able to focus my concentration, so I was relieved to hear the knock on the door.

It was Benny. Benny and I had been friends for years. We lived at opposite ends of the town, but we were in the same class at school. He wore glasses and smiled often. He smiled when a situation was funny, he smiled when it was hopeless. He smiled from embarrassment and he smiled when he was pleased, but even when he did not smile, the corners of his lips pointed upward a little more than most people's. One thing is sure, Benny will not die with a disappointed look on his face.

Benny's family, the Izsaks, lived in a tiny flat at the end of a dingy dark alley. Occasionally they invited me to Friday night dinner. The table was beautifully set, the *Shabbat* candles lit. Mrs Izsak, dark eyes shining with contentment and goodwill, greeted me as a much loved member of the family. She asked about my mother, she asked about me. Soon we gathered around the table. Mrs Izsak covered her hair with a lacy headscarf, her eyes with her hands, and started saying the Friday night prayer: '*Baruch ata* ...' and she thanked God for everything. The live-in helper brought in the chicken soup and the boiled meat and vegetables. Mr Izsak filled the glasses with red wine and said a blessing. By the time the dinner was over, Mr Izsak's face was even rounder, the pink in his cheeks nearly as red as the wine. The steaming chicken soup, the glass of wine, Mrs Izsak's beautiful smile, her softly spoken words, the *Shabbat* candles, all filled the small room with contentment and serenity.

It was night by the time I left the Izsaks. I felt blissful and tranquil, as if some of this family's contentment had been transferred to me. Did such peace spring from being religious, or from a good family life? Was it due to Mrs Izsak's calm personality, which was so unlike my mother's, or from never having to worry about money? I loved being there.

Yes, the Izsaks had a good life and perhaps Mrs Izsak should have been thankful to Mr Izsak for being so resourceful, for being such an accomplished life-artist. A quiet man, Mr Izsak was a signwriter and made picture frames for the officials. But he also framed pictures for his neighbours, the people who lived in the next street or further afield. Unofficially, of course.

Benny often came to visit. That day he had news. 'Mr Segal was summoned by the Militia. Their passports have been cancelled. Nobody knows why.' And Benny smiled, the smile he hid behind every time a situation looked hopeless. Mrs Segal and her dresses were stuck in town in an empty flat for an indefinite time. Suddenly not only the authorities, but the whole world, even the air we breathed, seemed deceitful.

Our own departure moved into the distant future yet again. Benny was more optimistic, but he too thought that we would be stuck in the country for quite a while, we would have to do the baccalaureate in Romania and he was off to study. And I? I would have to focus on the Romanian Insurrection. It was painfully boring and my mind kept closing to it like a tickled clam. Then there was the history of the class struggle in Romania, its poetical representation in literature, the theory of surplus value in Political Economy. I could not escape them.

Back from the market, my mother looked dispirited. She had heard the news. 'At least we have our furniture, and Stefan has a job,' she said as she unpacked her bag.

The games the authorities were playing with us had plumbed new depths and these, coupled with that boring Romanian Insurrection, felt like soul poisoning.

—◦◦◦—

The snow was gone from the streets and the hills, but Mount Paringu still shone white in the early spring sun. It was Sunday. Women holding their husbands' arms, children holding their fathers' hands, mothers pushing prams, girls arm in arm on the lookout for friends, filled the main street of Petrosani. All out for a stroll, out to smell the spring and feel the sunshine. And so were we, my father and I.

'Hello!' the Kleins greeted us. The conversation soon changed into German, the Kleins' mother tongue. They were both from Bucovina. *'Khrushchev und Gheorghiu Dej,'* then, *'Kennedy und Khruschev'*. I didn't understand a word, but I knew what it was about: the latest political events and how they would influence our chances of getting out of Romania.

'Who knows if we'll ever get out?' Mr Klein said in Romanian as we parted.

'We will, we will,' my father replied.

We kept walking, me on the lookout for friends, he deep in thought. He stopped to light a cigarette. 'I think the Kleins are expecting too much,' he said as we started walking again, 'I think all these people waiting for passports are expecting too much. Your mother is expecting too much.' He paused. 'Our life in Israel could end up a great disappointment, and then – then what would we dream about? People need dreams.'

My friend Addy walked past with a young woman.

The weeks rolled by. A thick fog of gloom settled on the Jewish community, the two dozen or so religious and secular families sprinkled around the town. Even Roza changed. The songs coming from the kitchen were rarely light and frivolous. She had not seen her sister Ella since 1946. 'I can still see her standing on the platform,' Roza said to me. 'She looked so beautiful. She was forty-two years old when she left, she is fifty-eight years old now. My God, she must be grey.'

Everybody's life was on hold. Some people wanted to have children. Should they or shouldn't they? Emigrating with a new baby could be difficult. Maybe it was better to wait, they said, maybe they would start to distribute passports again. The Cohens were getting

14

old. They had no children. Mr Cohen was not a well man. His days might end before the passport arrived, his wife might have to emigrate alone. And if bad luck struck, he would be buried in Romania with no one left to tend his grave. But the Cohens were religious, and emigrating to the Promised Land was a prophecy which they had to help come true.

Our lives were permanently temporary, and for our family, the bits of transitory life, the wait until the next month or the one after, added up to nearly six years.

But my mother kept waiting for the postman. 'Among those letters must be the one,' she hoped, day after day. She would soon be reunited with her sisters and brother, what remained of her family after the war. It was not as clear what my father hoped for, but he decided that he would abide by the will of the family to give a better future to his children, the two of us at least.

The third child, Tom, the son from his previous marriage to the glamorous Hella, was not living at home any longer. Six years had passed since I had last seen him.

We rarely talked about my half-brother, a young man with a limp and a feeble right hand, but his presence followed us like a shadow.

2

Another year passed. On Mount Paringu the snow melted again. Small streams gushed downhill, down as far as Petrosani, as far as the secret little street only minutes away from us where children played hide and seek and lovers kissed. On the banks of the brook the bushes were in flower, the bees at work. A warm sunshine lit the trees. Nature was rich with promise, but our lives were still filled with dreams of another country, against evidence and reason.

There had been no passports for months. The Segals were still in town. Mr Segal was working again. Their flat filled with the beginnings of another life: a newly acquired bed, a wardrobe, a table and chairs. 'It's only for the time being,' Mrs Segal said when we dropped in. Her georgette dress was still packed in the big chest, waiting to emigrate. The chest, covered with a colourful rug, sat in the corner of the lounge room. 'It fills the space, it cheers me up,' she said. Her optimism seemed like hard work.

I had passed my baccalaureate and was well into my first year university on that spring day in May 1963, sitting in Lecture Theatre One in the Mining Institute. Bright sunrays warmed the pages of my notebook resting on the wooden bench.

Mihai, the maths tutor, was showing us the proof of a theorem. A mess of x's and y's covered the blackboard. The students took notes, and as they bent over their notebooks the golden buttons of their black uniforms shone in the midmorning sun. Mihai turned to explain his reasoning, the sequence of if(s), then(s) and thus(s). His open jacket waved as he paced along the blackboard. His glasses glinted in the sunlight. He was a big man, about thirty.

I liked Mihai. He was good-looking, in a clumsy sort of way. Clumsiness goes with good looks, I decided, and sat there thinking of his grey eyes, and how he sought out my company at times – how he had singled me out the day before, talking to me as if the others did not exist. By the time my mind returned to the lecture theatre, Mihai had finished the proof. The student next to me put his hand up. Why and how something. A few more questions followed, then Mihai cleaned the blackboard and started on the next topic: differential equations. This was only a revision. He threw an equation on the blackboard. 'Any volunteers?' he asked and waited. Drawn-out silence. He looked at me.

'*Domnisoara* (Miss) Leitner,' he called, and I felt as if I had suddenly turned into a pretty young woman, a weightless being I never knew existed. Because no one ever called me *Domnisoara* in public. They called me Comrade Leitner. 'Would you like to try?'

I walked to the blackboard, my mind sharpened by Mihai's expectations. I was going to solve that equation; I was as determined as a gladiator to win a fight. I grabbed the chalk. I multiplied, I divided, I integrated. My mind raced ahead, my hand coding my thoughts, the elongated S for the integral, the pluses and minuses. I stopped for a moment, looked at where I was heading and kept going. It seemed too easy. I checked my working again. Everything was correct. Equals, I wrote, and underlined the answer. I turned to Mihai.

'Thank you,' he said. I floated back to my seat.

At the end of the tutorial he walked past my bench. 'Don't forget we're leaving at six.' He smiled.

The trip had been arranged the week before. Mihai and six of my colleagues were going up into the mountains that evening. The next morning four of us would go trekking, Mihai and the other three would return to town.

At six o'clock sharp the truck was waiting. Installed comfortably in the cabin, Mihai was talking to the driver. At the back, on wooden benches along the sides of the truck, my friends chatted, their faces lit with the expectation of a big adventure.

The sun was nearing the hills, lining up for its exit. The air was misty and tinged with pink. On the outskirts of town a man was fixing his fence. A boy waved. A cow stopped grazing and looked at us. A dog barked to prove who was in charge. Soon the houses were left behind and the road began to snake. We started climbing.

The black muslin of evening shrouded the mountains by the time we reached the chalet at the entrance to the forest. The door opened with a screech, and below the faint flickering light stood a slight man with a big moustache and a smiling lower lip. He had guests. Finally.

It was going to be a great evening and we were determined to enjoy every minute of it. We gathered in the dining room and drank and chatted, and when the wine was finished Mihai ordered more and there was more chatting and more laughter. Suddenly Mihai raised his voice and asked for silence. The chatting stopped. 'To add to the joy of this select gathering, I will sing a song. I dedicate this song to the young woman on my left.'

All eyes turned to me. My face burnt with embarrassment. But when I heard the first few notes of the familiar song, I forgot about the people around me. I was spellbound.

Mihai had a strong tenor voice, and the words of *Santa Lucia* reverberated in the wooden chalet. Line after line, note after note of the enchanting song escaped into the pine forest and rode away in the breeze. Startled sleepy birds swished into the shadows; squirrels pricked up their ears and ran away. The whole forest knew that Mihai was singing for me, that I was the queen of the evening.

'*Saantaa Luucia, Santa Lucia*', the song came to an end. Everybody was clapping. All eyes on me. Now my face glowed with happiness and joy. Lily was telling me something. I could not concentrate. She kept looking at me, her dark green eyes fixed on me more than I was comfortable with. Why didn't Mihai sing for her? For her well-shaped mouth, her beautiful black hair, her arched eyebrows, her olive skin? She looked like a goddess, she had been put on this earth to be noticed. And yet Mihai sang for me.

The evening was shading into night. The conversation had lost its earlier spark. 'Let's go for a walk,' Mihai whispered.

We left the gathering and walked into the forest. The full moon shone silver on Mihai's face. The pine trees merged into one dark mass, their tops jagged against the moonlit sky. We walked side by side, our arms nearly touching. From the corner of my eye I glanced at Mihai, the strong chin, the full lips, the wavy bushy hair, the well-shaped nose. He was taller than me, broad body, ungainly. Attractive.

I wondered what he was going to say, now that we were alone, but he did not say anything as we kept walking, and the moon shone cold and the forest was all around us. An odd stone rolled down the track. Something rustled among the trees, then silence. It was close to midnight.

'Beautiful night,' he said finally, 'but not a star above.'

'They're over there, look,' I whispered and pointed to the edge of the forest. I whispered because I did not want to disturb that moment. I wanted to stop the passage of time, the ticking of clocks. I wanted to preserve everything exactly as it was: Mihai next to me, the cool air, the resinous aroma of pine, the moon looking over us. And I waited for the sound of his voice.

He turned towards me. 'I know you have applied for a passport.'

Passport? My heart sank. Even here in the middle of the forest? In the middle of the night? For the first time in years I wanted to forget about emigrating, I wanted to forget the passport, I wanted to forget the free world. I wanted to be with Mihai for as long as I could.

He stopped suddenly. His face in full moonlight, his eyes fixed on me. 'They want to expel you.'

I kept walking. The path narrowed and turned sharply.

'I'm trying to sway them not to.'

The spring had gone out of my step. There was a swish among the trees. A night bird took off. Uneasiness crept up on me like a snake.

'You know,' he said after a long silence, 'one day the two of us will be walking just like we do now, somewhere even more beautiful, on the beaches of the French Riviera.'

My blood ran cold. A few weeks ago I had seen him on the street, walking with a man from the Securitate. He had greeted me with a smile, his head tilted slightly as always. The man might be his neighbour, might be someone he used to know, a casual acquaintance; I thought no more of it. But then I saw him again, with another Securitate officer. How was it that I hadn't put two and two together? Never drew the obvious conclusion? That he was a mole, a Securitate mole.

'You're in cahoots with the Securitate, I don't trust you,' I blurted. Then my mind guard, the censor that checked and filtered everything before it left my mouth, stepped in. *What? What got into you? How could you say such thing?* I broke into a sweat.

I needed to run. Away from Mihai and the Securitate, away from the treacherous world of the poisonous Santa Lucia. But where?

Mihai turned towards me. His moonlit face looked threatening. The tune of Santa Lucia resonated in my ears. It filled me with dread. I turned around and started towards the chalet as fast as I could, Mihai's steps behind me. Stones rolled down the path.

Back in the big dormitory, my friends were turning in. 'Good night,' Lily said with an all-knowing look. I pulled the blanket over my head. What had I done? I could see Mihai telling his Securitate friends about our conversation. An informer, a rotten informer ... But what if he isn't? What if what he said is true? But why the Riviera, why mention a world we are not allowed to pine for? Not allowed to say anything good about?

Everybody around me was asleep.

My thoughts kept going around and around. If he is not an informer, why did he say that I would be expelled if not for him propping me up? For favours? Was he drunk? He did not drink a great deal. He must be an informer.

I wanted to sleep, but I was cold and afraid and alone.

Next morning, Mihai and three other students left early. I did not see them. We, Lily, Addy, Eugen and I, said goodbye to our host and took the path up the mountains. The birds twittered, sunrays played shadows on the ground, the air was sharp with pine. The track started to climb steeply. My backpack weighed tons, my legs shook, my heart pounded. Even Lily started to show signs of tiredness. Eugen was the fittest among us. He could have climbed for hours.

Suddenly the forest came to an end. Abruptly, like a symphony. We emerged above the tree line in full sunshine. Green all around, as far as we could see – no, not quite: there was a white patch at the foot of the next mountain. On approach, the white patch broke up into grazing sheep.

Ion, the shepherd, a young man in his late teens, was happy to have company. He had been there for weeks. He pointed out the track leading to the next lake and from there to the highest mountain and the best scenery. Then he unwrapped a hunk of cheese and cut a thick slice for each of us. In exchange we offered him fresh bread and bacon. 'The weather will hold, there's no rain in the air,' he said as we parted. His speech was as slow as the grazing of his sheep.

We followed the track. I tried to join in the chatting and the laughter of my friends, but I had other preoccupations. I told myself that whatever was going to happen, would happen anyway. It did not make me feel any better.

The sun set. In front of our tent, strips of bacon sizzled in the fire. Above, a kaleidoscope of bright stars, some bluish white, some yellow, and all around, the mountains hiding in the dark, spying on us, on our stories and laughter.

Next morning we woke inside a thick cloud. 'Dreamlike,' Addy said, no longer the restless, nervy young man but a contented being. As I walked to the lake my thoughts kept replaying the conversation with Mihai. Maybe he was drunk. Maybe he had forgotten every-thing I said.

The water was freezing. My hands were numb, my face prickling from the cold air. I patted myself dry. To hell with Mihai, to hell with him and with the likes of him.

On the way back, the track followed the edge of the forest. Around us the last puffs of fog vanished into the blue sky. I could not believe

21

that one day I would leave all this behind. It was unimaginable that I would never see these mountains again. But I was determined not to let those thoughts or any others spoil my day. I did not want to think about the passport. We had wasted nearly seven years of our lives. It hung above our family like a curse. I am here now, I told myself, and as long as they leave me alone, I am happy.

———

The door shut behind me. I had just returned from my morning lectures. 'Benny was expelled yesterday,' I said to my mother as she put the latch on the door.

She abandoned the latch, turned towards me and fixed me with her green wide-open eyes. 'Expelled?'

'The State won't train him because he wants to emigrate.' I repeated the reason given by the officials. 'I'm next.'

'You are not. It's different with you.'

'Different, why?'

'You're too good. They won't expel you.'

I would have screamed if she had not been my mother and if the neighbours wouldn't have come running. Scream and howl: 'Can you ever acknowledge reality? Acknowledge the facts for once? And the facts are that in a week, or two or three, I don't know when but as sure as night follows day, they will expel me and I will have nothing to do but sit at home and argue with you. For months or years, or maybe for the rest of our lives, because there is no guarantee that we will ever get out!'

But I did not scream. There was no point. My mother could not face reality, could not look it in the eye. That's how she was, that's how she had always been, always.

Days went by. I could not concentrate in lectures. What was the point of studying? Of preparing for exams I would never have to take? Of working for a future which did not exist? I had strange dreams. Mice everywhere. As I started eating a yogurt a head poked out; they swam in my soup, they jumped out as I unpacked my books.

In the morning I woke up exhausted, feeling that something was wrong. *Today is the day*, was my first conscious thought. I reminded myself again that I didn't have the slightest interest in engineering, that engineering frightened me. I liked maths, but mention machines, forces, actions and reactions and I became paralysed with fear. I was at that university because we had applied to emigrate and no other university would accept me. I reminded myself that I was studying Mineral Processing to fill a gap in my temporary life, to give me something to do until we got the passports.

I was not the only one training for a profession that was of no interest to me. There were others, I don't know how many, who were at the Institute because of their 'unhealthy social origins' or whatever other incurable sickness the party had diagnosed them with. Whether they were born for it, or whether like me they had a blind spot for everything mechanical, whether they wanted to be doctors like my friend Eugen or architects like Benny, they would engineer mines for the rest of their lives. Even my much-loved Professor Dumitrescu, a midget with a hunchback and a doctorate from the Sorbonne, was there because he was not allowed to teach anywhere else. But that was exactly it. Expulsion meant I would no longer be with all those people, I would no longer learn anything. Expulsion meant living in an even more hopeless limbo than I already inhabited. Possibly forever. I tried to cheer myself – the following semester we would be studying mainly engineering subjects. If they expelled me, I would escape them all.

But it did not matter what I told myself, it did not matter what the arguments were and how many times I repeated them. It did not make it any easier. In one way I wished to get it over and done with. But then, what would happen then, when I no longer had to get up in the morning to go to lectures? What would I do then?

The mornings passed slowly. The days were too long. Each evening I breathed with relief. I did my sums. Four weeks had passed since Benny had been expelled. Maybe my turn had not come. Why would they remember me now? And why not? My anxiety was losing its edge, receding with every day. But there were word associations. Permanence implied temporariness, implied my situation, my situation there at university. The lecturer talked about what we would learn in two months. Not we, I will not be here then.

It looked more and more as if Mihai had not said anything to the Securitate, or I would have been in a worse predicament. Why he had said what he had that night in the forest, I didn't know and no longer wanted to know. He was definitely in cahoots with the Securitate; I had seen him again with their officers. It occurred to me that maybe he did protect me. If so, could he sustain it? We still had maths tutorials, but we had stopped flirting.

Two more months passed. Then one day I met Emil.

Emil had honey-coloured hair and hazel eyes. He loved walking me home after lectures. At times we walked in the hills behind the town, where there was nothing around apart from birds and bees and the odd barking dog. A grazing cow would chime its bell, and the sound would hang in the valley for a long, long while. At times the peak of Mount Paringu vanished inside the clouds and the breeze smelled of rain.

3

The meeting was about to start. The amphitheatre was nearly full. I sat in the first available seat at the back of the hall and said hello to the student next to me.

It was going to be a long, boring afternoon.

I thought of Emil. I thought of his beautiful eyes and the movie we had seen the night before. He had taken my hand, and as I felt the golden hairs on the back of his hand, shivers went down my spine. On the way home we stopped in our secret dark corner and kissed. I was still dreaming about his kisses and love when the din in the hall suddenly stopped. On the stage, three look-alike dark-suited men and my friend Addy emerged from the side entrance and sat down behind the big rectangular table.

Addy? *What was Addy doing there?* And what happened next is still with me, vivid and raw as if I am still sitting in that hall.

—⁂—

The official on the left stands. A deathly silence descends on the five hundred people in the hall.

I have not seen Addy for a couple of weeks, and as I look at his deathly pale face, I recall our last conversation. We were sitting in the lounge. My mother came in with a tray of tea and sorbet, placed it on the dining table, chatted for a couple of minutes and returned to the kitchen. As soon as the door was shut, Addy said that he had something important to discuss with me.

The suit on the stage is talking about the threat of imperialism. The USA, the greatest of all threats. Sitting on his left is Addy, his face

25

grey as a corpse, his eyes above our heads, gazing into the distance.

'We need to be vigilant,' the suit says, 'vigilant about traitors, vigilant about people like the man sitting on my left. Stand up. This is about you.'

About Addy? That's it. His plans! We had been sitting drinking tea. He took a teaspoon of my mother's sorbet and without lifting his eyes from his cup said, 'I'm going to run away.'

What? I thought, what is he talking about?

He looked at me. 'I'm going to go to the American Embassy to ask for political asylum.'

I was stunned, both by what he told me and by his carelessness in talking about it. To my knowledge, no one had ever succeeded in running away from Romania. We were smack in the middle of the communist bloc, surrounded by communist countries. Communist border guards, Soviets, Hungarians, Bulgarians, Yugoslavs were watching us from all sides. And then there was the Danube to swim across. Running to the American Embassy? Wasn't the American Embassy on Romanian soil? How could the Americans give you asylum, take you out of Romania, knowing that millions more would follow, that millions more would be on the Embassy's doorstep asking for the same?

And there was more. Addy's father was some sort of party official. He was not high up, but how would I have known how involved he was, what he really did?

'Come with me,' he added.

Fantasy, I thought. Madness. No normal man would dare do such thing; so I changed the subject. I should have talked him out of it, I should have warned him. But I was afraid. You never know who is a party faithful, who would denounce you, who would turn you over to the Securitate. The party is like an octopus with thousands of long, far-reaching tentacles. Invisible tentacles.

'A traitor. He ran to the US Embassy, he ran to our enemies and asked for political asylum.' The words of the official match up with the words Addy had said to me that afternoon.

26

'The Americans returned him,' the suit adds.

Impossible!

'Do you have anything to say?' the second suit asks.

Addy does not have anything to say. But he is not finished with yet, because the third suit has something to ask. Fear grabs me in its poisonous long arms, twisting my insides.

'Did anybody know about your plans?' the suit asks.

Eerie silence.

I break into a sweat. What if? They'll blame it on me. They'll say I poisoned his mind. I wanted to leave the country years before Addy even dreamt about running away. I will be stuck in Romania for the rest of my life. I will end up in prison for years. And my father? It will destroy him. It will destroy my father. They'll blame him for bringing me up as a traitor. My fingernails are piercing the flesh of my palms. My eyes are fixed on the ground. I cannot look up, because if I do, he might find my face in the crowd. He might give in.

'Well?' the suit asks again. 'Did anybody know about your plans?'

Addy's gaze is travelling above me. The wait is excruciating. Say something! I don't care what. Just say it. What are you waiting for?

'No, nobody knew about it.' The lifeless words cut the spine-chilling silence.

I collapse in my chair, a rag doll hitting the ground.

The meeting is being wound up. Addy is expelled from the university and will be allowed to do only physical work. Allowed? What does this mean? Condemned? But this is not a law court. It is not clear where, or for how long. Something else is being said but I don't register, it washes over me. Nothing else is relevant any longer. I take a last furtive look at his pale face. Will I be able to thank him one day?

My friends have spotted me. They are coming to greet me. I want to hide, but too late. They are going somewhere, I didn't catch where. I don't want to join them, I am going home.

My friends would not talk about what happened, because nothing had happened, nothing which could be argued or talked about. No one dared to question whether Addy deserved such harsh punishment. They would not even utter his name.

His file had been stamped 'Traitor to Romania'. A permanent stamp, everlasting. No years of hard labour would ever absolve him. He would remain a traitor to his country for the rest of his life.

I walked home slowly, as if life had been squeezed out of me. My legs weak and unsure.

The whole family was gathered around the dining table. 'How was the meeting?' my mother enquired.

'The usual.'

She wanted to hear details. I did not want to talk. What happened in that meeting would be locked inside me forever. She wanted to know where Emil was, how come he didn't drop in.

My father gave me a worried look. He must have sensed that something was not right. I faked unwellness and went to bed. My mind kept going around and around: What if? What if he had said *Yes?*

Two days passed. Addy was on my mind all the time. He was on my mind as I walked home along the narrow street that afternoon. On the other side, a familiar silhouette was coming into focus. Addy. A couple of paces behind him, a Securitate man. I kept my eyes fixed on the ground. We passed each other without acknowledgement, without even a furtive look.

That was the last I saw of Addy. I wondered where he ended up. For months. I never asked – I couldn't. I missed him. Did anybody else?

No one ever mentioned his name again.

4

Autumn 1963. A new academic year started. I was a second-year student and a year closer to becoming a Mineral Processing Engineer.

Emil was gone. He transferred to Cluj, to another university. 'My parents don't want me to have a Jewish girlfriend,' he said one evening as he was walking me home.

I did not reply. We kept walking, side by side, my hand no longer in his. I tried to console myself: we belonged to different worlds, I would emigrate and he would remain in Romania. It was better to end it sooner than later. But I wanted to know what his parents said, the exact words. Did they say, 'You have to break up with this Jewish girl,' or did they say 'You have to break up with this *Jidan*', the derogatory name we Jews were referred to by some? Those who blamed us for killing their God, those who saw in us the cause of all evil. And what did he say? Did he argue? Or did he just sit in silence? I wanted to know who was the man walking next to me. Who was the man who had held my hand minutes before, the man I used to kiss before we reached our street every evening? But I did not ask. It seemed pointless. The difficult questioning, the answers I wouldn't have believed, the unjustifiable justifications.

'I'll come and visit,' he added.

I kept walking.

It is well and truly over, I thought as I looked out of the window one evening, nearly four months later. A thick fog had descended on the town that evening. On the street, the trees stood bare in the faint lighting, like ghosts. The town was sad.

The world was sad. Kennedy had been assassinated. Lee Oswald, the young man who shot him, was dead too, shot by Jack Ruby the day before. And I? I had an inkling that the authorities wanted to see me. Someone had been looking for me soon after I left the university that afternoon. Someone from the corner office. But since I was not sure who asked and what, I said nothing at home.

'Jack Ruby?' Stefan pondered at the dinner table. 'Who is that Jack Ruby character?'

'Stefan! You're so naïve. What does it matter who he is, or who Lee Oswald is? What matters is who is behind all this,' Roza said, and the way she said it, it was clear who she blamed for that tragedy. Who else but our neighbour from the east, our great friend, the Soviet Union.

Roza blamed most unspeakable events in the world on the Soviet Union, especially if they were bizarre or shrouded in secrecy. Her assertions often sounded like fantasy, but sometimes her fantasy turned out to be right. Still, we didn't take her seriously.

'Johnson might have been the vice-president, but he is an unknown,' Stefan added.

'Not one to stand up to the Soviet bear,' Roza replied as she placed the pot of hot soup in the middle of the table. 'That's all we need. A weak US president, a stronger Khrushchev and an even more subservient Romanian president.'

Yossi was not interested in Kennedy or Khruschev. He was famished. He had been playing at his friend's house all afternoon. But food was imminent and he managed a few smiles. Roza placed two ladlefuls of soup into his bowl. At the sight of his dinner, the smiles on Yossi's face vanished.

'To each according to their deeds,' was the socialist theory, and Stefan absentmindedly swallowed another spoonful of his reward, caraway seeds floating in a lifeless floury broth. The steam wafted up into his face, his thoughts miles away, probably on the latest funicular design or the problems in the mine.

Yossi had resigned himself to his fate. He was pushing it down with plenty of black bread.

Next morning I was up early. Will it be today? I wondered.

Sure enough, at the end of my first lecture, just as I was packing my notes away, a student put his head in and called out, 'You're wanted in the corner office.' I knew the rest.

I took a deep breath and knocked on the door. Inside, from behind a table facing the door, two officials looked up at me from their papers. 'Please be seated, Comrade Leitner,' the wide-faced man said, pointing to the chair opposite. He quickly came to the point. 'Tell me, Comrade Leitner, why do you want to emigrate?' he asked in the friendliest of voices.

Why do we want to emigrate? Didn't we declare this seven years ago? If you needed further confirmation why didn't you ask then? Not me, I was twelve years old. Why didn't you ask my father? But I said none of that, I just regurgitated the much rehearsed argument from home: 'Because my mother wants to go, all her relatives are in Israel.' That argument was based on the tightest of logic – they couldn't punish her easily, she was a housewife.

He thought for a moment then looked at the other man. 'Do you realise that your father will not find a job there?' the other official asked. 'Capitalism has no use for people of his age,' and he made a note in his file.

I had no idea what my father's overseas prospects were because few people who left had ever written back, and those who did seemed to be managing. I only knew about his prospects in Romania.

He had been demoted. 'A man who wants to leave the country cannot hold a highly responsible job,' he was told. He was no longer responsible for the construction and reinforcement of the coalmines around the Jiu Valley, but he was still leading the most important and risky projects. For less money, of course.

Every time there was an accident in the mines, he feared being accused of sabotage. The mines were old, the workers unmotivated, money was in short supply, but none of these could be acknowledged officially. It was far more convenient to blame someone, and who better to carry the blame than someone who had applied to emigrate, someone untrustworthy ... my father. But there was more. While people respected him professionally, in the eyes of many Romanians he remained a Hungarian, a Hungarian Jew. His strong Hungarian accent was there to remind them that he was not one of them.

'If you emigrate you will miss out on a great future,' the other official said and circled something on his paper. He can't be serious, I thought, while in my mind's eye I saw myself, a young engineer in a coal flotation plant where workers looked like chimney sweeps, the air full of acrid smells and the ground deep in coal powder. I had been through three weeks of work experience, I found out what Mineral Processing really was. Of course a country needs coal flotation plants, but do they have to be such filthy, miserable places?

'Think about it,' the wide-faced man said. 'If the application is not withdrawn you will be expelled from the university.'

Withdraw the application? I had not the slightest wish to do so.

'I'll think about it.'

I had three days to decide.

My parents were worried. My father wanted to make sure that I had thought it over, that I had considered my choices, and whatever my decision, I understood its repercussions. 'We will accept whatever you decide.'

My decision was made.

'Are you absolutely sure?' my father asked for the last time.

'Absolutely.'

———⁓———

A week later I was sitting in the big hall. On the stage opposite, behind the big rectangular table, were three party officials.

Here we go again, I thought, remembering what happened to Addy.

'Comrades!'

'Comrades!' The grey suit on the stage demanded undivided attention.

I was sitting at the end of row fourteen; on my left was my friend Lily. No one else knew that the urgent meeting had been called for me, for my expulsion. It was announced at lunchtime: 'Meeting at six'. I had a few hours to kill. There was a chemistry laboratory at two o'clock. Why not? I thought. I would immerse myself in a chemical experiment at that university one last time.

I kept adding a solution from a burette to one in a conical flask, slowly, drop by drop. All of a sudden the solution turned turbid and a mass of white precipitate dropped to the bottom of the flask. It occurred to me that in a few hours I too would be rejected by this university, cast off just like that white sludge. I wrote down my observations, filled in the questionnaire and handed it in. I cleaned the bench and left. I rushed home, half running.

'It's today, at six,' I said to my mother as I closed the door.

'What's at six?'

'The meeting, the meeting for my expulsion.'

'Why a meeting?'

Why indeed? Couldn't they have said: Don't turn up tomorrow? That's what they said to Benny one day. No discussions, no cajoling, no meetings. Just, don't turn up tomorrow. Short and clean. But the authorities had something else in mind for me.

My father was not yet back from work. Yossi was doing his home-work on the dining table, next to him a pile of clothes waiting to be ironed.

'You should eat before you go, I'll get you a bowl of soup,' my mother said and returned to the kitchen. Food was my mother's answer to difficult situations. I ate the soup and started to relax. By the time I had to return, I was composed and calm.

—⁓—

So there I was, sitting among five hundred stone statues in black uniforms, barely breathing. Their faces frozen in neutrality, their eyes shifting occasionally from the officials on the stage to their shoes, then to someone's haircut to pass the time. Because passing the time is hard work when you have to listen to meaningless words.

The first suit finished talking. The second suit rose to his feet.

'Comrades, don't forget that the real danger is the enemy within. They are where we least expect them.' He kept talking, spreading bile and mistrust of the world. This was still only the introduction. He would have to move from the general to the particular, I thought, to the person in row fourteen. Like a lens which focuses the rays of the sun to a single point, he would concentrate his bile onto one person – me. And I waited.

The enemy within was finally identified. No longer a Comrade, but a traitor to the country, to the people of Romania. And then his vitriol moved to my father. My father who stayed in Romania after the war because he believed in communism, my father who donated everything he had to the state as soon as they came to power, my father who was considered by his wife a naïve communist sympathiser, was, in the eyes of the officials, the evil rich man, the enemy of socialism.

And the daughter of that evil man had to be made an example of to all those class enemies lurking among the people in the hall, the town, the country. A traitor? It was an official application. A response to a goodwill gesture by the government. It had been announced in *Scinteia* (*The Spark*), the mouthpiece of the Communist Party and the only newspaper in the country. Jews who had relatives in Israel, it said, would be permitted to leave, to reunite with their families. A week later my father joined the longest queue he had ever seen. The queue of Jews applying to emigrate at the Interior Ministry Office in Deva. They filled in pages and pages of official forms, every detail, to the letter of the inflexible and imbecilic rules of the authorities.

All of that was going on in my mind when the third suit rose to his feet. He called for a vote, the vote for my expulsion. A few hands went up, slowly, then more and more. Everybody's hands in the hall were up, all except Lily's and a couple of my friends' sitting next to her.

'Agreed unanimously,' the suit declared.

It was over. I no longer had to fear being called into the office, having to deal with authorities. I no longer had to fear expulsion every day. The weight I had been carrying for more than a year had suddenly been lifted.

The meeting was adjourned for ten minutes. I was to leave the hall. People stood up to walk around. Lily walked me to the door. My dear friend Lily! What courage! I could hardly hold back my tears.

Outside, the smell of coal was blowing from the mines. The air was cold, my breath visible in the moonlight. The first snow couldn't have been far. Cold, indifferent houses looked at me from the dark, as if saying, 'Who cares that you're a traitor? Who cares if you'll get out of this country? Who cares if you are stuck?' I do, and I will get out, I said to myself, but deep inside I was afraid. Afraid of tomorrow, afraid of the future.

My parents were waiting at the bottom of the hill. As we walked home, me recounting what happened, my father's arm around my shoulder, squeezing me from time to time, my mother holding my other arm, I realised how worried they must have been. They had been pacing around for a couple of hours, hoping to see me or someone else coming down the hill, someone who might know what was going on.

The following days turned into a roller coaster between the euphoria of relief and a thick fog of hopelessness. Our neighbour suggested that I take up knitting: 'It's good for the nerves.' Worried, my mother bought some white wool and I started knitting a jumper. For me? For her? Whatever comes out. I have two left hands.

Benny kept dropping in, encouraging me not to lose faith. If he managed to find work I would too, besides, it would be only temporary. The passports would arrive soon.

The whole community heard about my expulsion. The Jews were speculating. Maybe too many people wanted to leave, maybe the officials did not anticipate such an exodus, maybe they realised that if they played their cards right they could up their side of the bargain. There were rumours that Israel was paying money for each and every one of us. But what did I care if they sold us for pennies or for thousands of dollars? If they sold us like slaves? As long as they sold us soon, as long as we got out. Nothing else counted.

'Now they *must* issue your passports,' Steinberg said to me as he unpacked his pawns, queens and kings one evening. 'I heard there are others in the same situation, in other towns. There must be thousands; they cannot just leave you in limbo.'

Having analysed the political situation, the two men sat down to play. It was a silent game which went on and on while my mother, Yossi and I crept around quietly not to disturb them. I kept watching out for a smile or a frown, waiting for the game to end. A satisfied smile meant that the opponent had been tricked and a killing could follow any minute, but sometimes the smile turned to worry, a sign that there had been a miscalculation, the trick would not work.

'Check!' exclaimed Steinberg, shifting his eyes from the board to my father, whose concentration could nearly move his pieces remotely. Eventually Stefan picked up his knight and moved it in front of his king. Steinberg frowned, paused for a while then moved his bishop. 'Check!' he whispered. Stefan quickly moved a pawn to block the bishop and shelter his king. But Steinberg had a few more tricks and the game was on again. The air was heavy with tension.

'Checkmate!' Stefan exclaimed.

Steinberg was taken aback. He did not believe it. He looked at the board considering his options. A minute, two, four. There was no way out and he acknowledged defeat.

'Surely they cannot keep so many young people in limbo.' Steinberg repeated his prediction. 'The world will not allow it.'

The world? Why would the big world care about me? Why would it care about people who have no rights in this country, but are condemned to live here? But even if it did, what could it do?

The world seemed like the moon. It looked down on us, cold and uninvolved.

Then the ice broke. Two passports arrived in one day, one of them for the Izsaks. Benny was leaving. Now I was on my own. The Segals were going too, this time for real. There were rumours that more passports were on the way and my mother kept waiting for the postman. With more determination than ever.

I found work in the civil engineering office where my father worked. As a draughtswoman. The people in the office were all middle-aged.

Every morning my father and I walked to work together. Sometimes we talked, sometimes we just walked alongside each other quietly with our thoughts. He was under a great deal of stress. He had come around, he could see no future for us in Romania. He wanted to emigrate. Wholeheartedly.

'I think you should apply separately, the authorities will surely let you go,' he said to me one morning. I did not want to leave my family behind the Iron Curtain. I might never see them again. I was only nineteen years old. But every now and then, when I was down, when my situation looked utterly hopeless, I thought maybe I should. My Romanian friends had dwindled away, our lives had diverged. I was no friendship material, people were afraid to be seen with me. Even Lily had moved on. We did not have much in common anymore.

Will there be any news? I wondered day after day as I walked home. But every time I opened the door and searched my mother's face I saw the same expression: 'No, not yet.'

My father kept telling me to apply. We would be reunited eventually. They would not keep him in Romania for long. He had turned sixty-one.

Four months had passed since I had spoken to a young person. I had lost all hope. So one day I decided: I would go to Deva and apply for a separate passport.

I would emigrate on my own.

5

'He's dead!' My mother said breathlessly as she came through the door.

I was on holidays, sitting in the kitchen having a cup of tea.

'Who? Who is dead?'

'Gheorghiu Dej.'

I swallowed my mouthful.

'The President?' I asked, not because it could have been someone else, his was not a common name, but my mind refused to come along, accept the facts. All my life, well, ever since I could remember, Gheorghiu Dej had been in the realm of the communist leadership: party leader, Prime Minister, President. Gheorghiu Dej was as permanent as communism, as undying as his picture hanging on every official wall. A Romania without Gheorghiu Dej was unimaginable.

'Yes, him,' my mother replied. 'Of natural causes. That's what they said on the radio. Well, what could be more natural for a political leader than being invited to Moscow and be dead soon after?' She laughed.

It wasn't that soon. I think it took a few months. But my mother's assertions were not entirely phantasmagorical. For some Eastern European leaders, an invitation to Moscow was an invitation for a game of chess with death.

Gheorghiu Dej had been a Stalinist and a survivor. A survivor of internal and Soviet politics. He had been at the helm for nearly two decades. By the time of his death, Stalin was long gone and Khruschev had been deposed by Brezhnev.

Three days after his death, his replacement had been named, a little-known man: Nicolae Ceausescu.

'Who is he?' Stefan wondered, and he sat next the radio in the evening to listen to the news. But neither the Americans nor the Europeans could shed much light on the man. An old communist, a protégé of Gheorghiu Dej, they said. But did he share his views? Was he a sworn Stalinist? The pendulum of history had moved and we had moved with it. But in which direction? Closer to freedom, or away from it? Liberalisation or more bars on the windows? For the two dozen or so Jewish families in Petrosani, however, the most important question was: will Ceausescu let us out or will he lock the gates?

Three weeks passed. Spring arrived. On the main street, new green buds looked down from the tree branches. I was walking home cogitating. Soon it would be summer again, another summer. Three months had passed since I applied to emigrate on my own.

I felt feverish. Yossi had been sick with the flu for a couple of days, he must have passed it on to me.

'*Buna ziua*,' a neighbour greeted me in front of our block. 'Cheer up, *Domnisoara*, the sun is shining, it's spring again.'

'True, *buna ziua*,' I replied and headed for our entrance.

My mother opened the door and ushered me in. 'We got it,' she whispered. 'The whole family,' and pointed to the table. There, freshly out of the envelope, was the one-page letter.

I read it and read it again.

Comrade Leitner,

Your application to emigrate has been approved. Please present yourself to the Militia Headquarters ... to collect your passports.

I was still standing with the letter in my hand when the image of Mrs Segal trying her georgette dress flashed through my mind. I recalled the others who got their passports only to have them taken away a few weeks later. There was no reason to celebrate. Not yet. I will celebrate on the other side of the Iron Curtain. Or maybe in Israel. Yes, I will jump for joy there. I'll jump a dozen times.

'Stefan should finish work anytime now. Let's go and meet him.'

She told Yossi to keep warm, folded the precious letter, put it in her handbag and we were off. My throat was still sore, the fever was rising, but we had the release papers from Romania. In a few days we would have our passports and in a month we would be on the other side of the Iron Curtain. So I took my mother's arm and we walked up the main street, both of us determined not to say a word to anybody. Not yet, not until we had the passports in hand. Not a word to anybody? Not even to Mrs Steinberg? She had just turned the corner and was coming towards us. We would tell her, of course we would. But she had read our faces.

'You got it!' she said when we stopped. My mother tried to play down our happiness. Anything could still happen in the following few weeks.

Mrs Steinberg was happy, they were issuing passports again, Ceausescu had not locked the gates. The queue was moving. And now there was one less family to go. Soon it would be their turn.

Little did she know that less than a year later, her husband would be dead and she would emigrate alone with her teenage daughter. Alone to start a new life. Steinberg died of a heart attack. Some said he died of hopelessness.

There was always a price to pay to get out of Romania.

—⁓—

The news of our imminent departure spread fast. Another family with a passport, another family about to leave the country. People started to drop in, to see what they could buy. The physics tutor who lived in the block of flats opposite wanted to buy the big carved wood wall unit, dining table and lampshade. Someone else wanted the sofa. This furniture was brought to Romania from Vienna by my father's first wife, Hella. It formed the surroundings I grew up in. It turned our little flat into a home which was more Viennese than Romanian; it gave me a sense of belonging to a world away from coal, ashes and greyness. The carved furniture, the few brocades and laces which we managed to salvage during our many moves, fed my imagination. There was more to this world than utilitarian socialism. Hella, the woman I had never met, had brought beauty into my life.

People dropped in to pick up bargains. Our next-door neighbour wanted an iron. 'It's not for sale, not yet. We'll sell it just before we go.' She was happy to wait. As long as we kept it for her, she would give us a deposit. Even the old pots and pans were in demand. There was not much money in used pots and pans, but the cutlery and crockery would help towards one of Mrs Radulescu's summer dresses. The neighbour upstairs wanted the radio, my father's most valued possession. Maria the milk woman came to buy winter clothes. She came down from the mountains on her donkey loaded with two big milk containers. It was a big day for her. She could buy cheap clothes.

After communism took hold, my mother learned to sell our wares, to talk up the prices where she could. And while the donkey waited outside, Maria put on my mother's clothes and examined herself in the mirror, turned left, turned right and left again. My mother kept praising her: 'It's perfect, it wouldn't look better if it had been made for you.' But the worn coat which was knee length on my mother nearly touched Maria's ankles, its shoulders stuck out like the sides of a wide coat hanger. I could not keep a straight face any longer. I had to run out; besides, I was embarrassed by my mother's selling technique. She did not care. 'Romania has robbed us of everything,' she said later. But I could not see why Maria of all people should pay for other people's robberies. She was a decent hard-working poor peasant woman. 'At least she will have a warm coat,' my mother added, 'and it will cost her a fraction of what it would cost otherwise. She can always shorten it if it's too long.' One by one all our possessions were going. The day to say goodbye to Tom was approaching fast.

My brother Tom had been a taboo subject in our family for years, but on the day we got the approval to emigrate, the ice broke. Tom returned to our conversations again. I heard my father talking to my mother, deciding when to go to Cluj to say goodbye.

Apparently Tom lived in a small room in a school. Apparently, because I had never visited him, never seen his place.

41

'At best, he could take the chest of drawers,' my father said in one of the many discussions and ponderings, 'and he could definitely take the paintings and the jewellery. He can sell them if he falls on bad times.' And Roza packed the little box with the necklace, the signet ring, the pair of earrings and the beautiful rhombic ring set with diamonds and a red ruby. Its sparkle used to invoke in me another world, a world of fairytales, princesses and romances. None of that jewellery was ever worn. In our household, jewellery was kept in drawers and looked at and admired on rare occasions, behind locked doors and closed curtains. The authorities did not need to be reminded that my father had been rich once.

Nine years had passed since I saw Tom last, nine years since he left our family. The brother with whom I grew up, with whom I spent my childhood, had become the brother I used to have, long ago, in another life. I was apprehensive about our forthcoming encounter. My father must have been, too. He must have dreaded the day when he would say goodbye to his eldest son, because while nobody admitted it, no one knew when and if we would see him again. We tried to be optimistic. My mother kept saying, 'Tom will join us once we've established ourselves.' Did anybody believe it? I suspect my father wanted to believe it.

I wanted to believe it too, but right then I had other worries. We still had to go through Customs; we were not out of the reach of the authorities yet.

So one day, my father and I and Tom's meagre inheritance went to catch the train to Cluj. To say goodbye. It was a short visit. A couple of days only.

When I think about that visit, I am overcome by shame. How oblivious the young can be to the inner life of other people. And how unreceptive I was to those two men's emotions. I knew my father was preoccupied and sad and I understood why. But there were no tears, and wrapped up in the excitement of getting out of Romania, I only thought about the future, my future. There was no point in being sad – Tom would join us one day.

I did not grasp Tom's feeling of abandonment at being left alone in the country with no other support than his aunt, the busy Aunt Anna. True, he was no longer a child; he was twenty-seven years old and there had not been much contact between him and the family for years. But his father did write to him. His father had been there, always. Distant, but there, a train ride away. Now his father was emigrating to the West, a place which Tom was no more likely to visit than the moon, a place from where no one ever came to visit.

I had no inkling of how Tom felt. And I had little understanding of how my father must have felt when he said goodbye to his eldest son. The son with a limp and a feeble right hand. But the images of their goodbyes stayed with me and will probably never fade.

—⁓—

Finally our last day in Petrosani arrived. We said goodbye to our neighbours. Some asked to be sent medicines; Mrs Dumitrescu, the woman in the next block, asked for a shawl from the Promised Land. Yes, my mother said, she would send them, as soon as she possibly could, and extended her hand to seal the promise.

Our belongings were packed, the truck to pick us up was due any minute.

It was nearly twenty years to the day since my uncle, a Holocaust survivor, had left Europe. He was going as far as he could, to Australia, and had suggested to my father that we join him. He had one suitcase when he boarded the train. My father had replied, 'I can always leave with a suitcase, I can leave in twenty years' time.' So that morning, nearly twenty years since that day, my father must have remembered his words as he nailed down the lid of the wooden chest containing the sum total of our possessions, our clothes, linen, doonas, blankets and shoes. The fruits of his four decades of work.

We were leaving penniless; we were not allowed to take one penny out of the country. Our only investments were three salamis and two dozen cigarettes. Rumours were that they could be sold easily in Vienna, that we could make some pocket money, enough to look around that great city.

We were destitute but free. And nothing else counted. So when I heard the knock on the door, when I heard that the truck was waiting, I couldn't have left faster.

The door slammed for the last time and I said goodbye to my old life. With no regrets.

—⁓—

The Customs officers in Oradea looked bored by our worldly possessions. They must have seen tens of thousands of wooden chests like ours. More clothes, more linen, more shoes.

'Take out as much as you can,' one of the officers said to me.' I lifted the top clothes out of the chest. He rummaged under the rest, folded back the corner of the linen. 'And these too,' he said, pointing to the shoes. I lifted the shoes out and put them down next to the chest. He looked inside, then turned to my mother: 'You need to lift those sheets.' My mother obliged.

A second officer came to help. They kept searching, looking for valuables, for money or items which did not classify as allowed out of the country. Twenty minutes or so later the chest was through. To Israel by sea.

At passport control in Bucharest airport, there they were again, among clerks and procedures, a swarm of militiamen in their dark-blue uniforms. One of them could pick on us, things could still go wrong. I am not religious but I was praying, praying to all the gods of the universe. Let them be overcome by goodwill for once and let us go. I swallowed again as I handed my passport for another check and watched the clerk's face with trepidation. Another farce? But he let us through without a hitch.

Inside the plane I sat next to my father, with Yossi and my mother behind us. No one uttered a word. We were still in the land where thoughts could not be voiced. Through the window I could see two militiamen. I hoped it was for the last time. For the last time ever.

There was an announcement. We were about to take off. I

straightened up and fastened my seat belt.

The plane was running. Faster and faster. Lifting. Flying above houses, above Bucharest, above Romania, above all the misery I was leaving behind. In and out of clouds, from light to fog and light again.

Suddenly it was not the plane, but me, a bird just released from a dark cage, spreading its wings, flying for the first time. Higher and higher, faster and faster. Into the most brilliant blue sky.

6

Oh Vienna, how beautiful you looked to my migrant eye!

Even the airport toilets looked glamorous. Strong lighting, big mirrors. In a toilet? At the time, in 1965, they still had an old-fashioned Viennese touch. If the toilets look like a small ballroom, how is the rest of the city? I wondered. The rest turned out more beautiful than I had imagined: wide streets, exquisite flower shops, big baroque buildings, lights and more lights. The West was stunning.

Ten days later we found ourselves in an even more beautiful place, a place which rivalled heaven on that day of spring, Venice. Mass tourism had not taken on yet. The sun shone on the Piazza San Marco and its carpet of pigeons pecked the crumbs between the coffee tables where a few people sat and watched the passers-by. Further, on the big canal, boats sped up and down, their spray sparkling in the sun. But Israel was not Italy, and Tel Aviv was not Vienna, and when we boarded our ship *Enotria*, we knew that our glimpse of the heavenly West had been only a short interlude.

The engines murmured and buzzed as *Enotria* rolled on. Around us, the vast waters of the Mediterranean, above the most brilliant sunshine. The sunrays, the same sunrays which had lit the beautiful cities of Vienna and Venice, were now breaking in the deep blue waters of the sea. Bits of sunshine flickered in the small waves, like tinsel.

I was standing on the deck watching the sea, overwhelmed by its beauty, its power, its immensity. Its distant horizons belonged to a world unfamiliar to me, a world of huge dimensions and superlatives, so unlike the mountains I came from. On my left, lying on deck chairs, a couple of Romanians were speculating on what lay ahead. Three more joined in to offer advice. Nobody knew what awaited us, what to do once we got to Israel, where to live and how to cope with the heat. 'With wet towels,' said a plump woman in her early forties. 'That's what they do in Egypt.' In Egypt? But she is from Bucharest, how would she know? She was adamant, that's what they do in Egypt, she had heard about it from someone, 'a well-read reliable source'. Images of people walking around the street with wet towels covering their faces seemed ludicrous.

'We'll find out soon enough,' the woman sitting next to her said. 'We'll find out tomorrow.'

Tomorrow, I thought. Tomorrow is the start of my new life.

———※———

It was a hot and misty morning that day in May 1965, when *Enotria* entered Israeli territorial waters. The deck was full of people trying to catch a glimpse of their new country. But the Promised Land was hiding in the haze.

My mother squeezed me on the shoulder. 'Not long to go,' she smiled. There was apprehension in her smile.

'There!' someone shouted, pointing to a small strip of land barely visible in the distance. There was Israel. For me, not the Promised Land, but the country I had dreamt about for more than eight years.

The port and a handful of houses slowly emerged from the mist. They looked, well, probably like any other port. But the rest of Haifa was still hiding in the hot haze.

'Please form a queue for housing allocation!' came an announcement through a loudspeaker behind me, in some languages I knew and others I did not.

A table had appeared on the deck. Next to it, two middle-aged men, one with glasses, the second wearing a skullcap, both in shorts and open-necked short-sleeved shirts, started shuffling piles of papers. 'Israeli officials, Jewish officials!' my mother whispered and

47

I felt as if a weight had been lifted from me, a weight I had been carrying all my life and was not aware of. The edginess which gripped me every time I had to face officials was no more. I would no longer have to watch everything I said. They would ask questions and I would answer, frankly, without having to weigh every word, without worrying about its implications. I no longer had to declare that I was Jewish, because those people were just like me. No more questions about religion, no more shame for being different, no more weariness for standing up for who I was. I was in my own country. Hot and sticky, but mine.

The ship anchored. Through the mist, the hills of Haifa looked like a distant country, like a place out of reach.

The first Romanians, a family from Bucharest, had finished their negotiations with the two officials. 'We're lucky,' the woman said to her husband as they walked past us. 'Tel Aviv! Ah?'

As if overcome by the rising heat, the queue progressed sluggishly. More people peeled off the head of the queue and ambled past, discussing the locations of their new homes. Strange names, all close to Haifa or Tel Aviv. Of course, Israel is a small country.

The sun baked the mist, unveiling a few more houses on the docks, then blocks of flats standing tall on the hills. People stood and watched in silence. Did their dream match reality? Or were they as confused as I was? The city facing me was nothing like what I had imagined. Not that I had imagined anything concrete. But what did I expect?

'Beautiful,' whispered a woman. Nobody answered.

Finally we reached the head of the queue and the two unofficial-looking officials surrounded by piles of forms. They questioned my parents: my father's profession, what he intended to do, what I intended to do, the names and addresses of our relatives in Israel. The conversation was mostly in Romanian, with an odd word of Yiddish thrown in. The man with the glasses wrote as we spoke. His writing, from right to left, reminded me of pictures of ancient texts from my history books. Questions finished, the man leafed through his notes then raised his eyes to my father. 'Where would you like to live?' he asked.

'Kfar Saba,' my mother jumped in breathlessly, 'near my brother.'

The man leafed through his documents again. We waited. Will it be Kfar Saba? Or will it be the desert, or some other hot-as-hell part of the country?

He muttered to himself, then turned towards the skullcapped man and asked something in Hebrew. The skullcap agreed. The man with the glasses looked at us. 'You are lucky, we have some flats close to your brother, in Yoseftal.'

My mother could not thank him enough. The official wrote something in the ancient alphabet, pointed to a square on the form and asked my father to sign. 'By the way,' he said, 'Yoseftal is not far from Tel Aviv,' and wished us the very best for the future. In Yiddish.

Then the skullcapped official stood up. '*Bruchim haba'im l'yisra'el!* (Welcome to Israel!)' he said in Hebrew and shook hands with each one of us. Any misgivings Yossi might have had about our new country must have vanished. He had suddenly become important, he was now a man.

We grabbed our suitcases, with Mrs Radulescu's creations, the salami and the Romanian cigarettes – our investments which had turned out not to be in demand in Vienna – and joined the queue for the free taxi. The locals, young women in sandals, short skirts and sleeveless blouses, and men in shorts and short-sleeved shirts, walked past as if we did not exist. Mrs Radulescu's clothes, designed for a Romanian summer, were suffocating. My skin felt like an overblown balloon, my limbs heavy, my mind murky. But the queue was moving, we wouldn't have to wait for long.

'*Bruchim haba'im!*' called out a taxi driver. He took the form from my father, loaded our suitcases in the boot and we were on our way. As the taxi started out, a gale of hot air hit us through the open windows. Heavens above! Am I dreaming? This is purgatory.

'It's *hamsin* today,' the driver said in Yiddish. 'It's the hot dry wind from the desert,' he added and my mother translated. 'There are fifty such days every year.'

And the others? Are the other days much cooler? But my mother was busy talking to my father who was sitting behind her. Will the remaining days, the three hundred and fifteen days be much cooler? But I didn't ask, I couldn't. I didn't have the words.

The streets of Haifa kept flying past. On our right was the sea; on our left the hills dropped lower and lower then turned into feature-less land. Sprinkled here and there were clusters of flats. 'This is Kfar Gallim,' the driver said and my eyes started searching for a European town. Feelings of unease and strangeness were creeping up on me. But I didn't mind anything any more, nothing except the heat. The heat was unbearable.

Two hours later we arrived at our destination, Yoseftal, about twelve blocks of flats set out in a quadrangle in the middle of a grassy wasteland. The driver pulled up in front of a block and stopped. 'Over there,' he said pointing to the hill opposite, 'is Jordan, and those houses on the hill are in Qalqilya, an Arab village. And here,' he turned around and pointed to a window on the first floor of the block, 'is your flat.' He unloaded the suitcases, handed my father a key and shook our hands. '*Alles Gute* (all the best),' he said, hopped in the taxi and disappeared around the corner.

A demonic sun was burrowing into my head mercilessly. We picked up our suitcases and dragged ourselves to the first floor.

Our flat was so new, it looked unfinished. Except for the door to the bathroom, there were no other doors inside, not even door frames. Across the length of the bedroom walls, single army beds stood on the grey tiled cement floor. There was a small lounge room, a tiny kitchen, a bathroom and a balcony. On the floor of the kitchen stood a small paraffin stove. Next to the sink an aluminium saucepan and frying pan, a minimum set of cutlery, four glasses and four plates.

There was a knock on the door and, without waiting for a response, a woman walked in. She would not have looked out of place on a boulevard in Bucharest, but in Yoseftal? Miriam was from Romania. She was in her early fifties. She had long blond hair and an ample bosom, and as she walked, barely balancing on her very high heels, her big buttocks stretched her short skirt to its limits. She brought us tea, sugar, oil, bread, jam, flour and money for a week's food. And lots and lots of encouragement. Having advised and reassured us, she added, 'You have arrived home. Just have patience. If you have patience, everything will fall into place.'

The door closed behind her. We sat down on the two beds in what was now my parents' bedroom and looked at each other.

'It'll be all right,' my father said, wiping the perspiration from his pale face.

After the much awaited cold shower, my mother took up her duties. She placed a saucepan of water on the paraffin stove, squatted next to it, lit the wick, adjusted the flame and declared herself victorious. The water for the tea would be ready soon and there was the jam and bread Miriam had brought us. The salami destined to be sold in Vienna was green and mouldy. It did not matter. No one was hungry.

Our Romanian life was behind us, our Israeli life ahead of us, or so we thought when we ventured onto the street that late afternoon. On the only street of Yoseftal, which ran around the dozen or so blocks of flats, people were walking in a leisurely fashion. Nearly everybody spoke Romanian. If not for the heat and the strange surroundings, if not for Jordan a few hundred metres away, we might have thought we were in Romania again. Some people had been there for months, a couple for more than a year. They were eager for news of their native land. They encouraged us. 'We are managing and so will you,' they said. Meeting the Romanians lifted my spirits.

The sun had set. The night was settling in. People started to go home.

Back in the flat the air hung hot and heavy. We returned to the balcony to wait for a breeze. The street was quiet. A full moon shone on the wasteland in front. On the hill opposite, the lights of the Arab village of Qalqilya lit the dark sky. We were closer to Jordan than to any Israeli town. From time to time the eerie scream of a jackal pierced the silence of the night. Nobody uttered a word, not even Yossi. Memories of a different land played against the strangeness of our surroundings, the sinister noises of the night. And secretly I longed for Europe.

Our first day in the Promised Land was coming to an end. Settled in my bed I could hear Yossi's heavy breathing, but the rest of us were not so lucky. I wonder what my father thought as he lay awake in his bed in that empty flat. Romania behind him, Europe behind him, penniless and without a job at the age of sixty-one.

Mosquitoes kept buzzing in my ear. I tossed and turned in search of some comfort. But the bed was hot and the air was hot and the mattress burnt my skin. I felt trapped, trapped in a small, hot, airless room where my dream of eight years seemed a naïve fairy tale.

Suddenly an urge to run away came over me. Run away somewhere cool, where every breath of air is refreshing, where the cool breeze caresses the human face, where one can think clearly. But there was nowhere to run. I was caught between the howling of wolves and the cries of the jackals.

I took a few deep breaths. Scenes of my life in Romania flashed before my eyes. Going back was out of the question. The future looked hard, unbearably hard, perhaps impossible. But the road was only one way.

—w—

Next morning Roza counted the money Miriam left us, tried to convert it to Romanian money, but soon gave up. Whatever the name of the currency, working out how much she could spend per day was far more sensible. There was no fridge, so there was no point in buying more than a day's supplies.

Outside it was hot already, but less oppressive than yesterday. Luckily the two shops were only five minutes walk away.

In the greengrocer's shop there was only one customer, an elderly woman. The grocer, a small obese man, sat on a low chair in one corner like Buddha. Next to him a pair of scales. Piles of potatoes, onions, boxes of tomatoes, apples and bananas were spread around in no particular order. Flies were feasting on the small fruit and on the droplets of perspiration covering his plump face. Every now and then he raised a hand, waved the flies away then sat motionless, not quite asleep, not quite awake. Roza gathered a few potatoes and put them on the scale.

'Moshe!' The older woman called. She had finished her shopping. Moshe muttered something, then said, '*Eser lirot*' (ten lira). But it looked like *eser lirot* was too much for her and she showed eight fingers, and it looked like this was good enough for Moshe because he said, '*Yalla*,' and gesticulated something which I interpreted as 'just give me anything'. The woman bent over the boxes of vegetables and put the money in his small fat hands.

My mother weighed the potatoes, a few onions and tomatoes and signalled the Buddha. A show of fingers followed and of course, for Moshe's eighteen fingers my mother offered fourteen, but he was not happy; he wanted sixteen and my mother offered fifteen and he said '*Yalla*' again and the money was exchanged over boxes and flies and some half-rotten tomatoes. But she had managed to bargain in the Promised Land and she was happy.

I looked at my father. His eyebrows a tad higher than usual, he shrugged his shoulders as if saying, I have seen many things in my life, but clearly there is much more in store.

Inside the small shop next door there was a fridge with dairy products, and on one of the walls a few shelves with various items of merchandise the identity of which was secretly captured in the ancient writing which I would have to perfect in order to go to university. The flies, some probably from the greengrocer, were now settled on the fresh warm bread piled up in the window, intended to impress. The shopkeeper, a thin, slight man in his late thirties, greeted us: '*Shalom!*'

'*Shalom*,' we replied.

'*Romanim?*'

Roza nodded. He rolled into Romanian immediately. He was from Iraq. He had seven children, at least three always in the shop helping out. While we looked around to decide what to buy, I heard him talking Russian with one woman, then French with the next. My mother asked for bread. He pulled back the small dirty curtain, shooed the flies away, picked up one of the loaves with his hands, fingernails black with dirt, and handed it to my mother while he sent one of his children to get bread for the French-speaking young woman who turned out to be from Morocco.

Eggs, bread, toilet paper, soap. 'Twenty *lirot*,' he said. My mother tried to bargain, but the Promised Land was not uniformly promising; he would not give in and she paid out. 'Yogurt?' he asked his next customer, '*margarina*, hummus?'

We were about to leave. The Sephardi–Iraqi–Yiddish–Russian shopkeeper said, '*Iye tov, iye tov.*' Nobody understood. 'It'll be all right, it'll be all right,' he added in Yiddish and my mother translated.

Outside, the sun was baking the hot dusty street. It felt even hotter than the previous day. Every step was an effort; my legs were already heavy, my skin tight, my mind foggy. And it was only mid-morning.

Inside the flat, the air was hot and still. Utterly still, because the windows and shutters were closed to keep the heat out. I took a glass of water from the tap and sat down on the edge of my bed. The water was warm.

There was a knock on the door. It was Aunt Ella, my mother's oldest sister, and her son, David. 'Jacob will be here soon,' Aunt Ella said as she came through the door. She barely finished her sentence and my mother had her arms around her and they were sobbing like children. My father stood waiting for his turn. Embarrassed.

I had never met Aunt Ella, the good-looking woman from my mother's stories. She was in her sixties. Or my cousin David who must have been in his forties. They brought us crockery, cutlery, pocket money and four folding chairs. We took the chairs inside the bedroom and opened the shutters enough to see each other, and sat and listened to their stories. And laughed and cried. Droplets of perspiration kept rolling down our foreheads, but no one complained. 'David, you have to find Stefan a job,' Aunt Ella said. She was a matriarch. She had brought up six children on her own. They adored her and I had the impression that when she asked for something, it was as good as done.

Sure enough, within days my father had a contract for three years, supervising the building of the central bus station in West Jerusalem. East Jerusalem belonged to Jordan at the time. The central bus station was a small construction. Israel was a small country. It was a good enough job to start with. In time he would get something more substantial, we thought.

My father's job was five bus rides away from where we lived, two-and-a-half hours each way. But he had a job and there would be a regular income. To buy a fridge, furniture, a radio. He would get another contract when that one expired, somewhere else, closer to Yoseftal, or maybe we would move closer to his work.

Within a week, Yossi started school and I was off to a kibbutz to work and learn Hebrew. In four months' time I would start university.

Those were the first few days in our new country. The first pains of our rebirth. Locked behind the Iron Curtain, I was unable to imagine life in a hot country, a country where trees do not line the streets, the buildings are new but flimsy and shootings can erupt only a few hundred metres from the dinner table. But we were free and in a Jewish country. It was worth it, I thought at the time. And who could have predicted that seven years later I would take off again, to Australia, leaving my parents and Yossi behind?

Part II

Twenty-five years on

7

As our plane left Romania that day in 1965, I swore never to return. Like my ancestors of thousands of years ago, for whom every bolt of lightning was a punishment from God, I swore that I should be punished if I did not keep my promise. But here I was, breaking all my promises, infringing all my contracts, travelling to Romania. I am not religious but at times I can be superstitious, and the promise I had made a quarter of century ago amplified the apprehension and anxiety I already felt about this trip. But the pull was much stronger than the uneasiness.

I was here with my husband, Alex. I would not have dared to come alone. Our teenage daughter Tamara was with us too. I worried about her, I worried about both of them. I did not know what to expect from an ex-communist country.

We had planned to catch a train, but a swarm of Budapest taxi drivers surrounded us as we walked towards the ticket office. When they realised that I spoke Hungarian one of them said, 'Madam, I wouldn't do that.'

'Do what?'

'Go by train.'

'Why ever not?'

'I can see you're not from here,' the grey-haired moustached man said. 'Where are you from?'

The taxi drivers kept looking at me, waiting for the verdict.

'Australia,' I replied and then realised the local translation of what I just said: *Rich!* Too late, our fate was sealed.

'Well, that explains it,' one of the men muttered under his moustache.

'Explains what?'

He said nothing.

'Tell her, Bandy, go on,' the round-faced stout man on his right urged. Bandy obliged.

'Dear Madam, the trains are dangerous, Gypsies will rob you, they might even stab you. You don't know what it's like.'

As my gaze shifted from one man to the other, and there must have been at least half a dozen, each nodded in approval. I did not believe them, but what if they were right?

'It happens all the time. Trust me, Madam, I wouldn't take the train if I were you.'

The men nodded again. I was unconvinced, but what did I know? Twenty-five years had passed since I left that part of the world. Anything seemed possible. So why take risks? I turned to my bewildered family to translate. Whether they believed the stories or not, the prospect of sitting in a warm taxi looked far the best. So I sat next to the driver, Alex and Tamara at the back, and the taxi started eastwards.

We had been driving for hours, my reminiscences interrupted by the driver's worries about the economy, about his children's future, about Hungary. Barely a year had passed since communism had collapsed in 1989.

'Life is hard here, prices are going up and up. Some say it's the transition. Who knows? Who knows anything nowadays?' And he fell silent to contemplate the incomprehensible nowadays.

The wheels of the taxi kept swallowing the miles. The road ahead, flat and straight, chased the horizon in an endless pursuit. The *puszta* (steppe), green and teeming with life in spring, looked desolate that winter without the cover of snow. The contrast to my native land over the border could not have been greater.

Hills, mountains, small rivers making their way noisily among the trees. Romania! *What if something happens? What if they won't let me out?* I reached into my handbag for my Australian passport like an anxious child for her soft toy. I felt its comforting rough covers and started to relax. I would not get stuck in Romania again, I hoped. I hoped, because as irrational as this might sound, that fear had never left me. I zipped up the pocket where the passport was, then the main zipper, folded the top part of the handbag back on itself and clicked it in place. I was lucky, enormously lucky. I could cross borders … I was free.

'I'd better get some petrol soon,' the driver said, unaware of my little crisis. 'Who knows what it's like over there in Romania.'

As he debated with himself where he might get petrol and food, a small shed appeared next to the straight stretch of road which ran into the twilight. Stuck on one of its corners was an oversized sign: *Café*. All around was the unending *puszta*, a perfect scene for a sur-realist painting.

The bell chimed as we opened the door. Inside were three empty tables. Above the counter, bottles and bottles of heavy spirits. I looked for the table closest to a heater. There was no heater. The waitress, a small woman in her mid-twenties, did not seem to feel the cold. She was wearing a miniskirt and high boots. She took our order matter-of-factly, in a way which made it clear that she was there to serve, not to enjoy her job. And since customers meant work, there was no reason why she should be pleasant to them.

The steak turned out delicious, the chips a tad greasy, the pickles divine. My English-born husband couldn't have been more apprecia-tive. Tamara did not mind the food but she did mind going outside to the toilet in the sub-zero temperature.

We returned to the taxi.

The *puszta* had merged with the sky. The border seemed to be further than the driver anticipated and he was in no mood to chat. I was grateful for his silence. On the back seat, Alex and Tamara kept whispering to each other.

I was trying to recall my last meeting with my brother Tom, but the same few images kept displacing all others: my father standing with Tom on the platform, me climbing the stairs to our carriage. The sound of the whistle, the nauseating taste of smoke, the fear that my father would miss the train. My father embracing Tom again, then rushing towards me, Tom left behind, standing on the platform, my father climbing up, panting. The train moving, me and my father at the window, Tom standing in the same place, his image smaller and smaller, Tom a dot, then nothing. My father must have recalled those moments for the rest of his life. The dot turned to nothing, the past turned into the future and he never saw Tom again.

'Good road,' the driver said. 'Not sure about the other side of the border.' The road was still flat as far as we could see.

Suddenly a long queue of cars materialised in front of us. It was the border crossing. The queue seemed frozen, just like our surroundings. Some people stood next to their cars, chatting. We too stepped out to stretch our legs. A couple of hundred metres away was Romania. I was too anxious to have a conversation with anybody.

'Patience,' Alex said, 'patience.'

We got into the car again and jerked along in starts and stops.

'Look!' The driver pointed into the distance. The head of the queue was now in sight. On the right, three militiamen. Militiamen in long dark-blue coats with epaulets and dark-blue caps, the same uniform as when I left a quarter of a century ago, were walking up and down the queue collecting passports. I broke into a sweat. *Keep calm*, I told myself and took a few deep breaths. But I could not help it, the fear was overwhelming.

'What's wrong?' Alex asked.

'Nothing.' I could not explain what I felt. Not in a sentence, not in ten sentences. I wasn't sure a Westerner would understand it anyway, even if that Westerner was my loving husband. Besides, I did not understand it myself. The years of anxiety and dread seemed to have grown roots inside me. Insidiously, without me knowing.

I looked at the militiamen again. 'You need to bribe them,' someone had said to me back in Australia.

'Bribe them, why?' I find the act of putting money in someone's hand, when it's not asked for, when no transaction is taking place, impossible.

'They do expect it,' she said. 'Following the rules, letting one through the border crossing smoothly is in itself an act which deserves gratitude.' Again and again my mind went over everything in my suitcase: my clothes, Tom's presents – singlets, a jumper, salami, cheese. Nothing which could be construed as illegal. The food? No, not in Romania. Nothing illegal, I told myself again. Nothing. But there was still the unforeseeable event, the unpredictable logic, the logic which never made sense in that country. Alex and Tamara seemed blissfully unaware of my turmoil.

A militiaman came to collect our passports. 'There you are,' I said in Romanian and handed mine over. He looked at its cover a moment too long for my comfort, but nodded approvingly. Good start, I thought. He opened the covers and searched for the Romanian visa, looked at it for a while, then his face turned into a frown. 'It's not valid!'

My knees went soft. *Bribe them*, a voice in my head said, *bribe them*. I reached for my purse inside the pocket of my coat, my mind racing: should I put the money in his hand? His hands were busy leafing through my passport. In the pocket! In the pocket of a militiaman? *It's a trick to implicate you*, another voice said. I abandoned the purse and resolved to argue, convince him that he was wrong. Argue with a militiaman? No, never! You keep your head down and shut your mouth. Just do what you're told. I saw myself turning around, the long journey back to Australia. I saw Tom, the Tom of my childhood, waiting for me, checking his watch and waiting. An hour, two, three, waiting for my knock on the door. I couldn't do that, I couldn't let him down.

'What do you mean? Look at the visa: one month!' I pointed it out to the militiaman.

'One month from the date of issue,' he said slowly, emphasising every word. The visa had been issued six weeks ago.

'How could it be from the date of issue?'

As we debated what is a valid visa, a second militiaman arrived. He was courteous. He took my passport and disappeared into the shed. We stood in front of the small covered window, waiting. Behind, loud voices were punctuated by unending stamping. Whatever they were doing seemed to be taking forever. I kept shifting from foot to foot to keep warm, to dissipate the tension.

Finally the polite militiaman emerged from the shed and handed us the passports. Romania had agreed to let us in.

The taxi crossed the border. The road was dotted with potholes. Now and then a car drove past. The villages were sunk in darkness. Here and there a faint light inside a house, then night again. Was this really Romania? Had I forgotten what it was like?

Suddenly three big shadows materialised in front of our headlights, three women walking arm in arm in the middle of the road. Taken aback, the driver turned the steering wheel probably more than he intended, the car landed in a pothole and swerved sharply to one side. Shaken, he cursed the women, Romania and taxi driving. In the next villages more women appeared and disappeared in our headlights. Like ghosts.

The road smoothed over. We started climbing the Western foothills of the Carpathians. A few snowflakes met our headlights, then more and more. It was well and truly snowing. The surroundings were sunk in darkness. But in my mind's eye I saw my memories, the white mountains, a few wooden houses, thin smoke leaving the chimneys and trickling up into the air, scenery I have not seen anywhere else in the world. Not the pretty landscape of the Swiss Alps – the houses in my memory were not the fairytale sort, but soulful and moving, like an old woman's sad life. And yet, how I loved that scenery and how much I longed to see it again.

The driver stopped talking; he must have been tired. I hoped that he would have the stamina to take us to our destination and make it back home.

The road widened. A few houses flew past and then the sign *To Cluj*. The back seat had fallen silent but I was not going to initiate a conversation, not now.

It was past nine when we entered the city. The streets were frozen. A few lights in the centre of the town, then darkness. I was back in the Romania of my youth. Surrounded by dark buildings, I had an overwhelming feeling of being observed and listened to, of having to be careful what I said to the driver. The old communist Romania. But I knew it wasn't. Those were only emotions, which needed to be controlled.

The communist dictatorship had collapsed the year before. Ceausescu was dead, executed. We in the West had witnessed the ultimate proof: his body and his wife's, lying like rag dolls next to a concrete wall. Those of us who had once lived under that regime had to reassure ourselves that this was not a dream, nor Western propaganda. As impossible as such an event had seemed even a year before, it was real. Romania had shaken off the so-called communist regime. As I watched the news, I recalled my own transformation: a person who had never had a bank account, written a cheque or competed for a job, to someone tempted by choices and pulled around by market forces. Sure, there was everything in the West: jobs I could not get, cheques I could have written if I had the money in the bank, freedom to say anything but nobody would listen, open borders to travel but no money or time for it. In the end it all worked out somehow, but it took decades. Millions of Eastern Europeans would have to go through the same transition. It frightened me. I was twenty years old and full of energy and hope when I escaped the communist jail. I saw the neon lights of the West, the shop windows full of such abundance they took my breath away. But they, the millions of Romanians, had not escaped to a new world – they had to build it.

Romania was not the first country to break with the communist utopia. Hungary did it beforehand. It all happened suddenly. I can still remember the celebration in Double Bay in Sydney. Our favourite coffee shop owner, a refugee from Hungary, laid out a twenty-metre-long apple strudel in the street, free for anyone who wanted to celebrate the incredible event. A strudel running from the beginning of Knox Lane to the end of Cross Street in Double Bay was just as incredible as the dismantling of the Iron Curtain between

Austria and Hungary. You could be forgiven for thinking you were dreaming.

But now I was in Cluj. I got out of the taxi to ask for directions. Oh how good the winter felt! The snow, the cold air prickling my face, the sight of my breath condensing. I had not felt so alive for decades.

The young man whom I asked for directions seemed reluctant to tell me the shortest way to my address, but when I switched from Romanian into Hungarian he was more than helpful. The old Hungarian-Romanian divide seemed more pronounced than ever.

I pointed out to the driver which way to go. He turned into a major street and came to a stop in front of an official-looking three-storey baroque building. A private residence? I checked the address on the back of the envelope again. The address was correct, this was our destination. I paid the taxi driver his well-earned two hundred dollars and wished him an easy border crossing on the way back. My heart was too big for my chest as we climbed the steps leading to the huge heavy doors and I rang the bell.

I had not seen Tom for twenty-five years. We did not even correspond. Not until five months ago, when I sent him my first letter. As I dropped the letter into the red letterbox outside the Lane Cove post office in Sydney, I was overcome with a feeling of contentment. Where did it come from? What was going on? Was I reaching out to my roots? My brother? Was I reconnecting with my past which I had been so determined to erase? My native land? Nobody ever told me that you cannot turn physical distance into emotional one, you cannot forget your native country, you cannot give up your mother tongue. It deadens you inside. I always suspected but never fully realised what was happening to me. Until I posted that letter.

My spirits high, I waited for an answer. Day after day I drove home full of anticipation. But when I opened the letterbox I found only bills and advertising. A few weeks, a month, two months passed. There is still hope, I kept encouraging myself, but endless questions popped up in my mind, questions I did not dare to answer. Is he alive? Does he want to write to me? Why would he, after so many years?

Three months later Tom's answer arrived, by surface mail. Inside was a one-page, matter-of-fact letter: I am still working in a school, still a nightwatchman. Romanians are still poor ... I had expected more. But did I have the right? An invisible barrier, a quarter of a century of silence stood between us.

The reasons I had not written to him were many. My parents sent him letters from Israel and at first I added a few lines. Then I stopped. I was too busy with survival, first in Israel, then in Australia.

Years later I sat down to write, to explain my silence. Nothing I wrote conveyed the full story. So I gave up. Besides, I did not want to cause him trouble. The Ceausescu regime seemed vicious. Communication with Westerners related or unrelated could have been interpreted as untrustworthiness or worse. It all depended how much they wanted to persecute you. Life took over again, but Tom was never far from my thoughts. I missed him, I missed our times together.

The weeks passed and I was coming closer and closer to a resolution. We were planning to visit my mother in Israel. Maybe we could take an additional week and visit Tom. A month later I sent him a letter announcing the date of our arrival and we left before his answer arrived ...

So there we are, standing in front of the big door of an official building, waiting. Waiting for Tom to turn the key, the door to open and him to stand in front of me. But will he? What if someone else opens the door, someone who hasn't got a clue who Tom is? What will we do next? In Cluj, in the dark, among strangers, without a hotel room and no taxis in sight? What if the taxi driver's stories are true? Exhausted, my emotions keep bouncing from fear to hope, from fear that Tom is not there to hope that he will appear any minute, wondering whether he is waiting for us, or has forgotten that we are coming. *What if he does not want to see me?*

'Look.' Tamara pointed to a window with a dim light.

I pressed the bell again and waited. And then I heard the key turning. The big iron door crept back slowly. A small woman stood in front of us.

'Are you from Australia?'

'Yes,' I burst out.

She looked at me as if she had just seen a miracle and crossed herself three times. 'My God, I am so glad you're here. He's been so restless, he's waiting for you upstairs.'

Inside, enormous ceilings were supported by thick ornate Parthenon-like marble columns which stood in the freezing temperature. The cold of a crypt. There was a musty smell, a communist school smell. My guide switched on an odd light as we climbed endless stairs in the semi-darkness. At the top of the third floor she knocked on the only door. It was not locked and as the door retreated, a dim light shone on the high forehead, the receding hairline, the well-shaped nose with the round tip, the nose I always envied. My father's profile was resting on a much shorter man. He was clearing the table and putting something in his back pocket.

It all looked surreal, remote, as if I was watching someone on a stage. He lifted his eyes, turned towards me and took a couple of steps in my direction. The familiar limp, the awkward right hand. It was Tom. The Tom I remembered, the same short man, about five feet five, two inches shorter than me. His chest looked somewhat too big for his height. Or was it the knitted vest?

I didn't notice when the woman left or whether she closed the door. I was busy introducing my family, making sure that they were comfortable with each other. That turned out easier than I anticipated. In no time we were all talking. It was a two-way conversation with me in the middle translating. But exhaustion was catching up with me, words were evading me, in English, in Hungarian. It had been a long, long day.

Eventually Alex and Tamara turned to each other for company while Tom and I kept talking, talking as if I had never been away.

Tom lived alone in a flat in the top floor of the school, a converted corridor which betrayed its origin, long and narrow with enormously high ceilings, wall units full of books, paintings and more paintings, Persian carpets and photographs. He was a night watchman and read a lot. He seemed content. His fridge was empty but that did not seem to bother him.

I told him about us. Briefly. Some of it he knew from my first letter. I told him about my work as a scientist. He listened and smiled. He seemed proud of me.

That week in Cluj it snowed and snowed. On the street, pairs of women walking arm in arm, men, nearly all smoking, overtook us. An odd car drove past. The street went quiet again. Just like twenty-five years ago. But for Tamara who grew up in Australia under the big expanses of blue sky and sunshine, this world was new, the low grey clouds oppressive.

The sight of rows and rows of empty shelves in the supermarket which had only packets of dry mushrooms, biscuits and wine, one type of each, was something Alex would recall for years. When he suggested we buy some wine, Tom warned us: 'It probably tastes of vinegar.' So we walked out, my purse intact.

Around the corner people were queuing. 'Excuse me, dear Madam, what's for sale here?' Tom asked the woman at the end of the queue. 'Eggs, Sir, only eggs.' We joined in. Half an hour later and in possession of eight eggs, we walked on.

On our arrival I had changed five hundred dollars. The five hundred dollars converted into a briefcase full of Romanian notes. It looked like the proceeds from a bank robbery in a movie. But there was nothing to spend it on. We left it with Tom.

This was the world of my youth. Empty fridge, empty shops, cold school corridors. Romania of twenty-five years ago was frozen in time. But there had been a change, an important change: the fear had vanished.

We did have a white Christmas. We muddled through with minimum food. The lack of a common language was no longer a problem. Tom spoke Hungarian to Alex and he replied in English to his gesticulations. From time to time I stepped in to translate. The conversation with Tamara was somewhat easier. She cannot speak Hungarian but she understands some words.

Our short visit was coming to an end. I had learnt a lot about Tom, but we did not share any deep truths. He did not tell me about how life had really been for him all those years and I only told him facts about my life. We had had no contact for a quarter of a century. We needed to start trusting each other again, trusting each other enough to open up. We needed time.

The day before our departure we queued in the snow at the station to buy our train tickets to Budapest. We stood and waited like penguins minding their precious eggs on their feet. People kept chatting and before long, everybody knew that we were from Australia and I was Tom's sister. And I knew how many children and grandchildren the woman next to me had, where they lived and what they did for a living. We discussed the value of the dollar and what one can buy for a dollar in Romania. A lot, it seemed.

More than two hours later, we had the train tickets and headed back to Tom's place.

The snow was falling. Alex and Tamara were walking behind me. Tom was limping by my side, talking. And I realised how much I loved being with him. How much I loved being there, speaking my native tongue, meeting the teachers, the gatekeepers and cleaners in the school. They were friendly and unassuming, easy to talk to. I enjoyed the freedom of not being constantly sold to, of being able to cross a street not hassled by cars.

I realised that part of me still belonged there, to that land with its people. It had survived twenty-five years of denial, it had survived my merciless battle with myself to assimilate in two other countries. I would not bury it again. I would be back, I promised Tom and myself, as we boarded the train.

Part III

War the matchmaker

8

It was 2002 and I was on the way to Cluj again, to visit Tom.

After my visit in 1990, we had been back twice but only for short stays, on the way to Israel to visit my ageing mother. This time I was there alone.

I wanted no distractions; I wanted to get to know my brother again, to demolish the twenty-five years of separation which still stood between us like a wall of tangled weeds.

We did correspond. Infrequently. I wrote to him about my daughter, my husband and my work, he sent me one-page answers about politics, prices and the latest joke. He claimed he was well, the country less so.

Below my plane the rooftops of Transylvania slid heedlessly in and out of view. Men, women and children. Lives and history.

'I thought Transylvania is a mythical place,' a colleague said to me before I left.

Mythical place? Her words played against the long history of the world below me, the ancient Dacians who once lived there, the Romans who fought them in bloody battle, the Huns, the Visigoths and other barbarians whose names I could not quite remember. They came, fought, pillaged, and sooner or later moved on. The Magyars did not move on; they arrived in the tenth century and settled.

Through the following thousand years there were more invasions and 'liberations'. In the twentieth century, willingly or unwillingly, the country below me hosted the Austro-Hungarians, the Germans and the Russians. I thought of all those who lost their lives fighting there, those whose bodies fertilised the soil. Bram Stoker's mythical land could not have been more real for them. Or for all those who, like my father, lived through it all, worked, married, brought up children and kept hoping for a peaceful life. And as I reflected on all that, my plane landed.

It was early afternoon. Outside a pale sun shone tired and lifeless. I felt edgy. I always do when I am about to meet relatives I have not seen for years. Five years had passed since I last saw Tom.

So here we go again, I said to myself, and grabbed my suitcase from the only luggage belt in the small arrival hall. My heart was pounding. Above the exit, the clock pointed to 3:30 p.m. I had written to Tom that I would be landing at 1:30. Heavens above, he must have been waiting for two hours. If he does come. If he is well enough.

But there he was.

His face lit up as I emerged. I apologised for mixing up the times. He waved his hand dismissively. 'No problem, my dear, I'm no Westerner. My time is not money,' and he reciprocated my kiss unconvincingly. He was not a physically demonstrative person. Well, not with me. He looked thinner, slightly greyer, but essentially unchanged since my last visit.

Outside, in front of the arrival hall, parallel rows of old taxis were waiting for passengers, and as we tried to locate the head of the queue an enterprising driver opened the door of his taxi. 'Please.' He pointed to the back seat. He was a taxi driver-cum political commentator, and before long I was informed that the country was going down the gurgler and the communists were still in power. 'Under a different name, of course. A bunch of charlatans, dear Madam!'

Tom sat quietly smiling.

'Socialism? Capitalism? Which one is better?' I asked.

'They're all the same, dear Madam, just different ways of robbery. So one or the other,' he paused to change lanes, 'I couldn't care less. They wash over eventually.'

Political systems washed over the Samuel Brassai School building too, the century-old building where Tom lived. It had belonged to the Unitarian Church before the communists came to power, was appropriated by the socialist state and returned to the church again after the regime collapsed. There was religion, there was Marxism, and then religion again.

Stairs and more stairs led to Tom's residence. 'One hundred and seven to my door,' he informed me. Marble stairs, worn and polished by a century of service. Some sloping down more than I would have found comfortable on a wet day, but on that day it was not raining and Tom was going up confidently, proud to be able to conquer them at his age. But halfway up he stopped to rest his bad leg.

'God bless,' a student of about twelve said as he walked past, and whether it was the sound of my mother tongue, or he really meant what he said, his words triggered in me a sudden warmth for that school with its tall marble columns, its worn stairs and its modest young students.

Tom's flat seemed unchanged. The same furniture, the same carpets, the same cigarette smell. A miniature Buddha and two Chinese figurines sat on one of the bookshelves. The Far East had arrived in Romania.

Tom headed for the kitchen to put the kettle on. I unpacked my hand luggage, the tape recorder and the chocolates, and went to join him.

On the way, behind the floral cotton curtain which divided the lounge room part of his long and narrow flat from the bathroom, there was a novelty, a one-metre-wide Formica cupboard. And before I got the chance to ask what that incongruous piece of furniture was doing there – incongruous because everything else in Tom's flat was old and made of wood, Tom was back. He opened the door to the Formica cupboard and disappeared inside.

I was looking at his books on ancient civilisation when suddenly the sound of a flushing toilet reverberated from behind the Sumerians, the Hittites, the Etruscans, the Greeks and the Romans. Tom stepped out of the cupboard, a big smile on his face.

'It was installed three months ago.' And to the accompaniment of the filling cistern he declared, 'I am now the proud owner of a toilet. I have gone up in the world.'

'Brilliant,' I replied and held his gaze, but all I could see were my two bathrooms in Sydney. I tried not to blush.

It had taken three decades, but Tom's excursions up and down the one hundred and seven steps in the middle of the night were finally over.

At long last, a strong smell of coffee filled the flat. Tom put the cups on a tray, I added the chocolates, picked up the tray and headed for the small room at the back.

'Careful with those cups! They're for special occasions.' Something I could not quite pinpoint made me think that there were few of those, if any.

We tried to catch up on the years since my last visit. Tom asked about Alex and Tamara, but I couldn't help noticing that what he was really curious about was our Israeli family: my mother Roza, his stepmother, and our younger brother Yossi. The family which had nothing to do with him. He remained stubbornly interested in them. It was his childhood family.

We had been there before, on my previous visit. Sooner or later, Tom's enquiries about our family came to a dead end, a wall of silence which one day would have to be overcome. But it looked like that day had not arrived. Tom grabbed a cigarette and went out for a smoke.

I stood up to explore, to find out more about Tom. Most single men's residences look as if they are waiting for a woman to turn them into a home. Not Tom's. The furnishings, the rich colours did not speak of a man uninterested in his surroundings. Or of neglect. His flat felt like a home. Not a home suffused with the cosy smells of cooking, but a shelter from the outside world, a place for thinking and cogitating, a place where Tom could find solace among his hundreds of books, the paintings and the photographs.

As I surveyed his books, I felt as if someone was watching me. It was the photograph above the chest of drawers. A young woman in her late twenties, perhaps early thirties, was looking at me over her shoulder. Radiantly happy, big smile, perfect teeth, wavy shoulder-length hair 1930s style. She was wearing a clinging blouse or dress, impossible to say as only her top half was visible. I had seen that photo before – I remembered it well. It was Hella, Tom's mother. But the one next to it, her with a man, was a surprise. They were smiling and so very happy. He had a big crop of dark hair, a high forehead and dark brown eyes. He was looking at her, smitten with love. My father?

Below there was another photograph, a much younger Hella, maybe twenty years old, in a glamorous long wrap-around dress. The black and white photograph did not give much away, but the dress of that young woman might have been made of royal blue or ink navy brocade, or some other heavy rich material embroidered with golden threads. An actress? She looked far too serious, a young woman deep in thought.

My eye returned to the first photograph, and as I contemplated the metamorphosis of the young woman into the older one, I got a strange feeling that she was happy that I came, that I was there with her son Tom, my half-brother. I often refer to Tom as my half-brother. Half? Not really. Tom is my brother, no halves involved.

Something was not right though … I felt a sense of loss akin to pain. I recalled a photograph of my father with my own mother. He was older, pensive. My mother seemed happy, sort of. But my father? And as I stood there contemplating Hella with my father, I couldn't help thinking that in front of me, in that photograph, was a man I had never known. A man in love, a man besotted with that young woman.

I tried to concentrate on the titles in the bookshelf opposite, but ripples of sadness kept washing over me. I returned to look at the photos again.

The door slammed behind me. 'Old photos,' Tom said as he walked past.

Not for me, I thought. Not for me.

I felt tired. Emotionally. The meeting with Tom, the meeting with my parents' reality – not entirely new to me but it was the first time that I had seen the irrefutable proof. And there was something else. I had left Vienna that morning, the city where my father spent some of his young years, and every time I leave that city I feel as if I say goodbye to what he once loved. I feel as if I say goodbye to a part of him again.

I needed to clear my head. I needed a walk. Tom was happy to join me.

Tom used to wear a built-up shoe on his right foot, but today he was wearing sneakers and walked slowly and unevenly. He walked on his left foot and on a third of his right, the front part, his heel an inch or two above the ground and turned outward far more than the left.

Everybody overtook us. And as people walked past, I heard Hungarian, I heard Romanian, and with Tom limping by my side, I felt suddenly at home.

———

A week later, Tom and I were no longer talking about politics and prices; we were wholly immersed in the past. He seemed to be opening up; he was beginning to trust me.

'I don't think so,' I contradicted him on why he was left behind in Romania. Our recollections were diverging, the interpretation of events becoming partisan. It was his mother Hella against my mother. It was the mother he only knew from the photographs against the one who taught him to walk, to read and write, and who lost her temper easily. As she did with all of us.

Hella remained the beautiful woman in the photograph. War, communism, poverty, nothing could dim the radiant smile on her face. She cheated them all, she made her sad exit before they claimed their place on the stage of history. And before age would demand its dues.

I grew up surrounded by her furniture, her lampshades, her sculpted figurines. Everything connected to her was unusual and beautiful: the clothes she left behind which I wore on occasions made me the envy of the town, the heavily carved black furniture stopped people in their tracks with admiration. Her figurines, like the rotund balding man wearing an orange coat, head tilted to one side to avoid the big matronly bosom of his wife, made me smile every time I looked at them. I treasured her fine lace which lay on the black lounge room table at times. As a child I dreamed of being a princess every time I sat on her brocade upholstered chairs and looked in the Venetian mirror. Hella, the mystery woman who died so young, was omnipresent in my life. Tom was unaware of this. I never told him and I don't know if I ever will. Why? Because the current status feels just right. I feel as if I have stolen parts of his mother. In a strange way she is part of me too.

She was everything my mother, Roza, was not. On that point I had to agree with Tom.

'There's no hiding it, she was a peasant girl,' Tom said about my mother matter-of-factly. 'She married my father to go up in the world.'

I didn't know what to say, so I remained quiet.

'My father was rich. He was educated. And she wanted status,' he added.

Our conversation was starting to make me uncomfortable. I happened to be the daughter of that uneducated, status-thirsty woman with no redeeming features. I tried to stay calm and clear my mind. The reasons people marry are complex enough, but the reasons my mother, a twenty-three-year-old refugee from Hungary, married my father, a widower with a small handicapped child in wartime Europe, would be far more complex than either of us could imagine or will ever know. But I was not prepared to argue with Tom, not on that topic. His mind seemed made up, the conclusion final, as immutable as the laws of nature.

I wondered whether Tom still saw his mother as the young woman in the photograph or if she aged in his imagination. Could he imagine her face wrinkled by disappointments and struggle? I couldn't. Wrinkles were inconceivable on her; they were incompatible with her sunny smile. I took another look at her photograph with my father. I was nearly over my first reaction. I no longer begrudged his love for her, but I felt that he had lavished on her all the love of women he was capable of. There was not much left for my mother, Roza. I felt sorry for her. She had been cheated by life. In some ways I felt short-changed too. I was not the offspring of two people who loved each other, I was the offspring of necessity and compromise. Probably like most people on this planet, but I couldn't help wondering how it would have felt being the child of two people madly in love with each other.

Still, I was enthralled by this woman whose existence had affected our lives. I wanted to know more about her and I wanted to understand my father's loss. I was in luck. Tom was in storytelling mood. We sat and sipped coffee late into the night while Tom recounted their story, his eyes fixed somewhere beyond me, or maybe into the far-away past as the tale of his mother and our father gradually unfolded. And as he told the story of our father, Stefan, I remembered the stories my mother had told me. I also recalled some of my father's musings on our long walks, or at the dinner table, musings about Comandau where he spent his childhood, and about Vienna in the 1920s.

Tom's voice was warm and soothing. His words rolled out slowly as if he was breathing life into those long-gone years. And as I sat there among books and old photographs I saw my father, on that September day, a lanky young man, waiting on the platform in the small station of Comandau.

Next to him is his father nervously smoking his pipe, and his two unusually quiet sisters. A breeze ruffles the young man's disorderly hair as he looks at the autumn leaves of the oak trees opposite spiralling to the ground. A whistle, and soon a small locomotive with one carriage appears from behind the hill and fusses into the station.

Hurriedly, the young man kisses his teenage sisters, hugs his father and jumps on. Another whistle and the train starts rolling. With a heavy heart Stefan watches his waving father and sisters disappear into the distance. Moments later Comandau, the small settlement where he spent his childhood, the stories and the secrets, vanish inside the pine forest. And so does the grave of his mother whom he lost when he was fourteen years old.

'Not one day passed without me thinking about her,' he confided in me when he was seventy-one years old. I couldn't believe my ears. I realised how little I knew him.

When the train left Comandau, that autumn of 1922, Stefan must have felt apprehensive but excited. The long journey to Vienna had begun. A new life was waiting for him. Little did he know that Vienna would not only turn him into a civil engineer, but would change his life forever.

Four years had passed since the end of the Great War, the First World War. The Habsburgs were gone. Austria had lost a big part of its territory. The economy was struggling. Unemployment was high. Chauvinism and fascism were popular, especially outside Vienna. In Vienna, 'Red Vienna' as it was called at the time, the left-wing Social Democratic Party of Austria was in power. But not all Viennese were left-wing; there were plenty of fascists at work.

One day, not long after Stefan arrived in Vienna, hooligans hurtled into the lecture theatre throwing chairs and screaming: 'Jews out!' Many students abandoned their seats and ran to the door. Young men who, like Stefan, were in Vienna to evade Hungarian anti-Semitism and racial laws (the Numerus Clausus Act which set quotas on the number of Jewish students in Hungarian universities), realised that they had not escaped vicious anti-Semitism, they had not gone to a far enough country. In Vienna – once the cultural hub of Europe, the city where philosophy flourished, where one could hear the greatest music, where psychology was born – many people were as backward and anti-Semitic as the illiterate peasants of the Dark Ages.

That evening, the deaf Jewish landlady encouraged him at the top of her voice: 'It'll pass, anti-Semitism always bubbles up when people are not doing well.' And at the time people were doing badly.

Stefan was not sure about engineering. He wanted to be a journalist, but his father Ludovic would not hear of it. 'A man needs a profession so he can provide for a family. If you love writing, you can always write in your spare time.' But I doubt that he had any spare time that first year in Vienna. He had no spare anything. On Ludovic's allowance and with little German, Vienna was a hard, unforgiving city. And a politically polarised city, with left- and right-wing parties, each with a considerable following.

Tom took out a cigarette and held it between his tobacco stained fingers.

'My father befriended a number of left-wing students. No mere left-wingers, but students who were seriously involved in politics. Those were probably the roots of his left-wing leanings.'

I wanted to ask him not to smoke inside but I didn't want to interrupt; I might never get him back to this mood, to this rhythm, to his total involvement in the story as if something precious depended on it. His place in society? He kept describing to me all the events with their details, even those he knew I knew. And then he moved to philosophy and Wittgenstein. I tried to make him focus. I wanted to know how Hella and Stefan met. I wanted to move from philosophy to love, from Wittgenstein to Hella.

'They met at a fancy dress ball,' Tom said with a smile.

A friend took him. My introvert father had to be dragged along. As he entered the ballroom his eyes caught sight of this small Gypsy woman waltzing with a man twice her height, her feet barely touching the floor. My mother was a sort of dancer by profession, a dancer and a gymnast. Next to her twirled the queens and kings, the wolves and the cats. My father stood and watched. Eventually he worked up his courage and asked her for a dance. And now the story gets better.

Tom smiled his biggest smile.

A few weeks after the ball, my young father, wearing a shoelace in place of a tie as a protest against the rich of the world, rang the doorbell to my mother's home. A butler opened the door and asked him in. My father walked through the hall and emerged in this huge room, crystal chandeliers hanging from high above, beautiful furniture, opulent furnishings, paintings and works of art. He had been in Vienna for nearly two years but he was still a country bumpkin, though no stranger to nice surroundings. As you know, my father's father, Grandpa Ludovic, was well off. But my mother's parents, the Reiners, were of a different ilk. My grandfather was a banker, my grandmother a socialite.

'And his socialist views?'

'Socialist? Capitalist?' Tom shrugged his shoulders. 'He had fallen in love.'

Love which does not know boundaries, love which makes the socialist fall for the banker's daughter, the engineer for the dancer, love with all its highs, took hold of Stefan.

True, my grandparents were still rich at the time, but none of the offspring had the slightest interest in making money. They were artists. One was a painter, another a puppeteer, the third a sculptor; and as you know, my mother was a bit of everything. But there was something else too. My grandmother was a Christian, my grandfather was a Jew. They were both secular. Who was what, was not an issue.

As I listened to Tom I could not help noticing that he never said *our* father, as if I haven't quite made it, as if I was not quite the sister. As if we belonged to different families.

A few years later, in 1929 during the financial crisis, the fortunes of the Reiners took a turn for the worse. They lost their wealth. Their social life dwindled. Grandfather Reiner spent his life studying Chinese and my grandmother became sickly. But in the mid-twenties, their life was still good.

And my parents? If one's life is the result of the battle between good and evil, like the Zoroastrians believe, at the time good must have been ruling their lives. When my father had time they went to the opera on cheap tickets, standing room only, they went to lectures, museums, walks in the Prater. They went skiing in the winter. A perfect life, if you ask me, but evil was lurking in the shadows.

Art galleries? Walks in the Prater? Didn't we do just that, my father and I in 1965? We were in transit to Israel. It was spring in Vienna that day. The sun shone as we walked under the chestnut trees towards the big wheel in the Prater. Above us, an unending canopy of fresh leaves. My father must have been there many times with Hella, but he never mentioned her name to me, not then, not ever. It did not occur to me to ask how he felt coming back to that city nearly four decades later. Hella dead, the Jewish community decimated and he penniless on the way to a new country at the age of sixty-one with a second family.

With the pocket money given to us in the transit camp, we took a ride in the big wheel of the Prater and watched the buildings coming and going, stretching as far we could see, far into the horizon. From time to time my father would say, 'Over there is the Opera and there are the Schönburg gardens. Can you see that building next to the green cupola? It's the Politechnic where I studied, and not far from there is the Kunsthistorisches (Art History) Museum.' He knew the city so well.

We dropped into the museum. He showed me a few Peter Breughel paintings. I can still remember the delight on his face as he looked at those busy villages throbbing with life. (Ever since, every time I look at a Breughel painting I remember that day in Vienna and the smile on my father's face.)

On the way back to the train station we passed beautiful cafés, just looking in as we had no money to look out from such places. But I did not care, I was walking with my father on the streets of Vienna, past beautiful baroque buildings, churches and exquisite flower shops. I was in heaven. But how did my father feel? He must have thought of Hella. How could he have not? And he must have thought of Tom too, Tom his eldest son who was left behind the Iron Curtain.

'Three years later,' Tom interrupted my memories of that day, 'my parents married and settled in Transylvania, in Brasov.

> Brasov, a Saxon town with a large German-speaking population, high up in the mountains was an idyllic place to start married life. Grandfather Ludovic bought them a big house. When it came to ensuring that his son and daughters got a good start in life, he was very generous. Of course it was also the temper of the time, it was what the wealthy did. And Ludovic was wealthy. A self-made smart man. And a character, as you surely know.

A character? I never got to know him, I was the offspring of the wrong woman. But I had heard some of the stories. Sent by his religious parents to do rabbinical studies, Ludovic had a revelation on the road to Budapest: he had not heard God's calling – the only calling he heard was that of civil engineering. Five years later he was a civil engineer and had married a beautiful woman. Soon after, the couple moved to Transylvania and settled in Comandau where there was a major logging enterprise. The company needed roads, railways and bridges, it needed a good civil engineer, it needed Ludovic. Comandau made him rich. But life in the wild forests of Comandau was not for his wife. She became more and more depressed And one day she was no more. It was the end of the First World War. The families who survived the war unscathed rejoiced. But Ludovic and his teenage children were in deep mourning.

Whether it was love, desperation or pragmatism, a year or so later Ludovic took his young son for a walk and told him that he was going to marry his sister-in-law, barely ten years older than Stefan. The family re-established, Ludovic returned to his engineering and business affairs with even more energy. By the time Stefan and his young wife Hella arrived in Brasov, Ludovic was a very wealthy man.

> My mother arrived in Brasov with a wagon full of furniture, paintings, brocades, laces and Persian carpets. She set up

a beautiful house. She opened a school for dancing and rhythmic gymnastics. Everybody adored her. She became a daughter to my grandfather, a sister to my aunts and their husbands and even to my step-grandmother.

Tom kept talking, but I lost concentration. My mind was stuck on what he had just said: 'Everybody adored her.' They did not adore my mother, they didn't even make her welcome. Why?

'During the summer holidays, my mother was off to see her parents and to enjoy Vienna,' Tom interrupted my internal monologue.

After the financial crisis in 1929, Vienna was no longer the big attraction it had been. Sometimes she went to visit her sister, the painter who lived in Egypt. The sister who fell in love with the Middle Eastern light and the languid pace of life and settled there.

A couple of months later, a tanned Hella was back, renewed and happy, with shells, starfish, paintings and rings with mounted fossilised insects. But the world was far from renewing itself. It was going backward. Backward towards another world war. Grey clouds were gathering over Europe. In Germany Hitler became the Chancellor. In 1938 German soldiers marched into Austria. The persecution of the Jews started, expropriation of their properties, beatings, arrests. And then a ray of sunshine cut through the terrible darkness of the daily bad news. Hella was expecting a child. Stefan was ecstatic. Even Germany's annexation of Austria took a back seat for a short while. He believed that things would get better. They could not possibly get worse. Tom continued his story.

My mother went into labour in October, three weeks earlier than expected. My father was away on business, but the arrangements had been made months before. The doctor to preside over the birth was in place. It was made clear to him that when the time came, nothing should be spared to give my mother the best possible medical care.

Three doctors were at her bedside. The labour was difficult. Hours and more hours passed. She kept struggling. Eventually the doctors decided to pull me out. Not long after, she breathed her last as the three doctors looked on.

'My father arrived back in Brasov and headed straight to the hospital,' Tom said pensively, looking past me as if I wasn't there, as if I did not exist. Then he turned his gaze towards me and stood up. 'That's how it was.'

Ludovic, always the rational man, took charge. There in the hospital was a motherless baby. The baby was beautiful. He was called Tom, as his mother had wished. Two nurses, both German-speaking to preserve Tom's mother tongue, were immediately employed. The doctor visited every day to check on his progress. Weeks went by. Tom was difficult to feed, he had trouble swallowing his milk. The nurses force-fed him. Tom screamed. The doctors concluded Tom had been damaged during the forceps delivery. How damaged was he? Nobody knew. Stefan was shattered. Ludovic urged him to concentrate on his work. Everything which could have been done had been done.

And so the dancer was dead. Her son would never know the joys of dancing, or even of walking with ease. For a few years he would not even be able to walk. Tom went on:

> According to Aunt Anna, a year or so later, my father came to the conclusion that when it comes to major problems, doctors can't do much. Let's face it, they couldn't do anything for me and they couldn't do anything for my mother. I think it crystallised his attitude towards the medical profession for the rest of his life. He used to say: 'Out of ten sick people one dies naturally, one is killed by the doctor and eight are cured by nature anyway.' It was probably true in those times.
>
> Medicine failed but engineering might find a solution, he decided. Every evening he sat down at his desk to design shoes, braces, walking chairs. Something might start me walking. He sat drawing and calculating into the small hours. The chairs were built, the shoes were made, but nothing helped.

'This wretched leg,' said Tom pointing to his bad leg, 'was useless.'

I listened to Tom, but my thoughts were far away. I could not stop the flood of images: my father looking at his little son, Hella's smile on his face, sitting in a chair asking for toys he could not reach. Or his pain at the sight of small children running around with a freedom Tom would never have. Mourning for Hella. Alone.

The night was lifting as Tom reached the end of his parents' story. And I thought of my mother's story, amazed how the two converged.

9

By the end of 1940, the Second World War was raging. Germany had incorporated Austria, invaded Poland, Denmark and Norway, and had attacked Western Europe. The Battle of Britain was in full swing. In November Romania, where Stefan lived, joined the countries which had aligned themselves with Germany, the Axis. But Stefan had other worries too: two-year-old Tom still could not walk.

While Stefan was fretting about Tom, three hundred kilometres to the north-west, in the hills of Northern Transylvania, a young woman, Roza, was thinking of running away, escaping her small village, Jidovitza – 'the village of the Jew'. In August 1940 Northern Transylvania, and with it the tiny village of Jidovitza, had been taken from Romania by the Germans and awarded to Hungary, a pro-fascist and fiercely anti-Semitic country. Three months later Hungary too joined the Axis.

Life in Jidovitza used to be simple. The men prayed, the women cooked, gossiped and had children. They had as many children as God blessed them with. 'We were poor. Nearly everybody in Jidovitza was poor,' my mother told me at times. 'Most children didn't have shoes; they walked barefoot from spring to autumn.'

Most children? Did she? I wondered, but did not ask.

Roza liked talking about Jidovitza before the war, but not about the poverty. She was ashamed. She hinted that she might have been one of those children without shoes, but never actually said so.

'My father was a very religious man. He was a clerk in the council, either part-time or nearly full-time, depending on how much work there was. But he never missed an important prayer. Early every morning, he took his velvet bag with his prayer shawl and went to the synagogue. Late on Friday afternoons and on Saturdays he went to the synagogue again.'

Her father, my grandfather Josef. A few years ago his framed photograph appeared on my mother's display cabinet in Israel. From where? I have no idea. A man with a hat, a short beard and a slight twinkle in his eyes. No such photograph exists of my grandmother.

'My mother was a tiny woman,' Roza told me often. 'She wouldn't have reached my shoulder. She gave birth to thirteen children. Can you imagine, thirteen childbirths in those times? There was Ella and Izso and Adolf and Riza and Eszti and Luiza and Jacob and Fani and ...'

She would nearly always get stuck and start again, and as she added a name to the list she added another finger to her count. 'Yes, Ilona and Dora and me, the youngest of them all. The other two died soon after birth. And with all those children she still managed to earn some money. She sold what she could, soup, *tuica* (plum brandy), whatever she could make or could resell for a profit. A tiny profit. You didn't make much money out of peasants, they were poor too. They stopped at our house for a drink or for soup, on their way to Bistritza or to Nasaud. If not for my mother's extra takings, we would have starved. And while she cooked or served the peasants, my older sisters looked after the younger ones, me and Dora.'

Roza's brothers went to the *Cheder* to study religion. By 1940 they had all grown up, married and moved away. They found work, one of them set up a business.

'My father never stopped thanking God for his sons' luck,' said Roza, shrugging her shoulders. 'Well, that is what he did, that is how he saw it.' But Roza did not see it that way. She loved tradition, she enjoyed religious celebrations, but she blamed religion for the family's lack of education. '*Cheder?* she would ask. 'Is that education?

'Apart from the two of us, Dora and me, all the girls were married and had moved away. They came for the High Holidays, Rosh

Hashanah and Yom Kippur. And they came every time they fell out with their husbands. Ella and her six children were forever with us. Eventually she left her philandering husband, a beautiful man, a cantor with a strong tenor voice. He and the famous Joseph Schmidt sang together once in the synagogue. Anyway, when Ella went to the rabbi to complain about her husband's affairs, hoping that the rabbi would talk to him, the rabbi said: "He had six children with you? So what are you complaining about?"

'I loved the High Holidays at home. On Passover night I was the one who asked the question: *"Ma nishtana ha-laila ha-zeh mi-kol ha-leilot?* (Why is this night different from all the other nights?)" I was the youngest. Next to me sat Dora, a year older than me, then the others in order of their age more or less, and later when they married, they came with their families. We always clowned around and laughed. The Pollaks could laugh.'

True, my mother could laugh until tears rolled down her cheeks.

'By 1940, Dora and I were still single. We did have suitors, Christians. One of them, a handsome young man, wanted to marry me. He was a good man. My parents went into debt, nearly losing the family home. He bailed them out. But he was a Christian and they could not conceive of me marrying out. That's how they were. I cried for months. Did it help me? Of course not. But then, if I had married him, I wouldn't have left Jidovitza and I wouldn't be alive today. It was my fate to survive and theirs to perish.' And at this point my mother would stop talking. What else was there to say?

She told me stories as she ironed and the steam rose from my father's trousers, or as she washed the dishes or cut the vegetables for the soup. I listened without ever asking a question. I felt like an intruder into a time and a place I had no right to be. It was up to her how much she wanted to tell me. Those heavy topics – poverty, love, religion; the murder of her parents, four of her siblings and their families. I was primary school age, then high school, but even later as a young adult, I did not know what to say, how to comfort. So I let her talk.

91

'My father kept saying we, Dora and me, would marry when the right *mensch* (man) came *B'ezrat ha sheim* (God willing)'. But for Roza and her sister Dora, the right men failed to materialise.

By 1941 the war was moving closer to Hungary. Rumours about the suffering of the Jews in other parts of Europe reached Jidovitza. Everybody was afraid. According to some, Romania, while not a Jew-loving country and allied with Germany, was less vicious to Jews than Hungary.

'It's only over the border, I thought. Only one border to cross,' Roza recounted, 'but I didn't have the strength to leave. My parents were not young anymore. And Dora was not only my sister, she was my best friend. My mother kept saying, "Rozale, it's better if you go. There is nothing here for you." Even Dora wanted me to go. But I was not ready for it.

'One night I had a nightmare. Next morning, I only remembered returning home from somewhere, not sure from where, walking through the gate and not finding anybody, no person, no furniture. Even the *mezuzah* on the door was gone. The silence was eerie. A sense of dread hung over me for days. The dream was with me all the time. I told my mother about it. She was afraid.'

People in the village took dreams seriously. Roza was not sure what to believe, but if her dream had a meaning, it was nothing good. Nothing good was happening in the world either. Gloom had been enveloping the village for some time. What if the entire world was in for wars and destruction? What would happen to the Jews? They could only fare badly. They always did.

It was illegal for the Jews to cross into Romania and crossing the border looked quite impossible. But Romanian laws could always be lightened by bribes.

'We sat down one evening to discuss what to do,' Roza went on. My mother thought I should go. My father was not so sure. Crossing the border illegally on my own? Anything could happen. My mother thought that anything could happen to me if I stayed. At least if I went I might be in a better place. I might find a husband, I might even take the rest of the family out one day. If I went, they might all be in with a chance. Bit by bit my father came around. They would give me money, in fact they would give me most of their savings. Can you imagine? They gave me most of their savings.' And Roza could not hold her tears back any longer.

A few days later Roza packed a small suitcase, said goodbye to her parents and Dora, and slipped quietly out of the village.

She never saw them again.

I realise now that Roza never told me the details of how she managed to cross the border. Which train did she board? Did she sit down or move around to avoid the guards? How did she get past the Hungarian border guards? Every time she talked about crossing into Romania, she quickly reverted to that evening when the family decided to give her their savings, and the enormity of their predicament. Compared with her family, she had been lucky. She had survived.

She did tell me that when the Romanian border guards boarded the train, they came upon a Jew who did not have legal documents. He protested. His documents were all there, all legal. The guard was adamant: 'You can't go further. You can't enter Romania.'

The man would not get off. A guard leaned out of the window and called for a policeman. The policeman boarded the train, frog-marched the man to the carriage door and pushed him out. The man fell in a heap. He screamed, he begged. Roza's heart made its way into her throat. But there was no choice now. The border guard was close. He was gathering papers and passports. Roza scavenged in her handbag. She had papers all right, irrelevant papers, in the middle of which she had the family's savings. That was the only thing she could give him. How exactly the handover took place is not clear, but the Romanian guard took her papers, eyed the money and patted her on the back: 'Good Romanian lass.'

'I could not concentrate on anything. My mind kept repeating: I'm through. I'm through.'

Roza arrived in Brasov and found her way to the address of a distant relative. They put her up for a few nights and promised to help her find a job. But finding a job turned out to be difficult. She had no profession, and since the introduction of the anti-Jewish laws, Christians were not allowed to employ Jews.

A few weeks passed. Her prospects looked bleak. Then one day she heard about a vacancy with a Jewish family. Stefan was looking for a nanny for the two-year-old Tom. Roza had never been a nanny, but then she had never been anything. She liked children.

Not long after, a slim tall young woman with black shoulder-length hair and green eyes, not pretty but strikingly good-looking, rang the bell to Stefan's house. She wanted the job. She had no experience or references. As a Jew, Stefan could only employ Jews as full-time live-in workers. He did have a part-time cleaner and cook, but he needed a full-time nanny, always available. He gave her the job.

Roza treated Tom matter-of-factly, not as disabled but as a healthy child with a bad leg. With unending patience she encouraged him to stand up. Holding both hands she made Tom take a step, two. She walked him morning and afternoon. With a built-up shoe on his foot and an iron frame on his leg, walking for Tom was a big effort. Roza persevered. Tom kept walking, further and further. Months passed and Tom was really walking. What medicine and engineering could not achieve, Roza did. And yes, he had a bad leg and needed special shoes, but he was a happy child. He spoke well, always smiling, often laughing.

Stefan could not have been more delighted. And whether he loved Roza for what she achieved or for what she was, he decided to marry the nanny who was thirteen years younger than him.

What did Roza think? Did she fall in love with him or with his wealth, his beautiful house, the status of being part of a well-respected family, or did she marry him for lack of choice? Was it lack of somewhere to live, poverty, or just being stranded in a foreign country? No one will ever know. Did she marry him so she could pay for her parents and sister to escape from Hungary? Because if she did, she miscalculated. The border between Romania and Hungary was now closed, impermeable, no one could cross it any more. And her family could not be rescued from what followed.

'I sent them letters,' Roza recounted often. 'My mother answered. She wrote that she read my letter again and again. In the evening she took it to bed, put it under her pillow and cried until the pillow was wet with tears.' As was Roza's face as she spoke.

Stefan married Roza towards the end of 1941, as the Germans were progressing towards Stalingrad and secretly implementing their final solution, while in Eastern Romania (Bessarabia and Bucovina) Jews were murdered in their many tens of thousands. By 1944 that figure would escalate to hundreds of thousands. To the north of Brasov, only a few kilometres away, the Jews of Hungary feared for their lives. It would be nearly three years before they too would be deported and most of them murdered.

So only a short distance away from the death and destruction of the Jews, Roza started her married life in Stefan's beautiful house. But it wasn't Stefan's, it was Hella's: her furniture, her bed, her figurines, her sister's paintings. Drawers full of her photographs, her jewellery, her shells collected in Egypt. Wherever you turned you found Hella. Everything was preserved for Tom's sake and because there was a war on. And Roza continued to live in Hella's shadow for more than twenty years, until the family emigrated to Israel. But she never resented it. She never said a bad word about her. For us all Hella remained Tom's mother, the pretty, young, talented woman who died far too young.

Roza continued to address Stefan as *maga* for the rest of her married life. It was the respectful form of address which she had used as his employee. It had been etched in their relationship and it persisted for the rest of their life together. I now find it hard to reconcile my father's egalitarian attitudes, his socialist views, his general respect for the working class, with the hierarchical form of address in our family. I always found it strange – strange but not intolerable. We never discussed it. It looked like any hierarchy in the animal kingdom.

Willingly or unwillingly, my mother looked up to my father. It was the hierarchy I was born into – it just was.

While Hella was the darling of my father's family, Roza remained Stefan's wife, never acknowledged as a daughter or a sister-in-law. Was it because she was so unlike Hella, or because nobody wanted to see Hella replaced? Was it because of Roza's personality? Or was it because the family could not accept a woman with a much lower social status? Remarkable, since Stefan's sister, Anna, claimed to be a communist. Whatever the answer, it affected all our lives, but it affected Roza's life more than anyone else's. The young woman who had the courage to bribe her way across the border between Hungary and Romania during the war never had the confidence to prove herself outside our home. Not that she had much time, but through the years there had been a couple of opportunities to learn and to work. She would start, only to give up a few weeks later.

What should have been the happiest time in Roza's life was marred by worries and tragedy. The vicious anti-Semitism, the continuous worry about her parents, brothers and sisters, the bombing of Brasov and its surroundings by the Americans were the background to the first three years of Roza's married life.

Finally, in August 1944, the much-awaited Russian soldiers marched into Transylvania. Roza waited for news from her parents. She hoped that one day Dora would knock on the door. Some people returned within weeks. Others trickled through much later. Chaos and confusion ruled. She kept asking around, trying to find where they were last seen alive. The news filtered through, eventually. Her parents and her sister Dora did not survive, nor did her brother Izso and his wife, nor her sisters Fanny and Ilona, their husbands and their children. Iszo died in a work camp, the others in Auschwitz. The six surviving sisters and brothers left Europe. One of them emigrated to Australia, the others to Israel. But Stefan did not want to leave Romania. He wanted to stay, to experience the greatest miracle of all, an egalitarian society. He wanted to experience communism.

The two disparate people, match-made by the dreadful events of the time, made a go of their marriage. By the time I arrived into this world, Tom was six years old. For the next eight years he was my older brother who looked after me, took me around everywhere he went and got us into mischief.

Part IV

Under the gaze of Stalin

10

It was my second week with Tom. We had been to the market that morning. And what a surprise that was! There was probably more food on display in that one market than on any day in the whole of Transylvania during communist times. Stalls of fresh apples, pears, plums. Tables of tomatoes, capsicums and eggplants. True, everything was on the small side and less uniform than in the West, but in 2002 fruit and vegetables in Romania were still produced by small holdings with minimum automation and few if any chemicals. Further up were cheeses, thick and thin sour creams and meat, all kinds of meat. That market was the living proof of what free enterprise can do if not smothered by state control. Even Romanian free enterprise.

'Good grief, what am I going to do with all this fruit?' I heard Tom grumbling in the kitchen as I surveyed his Modern History collection. The fridge door closed. 'My God, why did you buy so many tomatoes? Far too many. You must be eating a hell of a lot in Australia. Very unhealthy.'

The mutterings stopped and Tom reappeared with a plate of plums, Bistritza plums which Romanians sell to other parts of Europe. I even saw them in a market in Helsinki, at a considerable price.

Tom had now been retired for nearly a year. Although he never said so, I think he missed work. He was still trying to adjust to his new life. He went out every day at least once, but he caught the bus more often, walked less, stopped every now and then to rest his bad leg and wait for the cramps to subside.

I kept looking at him, not quite believing how the years had passed, thinking that we had missed out on each other's life. Every now and then I drifted into daydreaming ...

Tom and I are back in the tiny Hungarian town of Kezdivasarhely. Tom the other brother, the slight boy with a much lighter limp, takes me with him wherever he goes, summer and winter, holding my hand.

It is snowing. Tom is leading me, pulling me along. Where, I don't know or care. I follow half-behind, my tongue out catching snowflakes. Each snowflake is different. Some are big and melt instantly, some are small and icy. The taste lingers. Around me everything is white. I am in fairyland. The snow is crunching under my boots. I feel his mittened hand holding mine tightly. I am snug and happy.

At the bottom of the hill Tom's friend, Miska, is waiting for us. 'You're late again,' he says. We are always late, but I have faith in Tom. He says something I don't understand, but Miska laughs and Tom laughs and I laugh not knowing why. On we go climbing, pulling our sleigh. On top of the hill Miska takes over. He turns the sleigh around, sits himself in the front and takes the reins. After considerable manoeuvring of his bad foot, Tom takes his place behind him. I squeeze between the two of them and we start sliding down the hill. The sleigh gathers speed; cold air is cutting my face. I grab on to my brother's legs. I grab harder and harder.

'Sook! Don't worry, sook,' Tom shouts in my ear.

The sleigh slows down, crosses the narrow street and comes to a halt. We go up and down the hill many times. Tom's limp is getting worse with every climb, but Miska and I show no sign of stopping.

The sun is about to set as we walk home. Tom points at the sky. 'Look at those grey clouds. It'll soon start snowing.'

'Again?'

'Again.'

My father opens the door, smiling. 'And how was today's snow?'

'Cold and slippery,' says Tom. 'And she never has enough of it.'

I take off my ice-caked mittens and sheepskin coat and show my red hands to my father. He rubs my fingers until the feeling returns. Then I place my hands on the hot dark-tiled stove in the corner of the lounge until it hurts and I can stand it no longer.

The lounge is warm and cosy. Although it's nearly two weeks since Christmas, the Christmas tree is still standing in the corner opposite the stove, a few lollies and glass balls hanging from its branches. The two small Christmas stockings, Tom's and mine, which were full of nuts and sweets, are empty now.

My father is back at his big desk surrounded by papers, slide rule in his hand. From the red velvet sofa opposite, I watch him concentrating. He must be doing something difficult because his eyebrows are knitted and he is thinking aloud, whispering words I don't understand, engineering words. It all sounds so complicated, so incomprehensible. But my father is a very clever man. I have overheard people talking to my mother about it. He must be; you have to be clever to speak such words. He puts the slide rule down, writes something, whispers again to himself, then his forehead smooths over and his face lights up. He must have worked it out. Warm and contented, I sit back on the sofa and would fall asleep if not for the hunger ravaging my stomach. But my mother is already setting the table. I watch her as she spreads the white damask tablecloth and sets out the silver cutlery, the beautiful porcelain plates with golden rims and the pink crystal glasses. The crystal reflects the light from the chandelier above and I am in a wonderful world where my father can solve all problems, Tom is always smiling and my mother is always cooking in the kitchen with Mary, our live-in helper.

We sit down to eat, me next to my father, Tom and my mother opposite. As we eat the soup, Tom is recounting our adventures in the snow and I am asked to bear witness, which I do. I bear witness to the whole truth and not quite the whole truth. My mother presses the little bell above the table and soon Mary arrives with the seconds ...

Those are some of the images of my childhood with Tom. But there are others. Stored somewhere in my mind are video snippets, before the video was even invented, some with a beginning and an end, others nanoseconds long, more like a snapshot, a moment in time: a smile, a gesture, a frown. Some I understood at the time, others I did not – stories and situations I was born into and not for me to question. Like the Christmas tree. The Christmas tree was mainly for Tom, as I found out years later. Tom's maternal grandmother was not Jewish so according to the Jewish religious rules he was not a Jew. Stefan, who had no time for religion of any kind, saw an advantage in Tom not being Jewish. He did not need another disadvantage in life. So Tom was brought up as a Christian. I knew that I was a Jew, and I sort of knew that he was a Christian. It seemed self-explanatory, no different from the fact that I was a girl and he was a boy, I had two good hands while he only had one. I was good at sums and Tom was hopeless.

Poor Tom. What bad timing to have come into the world in an era when maths, science and engineering were considered the only knowledge worth pursuing. And what bad luck to be in Romania at a time when public life had become riddled with lies and propaganda. Seeing what communism was turning into, my father decided that maths remained the only truth, and Tom had to attain a good standard in the only subject matter worth learning. By hook or by crook, he would teach maths to Tom.

'In our family, you did not deserve to live if you were no good at maths,' Tom said to me the other day. And smiled. We both knew what he was referring to.

My father gave Tom maths lessons regularly. Tom dreaded them. He must have felt like a man about to face a trial, a trial for which he knew the outcome already. Still, he kept trying. But he could rarely come up with the correct answer. Simple sums he did master eventually, but when he graduated to more complex questions, he was lost.

I still remember that afternoon, their last serious maths lesson. I must have been around seven years old …

Tom is sitting at the desk, on my father's left. I am sitting on the sofa, drawing. My father is explaining something about two cars, A and B, something about speeds, distances and travelling times.

'The question is, how many hours will it take for car A to meet car B? Is everything clear?' he asks for the last time.

Tom nods, takes a pencil and starts writing in his notebook. He rubs something out, then starts writing again. Then there is more rubbing and more writing.

'But Tom,' my father interrupts, 'if ...' and explains something.

'Aaah,' Tom says and returns to his calculations. My father is watching over his shoulder, waiting. I am waiting too. Finally Tom has the answer. He shows his father the results and explains what he added to what and what he divided by what. But something is not right and Tom starts writing again. After a while my father asks something. Tom cannot answer.

'Concentrate!' My father shouts and I see his right hand in the air then on Tom's face and Tom sliding sideways. My father jumps up to catch him. But Tom's chin has hit the wooden arm of the big carved chair. Oh no! Tom is bleeding.

'Roza! Roza I need your help! Quickly!'

My mother comes running, panic on her face. She takes a look at Tom and runs out again, then back with a small bottle and a few bits and pieces. She disinfects Tom's chin and puts a bandage on it. But Tom's blood keeps seeping out around the bandage.

'We'll have to take him to the doctor,' my father says, 'straight away.'

By evening Tom's chin has stopped bleeding. We are having dinner. After every spoonful of soup Tom tilts his head back as he swallows. When I ask him why he eats so strangely he says in a hushed voice: 'If I don't hold my head up, the soup will leak out through the hole in my chin.'

'Really?'

'Like an open tap.' He leans towards me and whispers in my ear, 'All because of maths.'

My parents are sitting in silence, no one says a word ...

Tom was full of mischief. He could not climb trees or run around like the other boys. His mischief was mental: wit, jokes, pulling my father's leg. He would stretch my parents as far as he could, as far as he could get away with.

I don't know what Tom said at school when he turned up with a bandage on his chin, but I overheard him telling our landlord, Mr Botar, that he fell against the arm of the big black chair. He did not say anything about maths.

Mr Botar lived in a bedsitter at the back of the house with no separate entrance. Every time he went out, he walked through our lounge room. He often stopped for a chat, mostly with Roza since Stefan was at work till late afternoon. He bowed slightly and kissed her hand. He talked to her in an old-fashioned sort of way, she a woman on a pedestal and he undeserving of her attention. 'He is a real gentleman,' Roza would often say. Many women must have thought so too, because getting married had never been a problem for Mr Botar. He had three marriages behind him already. But at the time he was single and settled.

More often than not, Roza offered him cakes, or the odd appetiser. 'Delicious!' Mr Botar would say, or 'This jam tastes of real strawberries.' Whereupon Roza would dollop another spoonful of jam on his small plate and he would eat it slowly, savouring every mouthful and taking great care not to drop the jam on his suit. Mr Botar always wore a suit.

He wasn't much of a talker, but every now and then he would say something which puzzled me: 'Satan is walking the Earth.' I did not know that Mr Botar, like many others, was a has-been, a has-been bank manager who worked as a clerk, a has-been official in the Evangelical Church who had to operate inconspicuously. Therefore Mr Botar hated the communists with a vengeance. The communists, just like Satan, had brought evil to the world.

One day, in one of his low moments, Mr Botar confided in my parents that he had organised a small religious convention on the quiet. Within days, five priests were due to arrive in Kezdivasarhely. He would have liked to invite them for dinner, but he had no wife and his bedsitter was not suitable for such an esteemed gathering.

'We have to help him,' Stefan decided, and volunteered Roza as a host. So one evening, five priests and Mr Botar installed themselves in our lounge. They savoured Roza's cooking, served by Mary with her swaying hips, drank our red wine and talked and laughed into the small hours. The evening was a success.

The following Friday night, Roza lit the candles as she always did, covered her face with her hands and murmured the Friday night prayer: '*Baruch ata* ...' Our Friday nights were sacrosanct.

But Roza was no longer religious. Her Orthodox parents had obeyed all rules, worshipped God daily and yet they were murdered. Still, she cherished the Jewish tradition to the end of her life.

I did not know what it meant to be Jewish, but I was ready to defend all the Jews in the world. I knew that some people did not like Jews, but in my mind they were not important, they were relegated to the bad people category. Once, when my friend from kindergarten sang a nasty nursery rhyme to me: 'The Jew in my house, the noose on his neck ...', I gave her a good slap on the face. She ran home crying. It felt great.

From spring to late autumn, Mary was always busy. The garden, the chickens, the pigs, the geese, cooking, cleaning and washing occupied her full-time. Roza got involved too, especially in cooking, gardening and making preserves. But late afternoon she would put on one of her best dresses, silk stockings and high heels, and go and meet Stefan coming home after work. Sometimes she took us with her. All of us, the children in front, Roza in her finest clothes holding Stefan's arm, would stroll down the main street of Kesdivasarhely. 'The handsome Mr and Mrs Engineer Leitner', the locals must have thought about my parents – the Engineer title was the usual form of address. But Mr Engineer Leitner, who used to half-own the Sportind factory which produced bathroom supplies, was now Comrade Leitner, no longer the factory owner but its manager, the manager of the Sportind cooperative. He and his business partner, Richter, donated the factory to the state before nationalisation began.

Stefan had been a communist sympathiser for years and thought that if he amassed some wealth while doing the work he loved, it did not mean he had to keep it to himself. Roza, far more realistic and less charitable, took time to convince. But she agreed, eventually. Although she came from a very poor family, she never believed in communism. Her philosophy was simple: what is yours is yours and nobody has any right to take it away.

We must have looked the ideal family, but my parents' marriage was far from perfect. I remember my mother packing a suitcase and Tom on his knees, begging her not to go.

'She wanted to walk out and take you with her. And not once,' Tom said to me during one of our reminiscences. 'It was blackmail. She knew that it would have destroyed my father. Your arrival was a special gift to the family.' From the way Tom said that, it wasn't just because our father could not have coped with a child being taken from him; it was because a certain child would have been taken away, the physically able one. When I realised what Tom meant, I had to leave the room. I felt really unwell. Suddenly I was overcome by the darkest of depressions. Why did Tom's words have such an effect?

It took me time to understand. It pained me that Tom's view was so distorted. It pained me that my mother was so desperate, that she hurt Tom so much, that she wanted to hurt my father. When I recovered, I wondered why she wanted to leave. Was she so unhappy? I don't know. But to this day the image of Tom on his knees, like a man in church praying for forgiveness, unsettles me to the point of feeling sick.

She did not leave. By late afternoon she was unpacked again and next day she was out with Mary, digging the garden and preparing it for the next harvest.

A week later a nauseating smell heralded the arrival of the magic fertiliser. Soon a horse pulling a cart full of cow manure came through the gate. The stocky driver transferred the load from the cart to our garden. The following days my mother and Mary were busy spreading, folding and raking the smelly dung into the earth. The garden was ready for sowing.

Within a few weeks the black earth, like a magician, turned the seeds we planted into green shoots. What other miracles could the earth perform? I wondered. The world seemed enchanted and full of mysteries.

The seedlings were replanted, some given to the agricultural college nearby. Roza's seedlings were sought after. She was one of the best vegetable gardeners in Kezdivasarhely.

By the time the garden was bringing up the next harvest, the trees and bushes in the front yard were covered with tiny green buds. Soon the lilac bushes surrounding our house were in flower. Even the hens looked happier as they pecked energetically in the yard. And I kept waiting to see the tiny chickens following in their footsteps.

The Baron, a friend of my parents, also took seedlings from Roza. The Baron was just another has-been. Once a big landowner, he now lived in the country under house arrest. Occasionally he could get away as far as Kezdivasarhely. He would arrive with his cart and horse. Sometimes he brought us wine, other times he invited the whole family to his farm, but once he invited only us children. And what a treat that was! …

The two of us sit in the cart, Tom all smiles, me with a sinking feeling in my stomach every time a second cart appears over the horizon. It seems to be coming straight at us and I am sure we are going to collide any minute. I pull closer to Tom.

'Sook!' he tells me off. But I do not budge, just sit quietly huddled up to him. 'Don't worry,' he says again as another cart approaches. I stay put.

The Baron urges his big brown horse on with an occasional gentle whip. We pass a village, a few more houses, and there is the Baron's home. In the front yard the walnut trees are in flower. Unperturbed by our arrival, a few turkeys are pecking the earth.

Inside the house the table is already set and my favourite cake is ready to be sliced. The Baroness, a tall, quietly spoken woman, asks about my parents. The teenage children are away somewhere, but what do we care, Tom and I? The goat is waiting in the yard. But when we try to catch him he runs away. 'Here, here,' Tom keeps saying to him, but he is not about to change his mind. The lamb is tame and friendly, its wool warm and inviting like a cosy house on a cold winter night. I feed the tiny golden chicks, watch the pigs slurping the swill and follow the Baron into the stable to check on the two horses. When it is time to go, Tom is not happy. He managed to tame the goat and now they are great friends. But he has to part, we have to return home.

'What well-behaved children these two are,' the Baron says to my parents as he sits on the sofa with a glass of sour cherry liqueur. But then my mother decides that we are not just well behaved: we are clever and I am super clever, so she asks me to recite a poem. I recite poems often. I know many poems; I learnt them by listening to Tom. He reads them aloud when he has to memorise them for school. My mother thinks that Tom is just trying to make a point of how hard he is working, but his mind is on other things the whole time.

'The noble man, the villain, who can't read and write …' I start one of my favourite poems. The Baron keeps looking at his feet. Finally I reach the last line: 'One day he and the others like him will get what they deserve, the ultimate punishment. Hanging.' I look at him, I look at my parents. No one says anything. 'I am so sorry,' my mother says to the Baron. 'That's what they teach them at school these days.'

I must have recited the wrong poem, I thought.

Tom and I were never parted, not until a rabies epidemic erupted in Kezdivasarhely. Grandpa Ludovic and our step-grandmother invited Tom to Brasov to keep him safe.

'They could not get used to the fact that Stefan married me,' my mother told me many years later. 'I could even understand that, but why would they hold it against their granddaughter?'

I could not go outside our yard. It was too dangerous. I missed Tom, but I did not fancy being with Grandpa Ludovic. He had visited us a number of times, each time for a few weeks. I cannot remember him talking to me, ever. He played chess with my father, talked to Tom occasionally or sat on the veranda. Rain or shine, he sat on the veranda and read. But what he really loved was a good storm. He would sit outside watching the lightning and listening to the roaring thunder. The bigger the lightning, the louder the thunder, the more pleased Grandpa Ludovic was. Was it the sheer power of nature which entertained him, or did he want to understand the science of it all? Apparently he was a brilliant man.

I was glad when he left. We got our veranda back. Why does he come to visit us? I wondered. Surely there must be clouds and rain in Brasov.

The epidemic continued unabated. It was rumoured that someone was bitten by a dog with rabies. People whispered that he went mad. Everybody was worried. I could not wait for Tom to come back.

Tom did return in mid-August, just in time to help with the harvest of the vegetables. Then it was time to make jam, pickle cucumbers, preserve goose livers, make passata. The house was frantic with activity …

Making the prune jam is a big messy job, so messy that it cannot be done in the kitchen, so Mary sets up the big copper pot above a small fire in the front yard and fills it with pitted plums.

She is wearing a dress gathered at the waist, and as she walks in and out of the house, her hips sway and the folds in her skirt move like waves. Mary adds a jar of sugar and starts stirring the pot with a huge wooden spoon. And as she does, she sings Hungarian songs to herself. The mixture is bubbling. The yard smells of hot sugar and plums. From time to time small blobs of hot jam jump out of the pot and fly towards the sky. She is singing my favourite, a playful song about the woman born in a rosebush. Men from nine villages try to court her, but she only flirts, teases and chooses as she pleases. I join in her singing and we keep repeating the last stanza over and over again, louder and louder, faster and faster, until we both burst out laughing and her big brown curls bob around her face.

Opposite, Tom has managed to climb up onto the wide wooden frame of the gate. How he got up there with his bad leg, I don't know. He is sitting and eating plums. Not the dark plums Mary is cooking, but little yellow plums from our garden.

'Tom, come down, I want to show you something.'

'I will – just go and get a pan from the kitchen.'

'What for?'

'You'll see.'

By the time I am back, Tom is already down. 'Follow me,' he says, heading towards the pigsty. We climb into the roof space, through the stairs on the side. The fence to our neighbour Mrs Nagy has a few palings missing and Tom can just reach the apple trees in her garden. Apple after apple from Mrs Nagy's tree ends up in our big pan. It's great fun, but what if she suddenly decides to come to the back of the house? With the pan full and Tom crunching in my ear on the juiciest apple, we descend to the pigsty. We are just walking back into our courtyard when the gate opens and my father walks in. He looks at us, he looks at the apples. He is furious.

'You take the apples back. Straight away!' he shouts. 'And don't come back until you have apologised!'

Tom tries his best to get out of this mission, but nothing he says helps. We have to go and confess.

We are hardly through the gate when Mrs Nagy's big dog starts to bark. Furiously, as if he can tell theft from a mere visit. Luckily he is tied up. Tom knocks on the door. No sign of Mrs Nagy. He knocks again. 'I hope she is out,' he whispers.

I don't even have the time to ask: and what then? because the handle turns and Mrs Nagy is standing in the door frame, her face one big question mark.

'*Kezi csokolom*,' (literally: I kiss your hand) Tom says. 'My father sent us,' and he starts to clear his throat. 'The apples,' he says and deposits the pan on her table.

'Are from here, you rascals! You have stolen them, you thieves. Shame on …' But we have already turned back and are going as fast

112

as Tom can manage. Back in our yard, Mary has finished cooking. The prune jam is cooling down.

In the coming days my mother and Mary keep making preserves. Tomatoes and cucumbers, capsicums and cabbage, apricots and strawberries and even goose livers end up in bottles or jars, for the coming winter.

I did not hang around the kitchen for long. I was not welcome. Sometimes I was in the way, but even if I was not, my mother did not want me in the kitchen. She wanted to make sure that I would not turn into a housewife, like her. That I would have a profession, an income and make my own decisions. That I would never depend on anybody.

It was still summer holidays, so in the afternoon Tom and I went to the movies. We used to go to the movies every time we could get money from my father. He was always the generous one. At times we went even if we had no money. We went without a ticket. Tom knew how to get us out of trouble if we were caught. He had lost the tickets, or dropped them in the toilet, or put them in his mouth and swallowed them by mistake. At times we went in through the fire exit. Inside the theatre I sat next to Tom and laughed with him. The Latabars, the Hungarian comedians, had him in stitches. I sat next to him without understanding a thing. Every moving car seemed to come off the screen and run me over. Terrified, I pulled closer to Tom. Occasionally I asked him to take me to the toilet. He thought that I did it on purpose. Always at the best time.

Autumn was near. The clouds chased the sky and the swallows were leaving again, flying south in perfect formation. A soft rain drizzled from time to time. Then one day Mr Botar was taken to the hospital. He never came back. Nobody ever again mentioned Mr Botar in my presence.

I turned eight, the academic year was about to start and at home the biggest event of the year, the event I dreaded so much, was upon us ...

One morning two butchers walk in, both of medium build with

big moustaches. After a short chat to my mother, they set up the sausage-making machine, sharpen their knives, place a big wooden board on the kitchen table and fill three buckets with water to wash and prepare the pig gut for sausages. Everything is ready. As the two men grab the sharp knives, a shiver of terror goes through me.

In the yard the death dance has already started. As if the pigs know their fate, they are running around squealing, their little short legs barely touching the ground. The men run after them, drops of sweat rolling down their foreheads. The pigs run faster and faster.

'Joska,' one butcher calls out and points to the slower pig, 'This one first!' They hound the tired pig from all directions. The pig's terrified screams are more human than beastly. Tom and I run to the back of the house, but there is no escaping the desperate sound.

Suddenly the sound changes. It is blunt and muffled. The pig is drowning in his own warm blood.

Just as we start to relax, the squealing starts again. It is the second pig. I cover my ears, but the sound is still there. Tom pulls my hand away. 'Don't worry, sook.'

By mid-afternoon the two pigs are open and cut up. The sausage-making machine is pushing the mince into the cleaned pig gut. Length after length of thin and fat sausages emerge ready to be hung up in the loft to smoke ...

By the time the weather cooled, the loft was full of smoked meat and sausages, the basement full of firewood and potatoes, and the pantry with preserves and wine. We were ready for the snow. But in the autumn of 1952, it proved to be the last time.

11

Evening. My parents are talking in the lounge room in subdued voices. The door to my bedroom is slightly open; a narrow strip of light cuts through the darkness.

'We have to move soon,' my father says.

'Timisoara is a big city,' my mother replies. 'It could be a good job.'

I remember thinking: move to a big city? Somewhere entirely different? We could end up going to more movies, have more friends and who knows what else we could do in a big city.

I was eight years old, but I knew about the Danube-Black Sea Canal. How and exactly when I heard of it first, I don't know. Those unutterable words must have made it into my consciousness through bits of conversations I overheard at times. Whatever the path, it got there together with an omnipresent fear, a fear that even my father could be taken away in the middle of the night and sent there. There, where people worked like slaves and many died. What I did not know was that the government needed people to finish the canal, and if they had something on you, you could wait for the Securitate at night.

By 1952 the Sportind factory, which Stefan donated to the state and now managed, had diversified into sporting goods. It had four hundred workers. Regular exhibitions showed off their products: gymnastics equipment, skis, footballs, basketballs, handballs, boxing gloves. The factory was a success.

According to Tom, who was fourteen years old at the time, one day two workers warned Stefan that at the party meeting someone was agitating against him. Tom could not remember the details of what they said, but it was something about how Stefan had exploited his workers in the past. So the two workers, whom he supposedly exploited for years, were worried. They warned him to be careful, that he could expect repercussions.

Sure enough, a few days later the Securitate called Stefan in. They brought up his unhealthy social origins: that he was well-off before the war, that he owned a factory, that he studied in Vienna and only the sons of rich families were able to do that. Stefan was now an identified class enemy – his file, with all the details of his life and his family's, was under the watch of the Securitate.

Stefan had never been a member of the Communist Party, but he believed in an egalitarian society. For nearly two decades, before the communists took over in 1948, the Communist Party was illegal in Romania, its members operated underground and the authorities pursued them viciously. Stefan gave shelter to some for months, to one for a whole year – a very risky deed that would have attracted a long prison sentence. But none of that counted with the Securitate. He was under their spotlight and Roza was terrified. She begged him to go to Bucharest, talk to two of the communists he had hidden before the war. They had high positions in the government, they could help him. But Stefan did not want to ask for favours.

'What if they arrest him? What if they send him to dig the Canal?' Roza fretted. How would she bring up two children? She had no profession, she had never had a job.

Stefan gave in. He packed a small suitcase and caught the train to Bucharest. The two communists advised him to move away from Kesdivasarhely. Move away as soon as possible. It is not clear how Timisoara came up and whether they helped him find a job there, but soon after Stefan returned, a telegram was sent to Uncle Jacob, my mother's brother in Timisoara. He was asked to look for a cheap flat.

'Bring only the essential furniture – beds, wardrobe, table and chairs, nothing else at this stage.'

My mother read Uncle Jacob's response again. 'Who knows what that flat is like?' she wondered, but then she decided we had no choice and started selling the yard and the pantry. Chickens, geese, preserves and newly smoked sausages disappeared within a couple of weeks.

We were packed in less than a month. Some of the furniture was coming with us, the rest would be left behind. The wall unit, the desk and a few paintings ended up with Mrs Somogy; the three golden brocade armchairs, the Venetian mirror and lots more with Mrs Gal. We would pick them up as soon as possible, as soon as we settled in our new home.

Mrs Somogy had tears in her eyes. She would miss us, she said. Mrs Gal was sad too. I was not going to miss anything. A big city was waiting for us. What an adventure!

12

And so we left Kezdivasarhely, me for a big adventure, my parents to escape the Securitate. It was September 1952, early autumn. The sun shone, the trees were still green. The trip to Timisoara seemed unending.

We had been travelling for hours. The small rivers which raced beside our train had turned away long ago. They turned south to join bigger rivers, which in turn would finish up in even bigger rivers, which would pour into the biggest river of all, the Danube. And as my father explained all this, it occurred to me that just like the small rivers, we too were moving fast towards some unknown place ...

The rivers are flowing south, but we are travelling west. The scenery is boring. I cannot keep my eyes open.

'We're nearly there,' my mother interrupts my drift into slumber.

'Wake up!' Tom pulls my sleeve. 'We've arrived.'

I join him at the carriage window. 'It's him. It's him!' My mother cries out.

'Which one?'

'Over there!' She points to a big man standing on the platform. The train slows and judders to a stop. 'Let's go!' But I am not moving. I have to take a good look at my first-ever uncle. He looks strange, like a child's drawing, put together from enormously long arms and legs and huge wide shoulders.

My father takes the two big suitcases and heads for the door of the carriage, the three of us behind him. My mother is waving in Uncle

Jacob's direction and within moments he is next to us.

He kisses my mother, embraces my father and Tom, and now, now it is my turn and I am not sure that I really want what follows. To be entirely truthful I do not. But Uncle Jacob's face is already next to mine, his prickly bristles on my cheek, his lips stuck to my face, and here it comes. A big, loud kiss. I reciprocate dutifully with a small faint kiss on his bristles.

As he straightens up my mother latches onto him, but not for long because the two men have to drop the suitcases at Uncle's place and will catch the next tram. They will meet us in front of the Opera in half an hour or so. From there we will go straight to the flat. I am very excited. I cannot wait to see our new home.

My mother, Tom and I start strolling towards the Opera as instructed. What wide streets! What tall buildings! Trams pass us in both directions. 'The Opera House,' says my mother, pointing to a beautiful big ornate building, so big it takes my breath away. We wait and wait. We look at the building, we look at the passers-by. Trams come and go. No sign of Uncle Jacob and my father. My mother seems worried, and when she is worried she is really worried. Then I worry that she is worried. This is a strange big place and we are marooned. Tom couldn't care.

Suddenly my mother stops pacing. Uncle Jacob is descending from a tram, followed by my father. We are on the way to our new home.

—⁓—

Our flat was in a three-storey building in Dumitrov Street, a short walk away. A square building, with a huge square hole in the middle. A square doughnut. The hole, which Uncle Jacob called the courtyard, was covered by an opaque glass roof. Squeezed between the end of the roof and the wall of the building was a narrow strip of blue sky.

Above the courtyard, two balconies ran around the length of the building, one on each upper storey. 'Each connects four inward-looking flats,' Uncle Jacob explained. 'Yours is on the top floor.' Door facing door, window facing window, the flats looked at each other and winked at the courtyard. We followed Uncle Jacob to the entrance of the building, into the windowless stairway. A weak bulb lit the first few steps, but further up the stairs were barely visible.

On the top floor there was daylight again. Uncle Jacob stopped in front of the second door, took a key out of his pocket and opened the main door to our flat.

'This is the kitchen!'

Kitchen? It was a tiny, tiny room. Bits of bread and other unrecognisable food were scattered on the floor. But Uncle Jacob looked as if everything was exactly according to his expectations. My mother just wanted to see 'the rest' and was walking towards the door of whatever 'the rest' was. Well, the rest did not take long to inspect – it was one big room and a very small second room.

'There is a shortage of flats here, in Timisoara.' Uncle Jacob barely finished his sentence when a strange insistent scratch came from behind. A mouse had stuck his head out from behind a cardboard box and scampered between two empty vodka bottles towards the corner close by. I grabbed my father's hand. Tom pointed to a second tail disappearing down a hole.

A short discussion followed on how the mice could be eradicated and then my mother reverted to what she saw as an even more immediate problem: 'How will we fit in such a small place?' The question hung in the air along with the cigarette smell.

There was a knock at the front door. An older woman, her floral dress barely containing her bosom, stepped in. She was our new neighbour, Mrs Pohl. She lived next door, so close she might as well have moved in with us. She wanted to know where we were from, what my father did, whether he had a job and where. There was no end to how much Mrs Pohl wanted to know. But I just wanted her to go, and I think Tom did too, and my father even more so. By the look of it my mother was getting impatient too, but you could not tell your new neighbour to leave, and we couldn't leave her there and go. Because that is what I really wished for. Lock her in there with all the mice and the rotten food and the bottles. Mrs Floral Bosom finally noticed our impatience, but she had another question: 'Why did you leave Kezdivasarhely?'

'For the children's sake,' my mother said. 'For their education.'

'Plenty of good schools here,' Mrs Pohl said, taking a deep puff from her cigarette holder. She slipped into a long pause. It looked like Mrs Pohl's blown-up cheeks would explode any minute, but no, she started blowing the smoke out of the side of her mouth, her face deflating like a punctured ball. She pointed at the rubbish littering the floor: 'Russian soldiers lived here. They left all of a sudden, a couple of weeks ago. They were sent home.' My mother nodded understandingly.

Finally the door closed behind Mrs Pohl.

'Sudden departure?' my mother burst out. 'A bunch of lazy drunkards, drunkards and thieves. As if I wouldn't know them.'

'Let's go,' my father said and we locked the door to the mice, the vodka bottles and the rotten food, and went to meet my uncle's family, Aunt Ilonka and my cousins, a girl Rita, about Tom's age, and a boy Ocsi, two years older than me. We would stay there until our flat had been cleaned and the furniture arrived. My mother was going to sort out the flat. My father was starting his new job next day.

When I recall that day in Timisoara, I wonder what my parents thought when they saw their new abode.

While the mice ran around our feet and my mother was wondering how we would fit in that small flat, three families lived in comfort in Stefan's big house in Brasov, which now belonged to the socialist state. That house was first expropriated by the fascists and then, in a nearly perfect handover with about three years' gap in between, was passed from the fascists to the communists.

The socialist state had swallowed his factory too. But Stefan always saw the funny side of a bad situation. In the years to come he would put his arm around Roza and say, 'It turns out that you married me for love, after all.' We all laughed, but Roza laughed the loudest.

With the move to Timisoara, Stefan lost the work he enjoyed: inventing new products, solving technical problems, running the

Sportind factory. In Timisoara he would be designing big civil engineering works. As he stood in the middle of that flat, among the rubbish and mice, with the threat of the Securitate still hanging above his head, he must have worried whether he would be able to handle his new job. But one way or another he had to succeed. He had four mouths to feed. Did his faith in communism finally take a beating? I don't think it did. Deep inside, he still believed in communism, in an egalitarian society, even many years later.

And Roza? Roza must have realised that the poverty which she knew too well from her years in Jidovitza had caught up with her again and would surround her like the web of a spider for God knows how long. In Kesdivasarhely she had everything she wished for: a nice house, a pantry full of preserves and smoked meat, and a full-time live-in helper. And she was somebody, the well-respected Mrs Engineer. Still, if living in that hole in Timisoara would spare her husband from the clutches of the Securitate, she was not going to complain.

Next morning she got up early, had a cup of tea and a slice of bread with jam, packed rags, soap and mouse poison into a bucket and left to clean the mouse-infested flat. By hook or by crook she would get rid of the mice, she promised.

So Mrs Engineer, a title which used to please her a great deal, chased the mice down holes and stuffed poison in every visible crack in the walls. She carried the rubbish and the dead mice down to the basement and washed the floor. On the evening of the second day she declared, 'All holes have been filled. The flat is as clean as it will ever be. As soon as the furniture arrives we can move in.'

Tom and I did not mind moving – well, we did mind moving to that flat, but not out of our uncle's home. He was a warm and friendly man but he had some strange habits, I thought. Every morning he wound a leather strap around his arm, put a little leather box on his forehead, opened his prayer book and started humming, or saying words I could not understand. I felt uneasy. Tom must have felt ill at ease too, because he behaved totally out of character. He did not utter a word, just watched in silence.

'He is praying,' my mother said, seeing the puzzled look on our faces.

We had never seen a Jewish man praying. I was used to my mother lighting candles on Friday nights and reciting a few foreign words, in Yiddish or Hebrew, but that was as far as my religious training went. Tom's religious Jewish training was even less important. He had been declared a Christian years ago.

Praying was only a small part of my uncle's religious practices. Midday Friday, he took us – my mother, me and a string bag with the *cholent* my aunt prepared that morning – to the baker around the corner, the baker with the big oven who baked huge bread loaves for the neighbourhood and had a shovel with a handle longer than he was tall. But we were not there for bread, we were there to leave the *cholent* in his oven. The baker took the earthenware pot containing our precious Saturday lunch, balanced it on his shovel and pushed it into the oven. It would remain there until midday on Saturday, when it would reappear somehow on our carefully set table, ready for my Aunt to serve the *Shabbat* lunch.

My Aunt Ilonka. She was a strange sort. She walked like a duck and she loved walking the streets of Timisoara as a duck loves swimming in a lake. All the time. Her hair always covered with a kerchief, and her lips with a smile. Was she happy, or was she silly? She was definitely a little odd. Bit by bit the reasons for the *cholent*'s travels – from Aunt Ilonka to the baker and back again – became clear. It was kept in the oven overnight so it stayed hot and Uncle Jacob did not have to set the fire in the stove on Saturday. 'Lighting a match is work,' Uncle Jacob said. 'It would break the Sabbath, a day of rest created by God.' To me, lighting a match did not seem real work, but what did I know about why God allowed religious Jews to do certain things but not others?

Uncle Jacob's family ate *cholent* every Saturday, a solid mixture of beans and barley. Good *cholent* is nice, it has smoked goose or some other meat, but poor man's *cholent*, the Timisoara *cholent*, was only barley and beans. I definitely did not like poor man's *cholent*, and neither did Tom; and I suspect my father hated it even more, but he would not have complained.

'I didn't realise just how religious Jacob is,' my mother said to me and Tom one day when Uncle and his family were out. 'I like it.' We looked at her as if she had made her way into our home by the back door somehow, a woman we had never seen before. 'It reminds me of home. It reminds me of my parents, of everything I left behind.' She was about to cry.

At long last the furniture arrived, and it was time to move out of Uncle Jacob's flat into our own. Tom moved into the small room, my parents and I into the big room. Tom only slept in the small room; the rest of the time he was in the big room with us where we ate and studied, Stefan designed roads and railways and Roza ironed shirts and darned socks. At times Stefan talked to her about his latest engineering design. It was mostly a one-sided conversation, Stefan talking a strange, incomprehensible language, Roza nodding and from time to time making a comment. Occasionally she asked a question. Shorter or longer, daily or weekly, the engineering conversations never ceased in our household, and in the years to come I often wondered how much Roza could actually follow. Follow or not, she sat and listened with patience and as much concentration as she could muster.

Sometimes she must have been too tired to concentrate. It wasn't only the daily queuing and the other household chores which soaked up her energy, it was the lack of running water in our flat. Either the pressure was too low to reach our floor, or in the winter the water would freeze solid in the pipes. With our buckets, she with two and I with one, we kept going up and down the five flights of stairs to the basement. We carried water for cooking, for cleaning, for washing clothes, for washing ourselves. She did not complain. It was the price she paid to escape the Securitate.

Had we moved far enough? Roza must have wondered at times. She was still terrified. People still disappeared at night. Stalin still ruled. Approaching steps could still be heard at night. The first time she heard them she froze with terror. Heavy steps, closer and closer. But then she worked it out: those steps belonged to one man only, whereas the Securitate always came in multiples. The steps on our balcony belonged to our own womaniser, Mr Otto Pohl who lived next door.

Otto Pohl was a tall and handsome middle-aged man. He lived with his mother, the cigarette-puffing Mrs Pohl. A few times a week, mid-afternoon, Otto Pohl put his best suit on, tucked a neatly folded handkerchief in his top pocket and departed like a tomcat in search of a female. We knew when he went out because he slammed the door and his heavy footsteps hammered the iron balcony, one and two and one and two. It kept trembling even after he was gone, a muffled one and a stifled two, weaker and weaker until Mr Pohl's steps finally died away.

Mrs Pohl did not mind her son going out, she just minded him not coming back at a civilised hour or not coming back at all. Otto Pohl would return in the small hours of the morning, trying not to make any noise, but the more he tried the worse it got, the slower he walked, the longer the iron balcony reverberated. On occasion he must have forgotten his keys, because he knocked on the door loud enough to wake us all up. His mother, who claimed that she could not sleep until he was home, took a very long time to come to the door. Once the door opened all hell broke loose. The Pohls spoke three languages, but they argued only in German. Maybe German is a good language to argue in, I thought. Tom knew German well, but I did not; my parents did not want me to learn it. Apparently Otto Pohl tried to reason that he could not stay home all the time, but his mother was not convinced. Every now and then he would decide that he had enough of his mother's prison, storm out and disappear for a couple of days.

Roza's fear of the Securitate subsided, but never vanished. She finally accepted that the events in Kezdivasarhely were forgotten and politically the move to Timisoara had worked. The eradication of the mice, however, had not. From time to time, one would make its way into our big room. Tom swore that there were more in his room, and occasionally a mouse ended up on his bed. He assured me that he did not mind them because he liked observing them. His newly broken voice was deep and convincing. It all sounded quite plausible, given that no matter how much we tried to eradicate the mice, there were always more holes in Tom's room than in ours. He said that when he sat up in his bed, the mouse would jump off and scuttle down a hole. At times it made its way back into his room and started to chew the wardrobe. 'Why?' I asked. 'To keep its teeth from growing too long.' I doubted Tom's stories, but I did not have the courage to disbelieve him. If I did, a mouse might want to prove me wrong and climb on my bed one night. I started to suspect that the mice didn't just inhabit our flat, they inhabited the building and probably the whole street, the suburb and, who knows, maybe the whole of Timisoara. In my mind's eye I could see them everywhere.

Tom told me off: 'Stop it! They only run around at night!' That was obviously not true, as we had seen enough of them during the day. But what if there were more mice at night? I went to school in the afternoon. By the time I came home it was dark. Would I step on a mouse? I kept asking myself. But all that worry and caution were wearing me out; besides, no one else had ever stepped on one, so I started to relax.

Tom was lucky, he went to school in the morning. During the week we saw each other only in the evenings. By the time I came home from school, the big room was warm and everybody was at home. There was no TV in those days in Romania. In the evening we congregated in the big room – Stefan would be working or reading, Roza busying herself with something, at times reading, Tom and I studying. At times Roza would say something, start a conversation or tell us stories from the past.

The soldiers who had lived in our flat must have brought back her memories about the arrival of the Russians at the end of the war. Not that she had ever forgotten them, but in Timisoara she talked about them often as she ironed or darned socks in the evening.

'Slivovitz, rum, they drank whatever they found, even eau de cologne. They had never seen a toilet. They didn't know they had to flush it. The paper piled up.'

Glad to be interrupted from his homework, Tom was all ears. And so was I – I could nearly smell the overflowing toilet's nauseating stink.

'When I showed them how to flush, they laughed. And then they flushed and flushed. Again and again. Like kids with new toys.'

Sometimes Stefan would remind her: 'Still, where would we be without them?'

Roza would not reply, just sit quietly darning. 'Maybe I shouldn't complain, it was heaven compared to what we had before. Not safe, but far, far better.' She picked up another sock. It was time for me and Tom to get back to our homework.

'The Russians stopped you on the street,' she started again, "*Davai ceas, davai dengi*," (give me your watch, give me your money,) they said, and you had better give it to them. One evening they banged on the door demanding money. I didn't open it, did I?' she asked Stefan to confirm.

He nodded.

'Russian soldiers were not ordered to kill. They just happened to shoot the odd man or woman. Just happened,' she said, putting on a funny intonation. 'Anyway, the Jews were no longer singled out, everybody was afraid. Equality at last. And now? Now they are stealing everything. Coal, oil, whatever they can take, trainloads heading east. I bet you they're on their way as I speak. This poor country has nothing left.'

She turned to me suddenly, as if she had forgotten that I was there. 'Just remember,' and she put her finger on her lips, fixing me with her green eyes, 'mouth shut!' She looked at me, checking for signs of wavering.

There was no need. I knew that home talk was different from outside talk. There was a prison in our street, a big oblong building with small barred windows. I knew that my father, or she, or maybe both of them, would end up there if I repeated her stories to anybody. I had the impression that she was very afraid, far more than my father.

Every evening as I came home from school in the dark, I walked past the big long building with the small barred windows and dim lights. It intrigued and terrified me. I tried to picture the men inside. I tried to imagine their cells. I wondered who those men were. What had they done? Did they just say the wrong things? Things like what my mother said all the time? Were they cold? How could someone live locked up for years? Without seeing the sun, without feeling the snowflakes melting on their face, without seeing their children? I wondered when they would get out again. Then I wondered about the windows with no light. Was someone in there? Or was the cell waiting for someone?

A few steps past the prison, my mind still on all those unanswered questions, I found myself at the entrance to our building in the pitch-dark. Four flights of spooky stairs were waiting for me. With my hand on the balustrade and my heart racing, I ran as fast as I could. I tripped often. My hand still on the balustrade, I picked myself up and started running again. On the first floor there was always a faint light from the flat next to the entrance where the stinking old lady with the dogs lived. I ran one more floor and emerged on our iron balcony. I saw the light at home. I had made it.

I missed Kesdivasarhely. The school, my friends, the big garden, the pigs, the chickens, the walnut tree, the lilac bushes. I even missed Mrs Nagy and her apples and plums. Not painfully but in a wistful way. Our life had changed and I understood that we had no choice but to accept it. Little did I know that there were even bigger changes on the way.

At the beginning of March, history decided to rearrange the deckchairs. It was a cold day. The sky was grey, the day was grey. At home the radio played boring classical music for hours. The music stopped for an important announcement.

'Stalin our great leader is dead …' Then the classical music continued.

Nobody said anything, not even my parents, as if what happened was too big, too incomprehensible for anybody to comment on. If the most powerful man in the world can die suddenly one day, anything can happen.

And it did. In 1956 at the Twentieth Party Congress, Khrushchev, the cuddly new Soviet leader, denounced Stalin's purges and self-glorification. In the USSR a less oppressive era was in sight; a waft of it would come our way. We hoped.

13

We had been in Timisoara for a year already. Life seemed to go on uneventfully. Sometimes a mouse still wandered around the flat; the Pohls still argued. We got used to it.

Tom had become a bit of a celebrity. He had written a few successful short stories. His Hungarian literature teacher enrolled him in the Union of Young Writers. My father corrected Tom's stories and typed them up on his typewriter. Tom's teacher was proud of him, his other teachers less so. His maths was still a problem, but it looked as though my father had given up trying to turn Tom into a mathematician. The two were concentrating on writing. They sat and talked about the stories Tom had written. My father seemed to know a lot about writing stories, at least that's what I thought at the time. Sometimes he told Tom to rewrite something and sometimes Tom objected. Otherwise he seemed content. Our life in Timisoara had reached an equilibrium of sorts. But it would not last much longer …

One evening I am lying quietly in my bed. In the opposite corner, in my parent's bed, my mother is whispering something. I sharpen my ears. 'He will be better off staying with them. They're in no need of anything, they have a comfortable life.'

Who? Who will be better off? I wonder. My father interrupts, but his voice is low and muffled. I cannot understand what he says. There is more whispering.

'Peter earns good money, university professors earn well. Anna earns well too, all journalists do.'

Silence.

'They're veteran communists,' my mother starts again. 'They're well looked after. They'll look after Tom much better than we can. We're struggling on your salary.'

So it's about Tom. Then I hear Cluj, then I hear Brasov. I drift to sleep.

In the morning my mother announces that she is pregnant. I am about to explode from the joy of it. She does not say anything about Tom, or about all those people who are better off than us …

Not long after, one Sunday morning, my father took Tom for a long walk. When they returned I was told that Tom would be going to Brasov to finish high school there. He was fifteen years old and nearly a man. It would be better for him to go to a boarding school. Our step-grandma would keep an eye on him. All arrangements had been made. His grandma would be waiting for him in Brasov. He was to leave in a week. Tom did not say anything. He did not seem happy or unhappy.

A week later Tom said goodbye to me and my mother, picked up his small suitcase, and my father took him to the station. I followed them to the bottom of the stairs and stood there watching Tom limping away alongside my father until they turned the corner.

That evening, my father sat quietly in his chair smoking. At dinner there were only the three of us. My mother kept chatting. Her tummy seemed to be poking out already. Is it a boy or a girl? I wondered.

My father ate in silence, his mind far away.

Soon after Tom departed, a letter arrived from Brasov. Tom had settled down well, my step-grandma wrote. Tom added a few lines to say that he was fine. Was he really? I wasn't. I missed his stories. Sometimes I played with baby Mary next door. Other times my mother told me things.

One morning she pulled the curtains shut, switched the bedside lamp on, took out a small metal box from a drawer and sat herself on the edge of the bed. 'Come and sit next to me,' she said as she struggled to pull the lid off the box.

'What's that?' I asked in a whisper. She did not answer. She was too busy trying to open the box. She turned the lid in one direction then in the other, then pulled with all her strength, grimacing until the lid came off. She poured the contents of the box onto the bedspread: a gold necklace, a pair of gold earrings with little diamonds and rubies.

'These earrings are yours,' she said, 'but for now it's better not to wear them.' She tipped the box further. A solid gold ring, a man's ring, fell out, then a ring with lots of little diamonds and a red ruby in the centre, mounted in a rhombic gold setting. My mother put the ring on her finger and turned it from side to side. As the light from the bedside lamp fell onto the ring the diamonds sparkled, the ruby shone and I was no longer sitting in semidarkness in a flat in Timisoara, but in a palace, among princesses and beautiful dresses, with dazzling earrings and rings. But the ring in front of me was the most beautiful of them all.

'Don't you ever say anything about this jewellery to anyone,' she said.

'Of course not.'

I was still thinking about that ring as I put my pyjamas on. I hoped I would dream about it, and about many other beautiful things. I wished I could dream forever.

Next morning after breakfast I did some homework and went to play with baby Mary next door. Mr Popescu, Mary's father, was a militiaman. My mother didn't like me playing with Mary, as I found out later.

Mary had just been fed and was happily burbling. Mrs Popescu showed me how to change her nappy and while she did, she asked me about my school and my friends. I had no friends, but I wouldn't have told her that. Mrs Popescu left me with Mary and went to wash the dishes and prepare lunch. Mary was happy for a while but then she must have got bored or maybe she noticed that her mother was not there because all of a sudden her face twisted in a miserable grimace and she started crying. Nothing I did would stop her. I returned her to Mrs Popescu, we chatted for a while and I headed back home …

My mother is in the kitchen. She is furious. I don't know why, but I am used to not understanding my mother's moods. I hurry into the big room to finish my homework. I am about to close the door but she is straight behind me. She wants to talk to me.

'Did you tell Mrs Popescu about the jewellery?' she whispers.

'Of course not.'

She saw me talking to Mrs Popescu for a long time. She wants to know what we talked about. I tell her that Mrs Popescu taught me how to change nappies. I need to learn now, now that I am going to have a baby sister or brother.

'Is that all?'

I try to remember. We talked about the silly noises Mary made and about my school. I tell her so, but she is not convinced. I was there for more than an hour and she is sure that we spoke about other things. I cannot remember anything else.

'Did you tell her about the jewellery?' she asks again.

'No.' And seeing that she is not convinced I repeat: 'No!'

She is furious. When she looked out, Mrs Popescu was showing me the back of her hand. 'Why? Why did she?' I cannot remember.

'I need to know!' she whispers menacingly in my ear. 'Do you understand?' And she slaps me on the face. But I have nothing else to tell her. She slaps me again. I am bleeding, but she will not stop. I give her my word again and again, I did not say anything to anyone. She is deaf.

Tears mixed with blood roll down my face. I am the most miserable being in the world, because my mother does not believe me, because Tom has gone away, because of that awful school I go to every afternoon, because of the cold and the mice and the grey home and the iron balcony and the dark stairway and the stinky old lady with the dogs I have to avoid all the time and even Mrs Pohl.

My mother stops suddenly. But I don't care anymore. I wish I could be away from her forever. I wish Tom was back, I wish my father was home. She washes my face with a wet towel and puts a cold compress on my nose. I hate her. I have not said anything about the jewellery. I wouldn't have. She has been utterly unfair to me.

She helps me pack my books and sits me down for lunch. I am not hungry. Besides, I cannot go to school feeling like this, but I don't want to be with her, I don't want to be in Timisoara, I don't want to be in this world.

The afternoon passes slowly. After school I walk home as slowly as I can. I don't want to be with my mother alone. I will wait until my father is home from work. My father will believe me. I know he will.

I will not go to play with Mary again. Anyway the baby is due soon …

—⁂—

One mid-summer day, my baby brother Yossi decided to join our family. It was a hot day. The glass roof above the courtyard had trapped the heat inside the hole of the doughnut and turned our flat into an oven.

For more than a year we had put up with the noise of our neighbours, the clanking of dishes, the arguments next door, the crying of baby Mary a couple of doors further down. It was payback time. And Yossi was born to show them what it was like to have noisy neighbours. He cried all the time. It was especially bad when I was left to look after him on my own. My mother went regularly to the flea market to sell whatever we could spare, whatever was not crucial to our lives. We needed money for food, especially the week before payday. As time went by, my mother sold our china, the silver dishes, her fur coat, a couple of paintings. I wondered what would she sell when everything was gone. At least I would not have to babysit my baby brother.

On the day of the flea market I took a day off school to look after Yossi. My mother gave me instructions on when to feed him, how often to change him, then packed as much as she could carry in her sack and departed. I did not like being left with Yossi. I thought he had it in for me because as soon as my mother was out of earshot he started screaming. The first time it happened I tried to push a dummy into his mouth, but that aggravated him no end, and when I gave him the bottle he turned his head. He continued screaming for what seemed to me hours. Going to school, even doing schoolwork and tests, was easier and preferable to having to look after my baby brother.

Yossi had no cot or pram; he slept in a drawer. The Yossi-containing drawer sat on top of the chest of drawers most of the time, but when my mother was away it was left on my parents' bed so I could reach him, so I could pick the little terror up and cuddle him to sleep. Sometimes it helped for a few minutes, then he started again. Soon Mrs Pohl started shouting too: 'Can't you do something with that kid? He's driving me crazy!'

I tried singing to him. I made faces. I never knew I could make so many faces. Nothing helped. I picked him up and kissed him. He fell silent. I put him down and went to get my school books. Yossi started crying again.

'Bastard,' Mrs Pohl shouted. 'Bastard!' She banged the wall. And as if to spite her, Yossi screamed louder. I picked him up again. I cuddled him for a while. I hoped he would get tired eventually and maybe, just maybe he would stop. At last Yossi's eyes started to droop. I put him back into the drawer as gently as I could. Finally he fell asleep and Mrs Pohl went dead quiet as if she had departed to a better, more silent world. I hoped she had. Now I could sit down to do my homework.

Buried in Romanian grammar, writing declensions of nouns: *scoala* (school), *casa* (house), *mama, tata, frate* (brother). Nominative, genitive, dative, accusative and so on. The word *brother* had become the most hated word in my vocabulary and as I was declining the word, linking it with death and destruction, I heard the familiar scratching in the corner. A mouse! I stiffened. What if it comes out? What if it crawls onto the bed? I had never seen a mouse on the furniture, but Tom's mouse stories were never far from my thoughts. Anything could happen. I could not get help from Mrs Pohl, not after all Yossi's screaming – she would not want to save my baby brother. I had to save him myself. I hated my brother, but I had promised my mother that I would look after him and I felt duty-bound. I would defend him no matter what.

Wow! The mouse was out and running across the floor. I held my breath until it disappeared in the opposite corner. Terrified, I stood up to investigate. I found the hole and pushed a small suitcase against the wall. It woke Yossi up. He began to cry. He cried and cried. Louder and louder. Mrs Pohl started banging the wall again. And so it went, on again, off again until my mother returned. She was always tired when she came through the door, but if she managed to sell most of her wares and make enough money, she was happy. She could see us through until the next payday. With every market day my much-wanted brother was becoming more and more of a curse. I would never have children, I promised myself. Ever.

Tom wrote occasionally, short letters only. According to Roza, he was better off than us.

Yossi was growing up. He was approaching his first year on this earth and we were approaching two years of life in Timisoara. Some days I still missed Tom, some days the water still struggled to reach our second floor, and the mice still shared our flat. But there had been a change.

'There is nothing left to sell,' Roza said to Stefan one day. 'From now on we'll have to manage on your salary.'

I was ecstatic. My market days were over. And Mrs Pohl's bangings? My mother could deal with them. I would be at school.

The caraway soup was no longer the month-end soup, it reappeared at all times, like a disease which refuses to go away. Some days it was followed by beans or potatoes, but the day before payday the potatoes and beans were no more. At breakfast, Roza boiled the milk, scooped the skin off and spread it on the bread. Yossi had a great appetite, but at the sight of such a breakfast his mouth contorted in misery. Rubbing his eyes with his cupped little hands he sobbed, but he ate it just the same. There was nothing else and he was hungry.

One morning I overheard my father saying, 'I can't work. I'm hungry all the time.'

'I don't know what to do anymore,' my mother replied. 'You'll have to find a better job.'

Who knows, my father might get a better job soon. Maybe the caraway soup will vanish from our table.

A few days later he said to Roza, 'Mining towns are looked after by the government. They are better supplied with food, they have better housing. Even the pay is better.'

Mining towns were working-class towns. Valea Jiului, with its capital Petrosani, was the coalmining centre of the country. If a better life could be found anywhere in Romania, Stefan reasoned, it had to be in Petrosani. Once Roza heard about the better pay, she could not be held back. She was ready to move. And so was I.

14

'Tom, was it true that in Timisoara you had mice on your bed? Remember the stories you told me?' They had been nagging me for years.

'Well,' Tom shrugged, 'I don't remember, but yes there were mice and the odd one might have ended up on my bed. It prepared me for what was coming. I learned not to be afraid of mice. It came in handy later when I worked in animal breeding. There was no shortage of mice there.'

'I still don't understand what happened in Kezdivasarhely – why did that worker complain to the Securitate about our father? I doubt that he was unfair to them. I doubt that my father exploited anybody.'

'Exploited them?' Tom laughs. 'My father? Don't you know what happened?'

'No.'

'He wanted the house we lived in. A few weeks after we left, he and his family moved in.'

We were having lunch in the Laughing Monkey café restaurant, popular with people in their late thirties and forties, opportunists who after the fall of communism caught the entrepreneurial wave unleashed by the new freedom. Some set up businesses, others were speculating on whatever they could.

Tom was enjoying his *mititei,* a charcoal-grilled mince, light and spicy. I was enjoying them too; you don't find Romanian *mititei* in Sydney.

At the next table, two men and a woman were discussing real

estate. I heard Brasov, again and again. 'It's a ski resort. It'll be a good investment,' the younger man said, pouring himself a glass of mineral water. Then I heard dollars, euros, the EU. 'The prices will skyrocket once Romania enters the EU,' he added. His companions nodded in agreement.

The older man was ready to invest, buy a couple of houses and take it from there. He would check out the market as soon as they got there. Once they finished their lunch they would be on their way, driving to Petrosani then east to Brasov. 'Petrosani,' the older man said, 'has tourism potential if only they would clean those desolate high-rise flats. Many are empty now.'

Petrosani, our last residence in Romania. The coalmining town which back in Timisoara was our hope, our escape from mice and poverty. We definitely escaped the mice – the flat we moved to was new. It had two rooms, a small kitchen and a bathroom, and was big enough to accommodate the beautiful wall unit we had left behind in Kesdivasarhely. The rest of the furniture, the big desk, the brocade covered chairs and sofa, the Venetian mirror and the other odds and ends, remained there. Nobody knew for how long, probably forever.

As I savoured my lunch with Tom, my mind replayed snippets of our life in Petrosani. My mother singing in the kitchen, my mother cooking, my mother ironing, my mother crying. In the evening my father joining in, playing with Yossi: five fingers, four fingers, button here, button gone, Yossi's puzzled face, Yossi laughing. Later, when Yossi has gone to bed, the three of us talking or me doing homework, them reading, my father lifting his eyes from his book every now and then and losing himself in contemplation.

In the middle of all that, Tom arrived home one summer day. Tom with the baccalaureate. Tom, nearly a man, with an evening shadow and a more pronounced limp than I remembered. He hardly said anything to me and I hardly said anything to him, because even if I did, it turned out to be inconsequential, nothing to laugh about or to be scared of.

A few weeks before his arrival, Aunt Anna, Stefan's sister, had decided that it was time for her to take Tom's education into her own hands. To Roza's dread, because there was never anything pleasant in them for her, Aunt Anna's letters ceased to be a rare event. In her latest, she offered to help Tom and implied that she might do a better job in guiding him through this important part of his young life than my parents would. By my parents, she apparently meant Roza, who saw red when Anna's name was mentioned. There was no love lost between the two women. Except for an odd dig, Anna took no notice of Roza or her offspring, Yossi and me. Roza felt that it was her duty to point out from time to time that in pursuing her interests, she had abandoned her two-year-old son with her first husband and did not see him until he was a teenager.

So what motivated Anna's decision? Did she want to help her brother Stefan who could hardly feed his family, or did she feel especially loving towards Tom because she had been close to his mother Hella? Roza did not believe in Anna's good-heartedness. 'She did not trust me. She thought she could do better.'

The more my mother got worked up by Anna's letters, the more fascinated I became with my aunt. I became intrigued by this short woman whom I had never met. A journalist, a writer, a woman who had lived overseas for many years. Overseas? Only ambassadors went abroad in those days. True, she went abroad before the war when the borders were not closed. Still, a woman on her own, in foreign countries?

By the time she ended up in England in the late nineteen thirties, she had left behind two husbands and a young child. In England, Anna the journalist became a house servant and, during the war, a worker in an ammunition factory. When the war ended, she got a job with delinquent children, married for a third time and a few years later returned to Romania to live in her native land under communist rule. Both she and her husband were committed communists. Their convictions were not born from a life of poverty or years of imprisonment; they were the result of a belief in a theory.

They revolved among academics and writers only. They did not have one working-class friend.

But at the time I thought: what a woman, she has done it all.

When Aunt Anna's letter arrived saying she could turn Tom into a real man and that she had worked with far more difficult young people, my mother was furious. 'What is she on about? Tom is not a delinquent and I hope she is not Makarenko.'

Makarenko was the Soviet pedagogue, famous for his success in disciplining difficult young delinquents. But my mother had a different take on why Makarenko was so successful, if indeed he was.

'In the beginning he used to walk around with a gun and if someone misbehaved he shot him. That fixed the discipline. Nobody dared to misbehave, but if there was an odd fool who did, he pulled out his gun and poked it in his face.' As usual I laughed at my mother's original interpretation of communist heroes.

After another of my aunt's letters, my mother declared, 'She can do a better job? Well, we'd better take up her offer.' It was decided that Tom would go to a university in Cluj and do a degree by correspondence. He would get a regular sum of money from home, but he would have to work to supplement it. Tom would live close to the university and libraries, and close to Aunt Anna. Aunt Anna would keep an eye on him, she might even help him financially. It all started to look quite rosy. But my father had doubts. 'Will Tom be able to motivate himself? Will he persevere with a correspondence course?' My mother reassured him, 'Anna will keep an eye on him. It's the least she can do.'

The visit ended. Tom said goodbye, kissed each of us matter-of-factly and departed. Two weeks later he started university.

—~~—

While Tom was studying Biology at university, I went to school in my navy uniform with its replaceable white collar, under which I dutifully tied my freshly ironed red cravat of the Pioneer. But I did not go to school to learn new things. That I did at home. With the exception of Maths, I could never concentrate on anything the teachers said in class.

I read a lot. I graduated from Alexander Dumas' *The Three Musketeers* and *The Count of Monte Cristo*, the warm stories of loyalty, friendship and uncompromising love, to Sir Walter Scott. But *Ivanhoe* unsettled me. The portrayal of Jews, of Rebecca the beautiful Jewish young woman and her father, made me wonder whether that was how people perceive Jews. Rebecca and her father were condemned to remain strange and foreign in their own land, condemned never to belong. Was that what would happen to me? Eventually I put those thoughts out of my mind. I had a number of friends; surely I was not looked upon as Rebecca was. But I never forgot her, and her portrayal as a foreigner, someone with no chance to belong, resurfaced from time to time all my life. I read other books, Stendhal's *The Red and The Black*, Flaubert's *Madam Bovary*, stories of more recent times, more convincing, the feelings more intense. During Ancient History lessons under the watchful eyes of Marx, Engels, Lenin and Stalin – whose pictures adorned the wall above the blackboard in every classroom – I contemplated Charles Bovary's love for Emma Rouault while the teacher talked about the exploitation of the slaves in ancient Rome and Egypt.

Months passed, the snow melted, the swallows returned, the branches of the oak tree outside the classroom window became covered with buds, and the buds gave way to green leaves as I progressed from one author to another, from one story to another. I lived every story I read. I was no one in particular, just a bystander who could hear all the conversations, see all the actions, follow the intrigues and wish for love and loyalty to triumph. Sometimes heroines died, sometimes the odd schemer got away with far more than he should have, but there were always honest and uncompromising characters, and I loved those.

The world of Ancient History did not interest me – it was full of wars, exploitation and helplessness. I did not doubt the inhumanity of the owners towards their slaves whose lives seemed to be worse than those of animals, but exploitation was such an overused word, I could not engage with any lectures on the topic. Besides, love with its intensity and lack of compromise was so uplifting.

School was for friends and fun. Back at home, later in the afternoon, I opened my Ancient History textbook and read the text the teacher had been talking about. It was totally unfamiliar, as if I had never heard a word about the topic. Learning from books, which I perfected at a young age mainly to avoid listening to boring propaganda, came in very handy in my later life.

While I read about love, I knew nothing about its physicality. But luckily Mrs Luca, our upstairs neighbour, decided that it was time for me to find out how babies are made, 'the facts' as she put it. So one afternoon, while my mother was cooking in the kitchen, the two of us sat on the sofa in the lounge room and Mrs Luca told me the facts about the physical love between a man and a woman. About the mechanics, not the pleasure. I would not have believed her, but who could have made such things up? Definitely not the beautiful Mrs Luca; besides, the way she talked, in hushed tones as if she was divulging the world's greatest secrets, convinced me.

Mrs Luca lived in the flat above us. She lived there with her older husband, a big taciturn man. She must have been in her late twenties, maybe early thirties. She was tall and slim and her white skin reminded me of my favourite porcelain plate, the one salvaged from being sold.

'If marriages are made in heaven, heaven got it terribly wrong when it paired up those two,' I heard a neighbour say. 'She is full of life, he is quiet and grumpy.' I did not think that marriages were made in heaven. I did not believe in heaven, and anyway how could a marriage be made in heaven when we lived on earth? The transmission mechanism was missing.

Clearly the Luca's disastrous marriage was not heaven's fault, it was the grump's fault. Among his other faults he was also balding. Mrs Luca had enough hair for both of them, beautiful auburn hair, half of which she gathered above her head, puffed up and turned

143

back on itself until it looked like a bird's nest; the other half fell down past her shoulders.

Mrs Luca dropped in often. She talked to Roza, or if Roza was busy she talked to me, and when she was cheerful she joked and laughed and her big brown eyes narrowed down to a slit. At times she looked ravishing, but other times she looked pale and sad. It was all because of him: *The Brute!* That was his unofficial name. Who exactly invented it I don't know, but what else would you call a man who regularly beats up his beautiful wife? The beating would start with a muffled thump or thud, then we could hear things being thrown around. You never heard his voice, just the impact of things banging against the wall or the floor. Panic gripped us as her screams came through the ceiling. 'How will it end this time?' we wondered. After a major fight she would not be seen for days, but one day she walked down the stairs, bruises and all, down to the storeroom in the basement, saying hello to whoever happened to cross her path. From that day on, she never hid her bruises again.

'This is her destiny, the poor thing,' a neighbour said to my mother.

'Romanians believe in destiny,' my mother explained to me later. I wasn't sure if I should believe in destiny, but I knew that she did. When she talked about her parents or her sister Dora, she always finished up with: 'It was their fate, their destiny.'

Just as we decided that things could not get worse upstairs, one Sunday they did. The Luca flat had been quiet for weeks. We all thought that Mrs Luca's life had turned the corner, but it must have been only a small corner, because the banging started again ...

My father is sitting at the dining table, writing a letter to Tom. I am trying to do my homework. I cannot concentrate because Mrs Luca is crying. Yossi is asleep. That boy can sleep through everything.

I am preparing a Physical Geography lesson, trying to understand cloud formation. Water evaporates, the vapour rises up into the sky, condenses and sometimes turns to crystals. The crystals turn into clouds. Will Mrs Luca's tears evaporate and rise? How many tears make up a cloud? Will Mrs Luca's tears fall back to earth? Rain, or snowflakes of unhappiness. The thought of it makes me want to cry too. I cannot study. My father is no better; he has stopped writing and is looking troubled. Even my mother is lost for words. We sit and listen. What's going to happen? Suddenly Mrs Luca's scream cuts through the ceiling. Then a howl pierces my whole being. Heavens above! The Brute is killing her.

My father jumps up and runs to the door, my mother after him. I close my notebook and run after my mother. As I reach the second flight of stairs, my father is leaping up the last two, my mother behind him. The door to the Luca flat is half open.

'Go back!' my mother screams. 'Immediately!'

By the time I am back downstairs the screams have ceased. Yossi is awake and crying. Soon my parents are back. They look troubled. They found Mrs Luca lying on the floor, her face covered with blood. Her nose was bleeding intensely. While my mother washed Mrs Luca's face, my father had a firm word with The Brute.

After that Sunday the flat was quiet for weeks. Mrs Luca became my mother's best friend and she spent a lot more time with us, but only during the day when her husband was at work.

One day the most unusual thing happened, unusual for those times. I was on holidays. My mother was in the kitchen peeling potatoes and singing a Lehar song. The chicken she bought that morning was on the cutting board, feathers and all, waiting for the water in the big pan to boil. Well, the chicken was not waiting for anything anymore, my mother was. She seemed happy. She checked the water again. It was nearly ready. She washed the potatoes and put them in a bowl of cold water.

The steam started rising from the big pot. My mother was ready for action. She grabbed the chicken by its legs and immersed it in the scalding water, then took it out, placed it on the cutting board and started pulling off the feathers. The smell of guts, excrement, wet dirt and scalded limp feathers made me feel queasy, but I loved watching my mother busying herself in the kitchen, it reminded me of Kezdivasarhely. She stood in a fog of vapours, her agile fingers moving quickly. The feathers came out easily, as if they had hardly been attached. Bits of bare chicken emerged one by one, the breast, the thighs, the back. The feet got an especially long scalding so the rough skin could be pulled off.

Above us, in the Lucas' flat, the furniture was being pushed around. Suddenly the noise stopped then re-emerged in the stairway. Bang! It was our door. 'Careful!' a man shouted. Bang!

'Have a look,' my mother said worriedly, as her sharp knife cut along the breast of the chicken.

Outside the door, two men were taking a trunk down the stairs, sweat running down their foreheads. I followed them into the street. A truck was parked in front of our block. The two men placed the trunk on the truck and returned upstairs to the Luca flat. I returned to tell my mother about the goings-on. The men were on the way down again, with a suitcase each. There was no sign of Mr Luca. He must have been at work.

My mother was waiting for me in the doorway. Above, the door slammed and Mrs Luca appeared on the flight of stairs leading to ours. She looked unslept and uncared for. She stopped by us to explain. She was leaving her husband, she was moving back to live with her parents. We couldn't believe it. Mrs Luca going? She will not be dropping in again? We will not hear her stories and laughter? I couldn't imagine our life without her. But I was comforted by the thought that The Brute would get his punishment. He deserved to be on his own for the rest of his life, and I had visions of him on his deathbed. Alone and screaming, just as Mrs Luca used to do. Justice at last!

A couple of weeks later I took Yossi by his trusting hand and went to meet my friends. It was nearly summer. While Maria and I were playing with the ball, Yossi was mothered by the other girls. Everybody liked him. He was a beautiful little boy with big green eyes, pink cheeks and black hair, and provided he was not hungry he was no trouble.

A truck tooted us. I ran to grab Yossi and we retreated to the side of the street. The truck pulled up in front of our block of flats. Maria and I returned to our game. In front of our block, two men took a trunk off the truck and walked towards the stairway. Yossi called, wanting to go. I took his hand and headed for home.

Our door was open. Mrs Luca was talking to my mother and sobbing. 'My mother sent me back,' she said. She looked desolate. '"A woman's place is with her husband", my mother said, "it's her duty".'

It seemed to me that Mrs Luca's duty was to die at her husband's hands. I was disgusted with the whole world.

'You cannot live with your parents at your age,' her mother had said. 'You have to be self-reliant and if misery is part of it, you'll have to do the best you can. Life is hard for everybody, but we all manage.'

She had a good-looking husband with a good income, a furnished flat. She had to be grateful for the life she had. That's how her mother saw it.

The Luca flat went quiet again, but Mrs Luca was a changed woman. There were rumours that she was having an affair with the disabled teacher who lived on the other side of the street. I was glad. He was disabled enough not to be able to beat her up. He could hardly walk. He was an ugly man, but it looked like this did not bother Mrs Luca. She seemed happy.

In the afternoon, when The Brute was still at work and the teacher had finished teaching, they stood in front of his block of flats, talking and laughing. Sometimes they disappeared inside for a while. Later, when The Brute was back, they waved to each other from their respective windows. Everybody knew, everybody but The Brute. Mrs Luca was taking her revenge and we kept laughing.

The Lucas' life was one big drama, but most families around us lived peacefully; some even seemed contented, and no one more contented than Mr Bogdan. Every afternoon, Mr Bogdan, a pensioner, took his newspaper and sat on a big wooden chair in front of the main entrance of our block. The birds chirped, the children played and Mr Bogdan basked in the summer sun, reading the paper. As I walked past him one day, I noticed that Mr Bogdan did not seem to turn the page. He was on page two when I went out and on page two when I returned mid-afternoon. I stayed in for a while, had an apple and went out again. Mr Bogdan was still on page two. It dawned on me that Mr Bogdan was not reading. He was just staring at the paper. I followed Mr Bogdan in his lack of action a few more days. He was definitely staring at the paper. Eventually we worked it out. Mr Bogdan was illiterate.

There were no illiterate people in Romania. I had never met anyone who could not read. Everybody had to go to school for at least seven years, but everyone I knew had finished high school. If you were educated everybody looked up to you. So discovering Mr Bogdan's illiteracy, discovering that there were people in this world who could not read, was a shock.

'Before the war, when Mr Bogdan was a child, school was not obligatory,' my father explained when he overheard me joking about Mr Bogdan with my mother. Mr Bogdan missed out on one of communism's greatest advantages, basic education for all.

Most people I knew went to university, real university, not correspondence courses like Tom. Judging by his letters, everything had worked out well for Tom. But my father must have had doubts. One day he announced he was going to Cluj to see how he was set up, talk to him about taking his studies seriously. And two days later he was on his way.

Part V

Ripples of 1859

15

The days of my visit kept trickling along.

We were about to go out and Tom was looking for his small bag, the bag with his bulletin, the identity book everybody always had to carry during communism. Thirteen years had passed since communism fell but Tom would not leave the house without his bulletin.

'What use is it now?' I asked. 'Communism is gone and buried.'

'You never know, it's best to have it on you.'

The bag was next to the door. But Tom was not ready to go yet. 'Just one smoke,' he said and looked at me, trying to work out whether he could smoke inside. He could not understand why, if most Romanians smoked unbothered, his sister, admittedly a Westerner now, was so troubled by it. I suggested he open the window and sit close to it. He agreed, grudgingly.

Tom lit a cigarette and leant back in his seat with obvious pleasure. I looked at him, thinking that two weeks had passed but I had hardly learned anything new about him. How did he survive communism? Life had stamped him with a physical handicap, communism with a social one. He couldn't have done much worse. Why did he fail that first university year?

I remembered my father going to visit him to check if he was well set up. 'Tom is doing well, he's turning out into a fine young man,' he said upon his return. But what happened next? I wanted Tom's version of the story.

Tom could still remember his father's visit.

He arrived one Saturday. I showed him my room, I showed him the Palocsay Research Institute where I worked. He was very interested. He was interested in everything, but when it came to inventions, to creating new things, his ears would prick up. He wanted to understand why and how. You could hear his brain ticking. And when it came to the research work at Palocsay there was plenty to be interested in. The Institute was famous, famous not only in the communist bloc but the whole of Europe. They crossbred roses to create exotic colours, unusual fragrances. They crossed tomatoes with capsicums, plums with gooseberries, aiming for the best characteristics of both. I told him about all these. He kept asking questions. I didn't know much at the time. I wasn't a researcher. I was just a high school graduate, so I became a storeman.

I recorded what went out and what came back, and of course I ate the odd experimental tomato or capsicum. I was hungry. I was always hungry. Once I ate a handful of gooseberries. Experimental ones of course. They caught me and took away a whole week of my salary. Do you think they were the ultimate plum gooseberries? I can assure you they weren't. They didn't taste like that to me.

That Sunday we had lunch at Aunt Anna's. She assured my father that I was fine and she would always be there to help. In the afternoon my father and I went for a walk over in the park, next to the Laughing Monkey café restaurant I took you to the other day. It was cold. Early December? Not sure. But I remember the cold. The slanting rays of the sun had just retreated behind the horizon. We talked for a while then sat in silence. I thought that there was nothing else left to say. I thought that if I was cold, he must be too and that we were only there to say goodbye. But he was not about to go. He took out a packet of cigarettes, offered me one and lit one himself. When we finished smoking I stood up. He asked me to sit down, put his hand on my knee and said, 'Take your studies seriously, my son.'

'Of course,' I replied, thinking, oh, not again.

'You've surely worked it out by now what I am going

to tell you,' he said, and paused for a while. 'You're a clever young man, but you have a physical disadvantage. Life for you will be more difficult than for most other young men. You will have to work hard, get a good degree. If you do, you will have a much better life. If you don't, you will struggle for the rest of your life.'

'I understand,' I replied, and seeing his concerned face I reassured him again: 'Don't worry father, I understand.' We walked down to the station and as the train to Petrosani pulled in he gave me a hug and said, 'Good luck, my son, and remember what I told you.' And I did. When things did not work out, the most difficult thing was to gather enough courage to tell him. My greatest worry was not what I was going to do next; my overwhelming feeling was guilt and shame. I had let my father down. That's what hurt me most.

Tom took a last drag of his cigarette and extinguished the butt in the ashtray. He sat pensively watching the sky. I wondered if he was going to tell me more or would he declare that it was time to go. But he started talking again.

The work at the Research Institute did not leave him with much energy to study. He didn't just work in the store. When there was a shortage of people, which was often the case, he was called to help. Fertilise the soil, sow the seeds, gather the harvest. On cold days he was happy to join in; moving around kept him warm. But he didn't help only on cold days. He worked in the fields often. And what the others did with two hands he had to do more or less with one. His right hand was only for show, it had no strength, but Tom rarely invoked his physical handicap as an excuse.

Late afternoon, when I finished work, I went home to study. The fresh air, the heavy physical work caught up with me. I was exhausted. After dinner I could not keep my eyes open. The exams were approaching. Well, that's how it was.

He fell silent.

'Well? Are you going to tell me more?' I asked after a while.

'More?' He shrugged his shoulders.

153

I did have fun too. But studying was not part of it. A friend of mine, a good-looking young technician, used to come in and if there was a pretty young woman in the storeroom, he gave her a squeeze or a kiss when she least expected. The woman would push him away, laughing. A day or two later he might come and tell me how he took out such and such a girl in the evening and what else happened. I was very impressed. When it came to girls I might laugh with them, tell them a story, but I never touched anybody, I treated them with the greatest respect. Beautiful girls were like a melody, untouchable. They were in a world of their own, a remote world to which I never found the door. I was seventeen years old and like most young people in those times, I knew little about life. Women taught me eventually; they brought me up.

One day my friend said to me, 'Is this how you want to find a girl?'

'How else?' I asked.

'You'll never find a girl if you treat them with too much respect. You have to impress them, prove that you are a man. That you are in charge.

I hesitated. 'I'm not sure I could.'

'Could what?'

'Just squeeze a girl, like you do, suddenly. Someone I don't even know.'

'The first time is difficult. But trust me, the second time is easier and by the third time you lose all your inhibitions.'

A few more days passed. He kept prodding me. 'I'll give you a clue. You decide that tomorrow, or the next day, or the day after, whichever day, you will make a move on the first woman who comes in here. Just make sure she is young and smaller than you. That's all.'

I thought about it. I sort of disliked his methods, but they seemed to work. None of the young women got really upset. They sort of complained, but soon laughed it off. I could not see myself following his advice, but I was longing to find out how it felt to hug and kiss a woman. He kept urging me. Finally, I decided to try it out. I would make a move in a

154

couple of days. And just to make sure that I would go ahead with my plan, I swore to myself that hell should descend on me if I didn't.

The big day arrived sooner than I wished for. I was in a frenzy. I could not eat, I left without breakfast. Today is the day, I kept repeating to myself.

First a couple of young men came in for their tools. Soon after, a big middle-aged woman walked through the door. I sighed with relief. And then this cute young woman, whom I had never seen before. She was small, she was pretty. Oh boy! Did she qualify! All hell will break loose if I don't, I reminded myself.

She asked for two boxes for seedlings. Her voice chimed like fine little bells. Just a moment, I said, and went to fetch them. I returned with the two boxes, walked out from behind the counter, put the boxes on the counter and when she turned to fetch them I found myself in just the right spot. My knees went to water. NOW! The silent voice screamed and I grabbed her with my left arm as tight as I could.

'Go away!' she shouted and pushed me, but I was not going to let her go yet. 'Go away!' But there was one more thing to taste and I planted a kiss on her cheek before I let go of her. With her newly regained freedom she raised her hand and gave me such a slap on the face that I felt my eyes rolling out of their sockets. She took her boxes and walked out. I walked back behind the counter and tried to recover from the shock of the first kiss on the pretty woman's smooth cheek. My face was burning. My heart was racing. But I had done it. Didn't he say that it would be easier the second time?

Later that day I wondered if it was the same for my friend, if the first time he had met a similar reaction. But doubt started to creep over me. Next morning, I told him what happened. He stared at me with disbelief and burst out laughing. 'She's the new agronomist!' He kept laughing. 'You don't go for those.' But he must have noticed the horror on my fallen face. 'Don't worry, you've done it.' And kept laughing.

I did not sleep that night. How could I be that stupid? I

resolved that next time, I would take time to work out who to target. But there has never been a next time. It was not my style.

She did turn up again and I served her. She thanked me and left. But every time she appeared I could feel the slap on my face and blushed intensely. Yet as she walked out the door I felt her smooth skin on my lips. It was worth it.

That was the fun part; meanwhile the end of the year was approaching.

The exams were three months away and Tom was hopelessly behind with his studies. When Aunt Anna realised his impending doom she went into action. She decided that Tom had to change jobs, and what better job for a correspondence student than being a gatekeeper? A gatekeeper at the university where he studied. He would have plenty of time to study. He would be close to libraries, professors and tutors. A perfect arrangement.

Soon Tom left the Research Institute and was sitting in a small office at the university gate, and between 'Can you please tell me where is …?' and 'Can I leave my bag here?' or 'Have you seen professor such and such? Has he left for the day?' he read and studied. At times he got carried away talking to someone. It was tempting. Reading heavy textbooks was hard work. It was like climbing hills – just as he got to the top of one hill, there was an even higher one to climb.

I read through the prescribed material once to have some idea of what the course was about, hoping that something would stick and second time it would be much easier. But the further I progressed the more incomprehensible it all became. I felt more and more lost. Like a little boy in a big city, out for the first time, trying to find his way home. My father's letters arrived with an embarrassing regularity. He kept encouraging me. And I was at a loss what to write back.

As Tom read the letters he must have remembered his father's warning. That his life would be far more difficult than the life of others. The others who did not have his physical handicap. These warnings must have rung in his ears as he saw students walking past

156

the gate where he sat, those who were privileged enough to go to lectures, listen to discussions, understand what they would later read, and the others who walked past the gate holding the hands of beautiful girls.

He persevered but by the end of the semester he only felt confident enough to go for one exam. He passed. He did not even attempt the others.

> Getting a degree by correspondence looked impossible, I was
> not going to try it a second time. Or ever. But now I had to
> write home and confess: I failed the university year.

But Tom didn't just fail the university year, he failed his father's only hope to make something of himself. Tom had failed his own future. And Stefan was distraught. Roza tried to convince him it was not his fault, it was Anna's fault: she should have supervised him more closely, helped him. And it was Tom's fault for not even attempting the other exams.

Stefan kept agonising. Without a profession, Tom would be condemned to a life of poverty on the edge of society. Tom should not remain a gatekeeper. He would get used to sitting all day. He would become even more disabled than he already was.

One day he sat down and wrote to him: 'My dear son. Don't be a gatekeeper, it is not for a young man to sit and do nothing all day. Come back, I will help you to find a job and you can finish your correspondence course from here.'

So Tom took the train to Petrosani for another try at living with the family. This time he might be lucky, he thought.

16

It had been raining for days. The yellow and brown leaves which swished under my feet the week before had turned into a mire. Tom was due to arrive any time. I was standing at the window watching the street.

Opposite, below the eaves, a line of fluffed-up sparrows was looking at the pavement, waiting for the rain to stop. In the next block the curtain slid sideways. Mrs Dumitrescu opened the window. I liked the soft-spoken Mrs Dumitrescu and her son, the physics tutor who wrote poetry in his spare time. He always said hello and smiled. In the winter he often stopped to watch me slide on my sleigh. He looked as if he wouldn't mind having a go, but at his age one has to be serious, enjoy life less. My mother thought that he had inherited Mrs Dumitrescu's gentle nature, that's where the poetry came from. Well, how would my mother have known? Nobody had ever seen a Mr Dumitrescu; he did not seem to exist.

Mrs Dumitrescu bent over the window sill, flapped out a tablecloth, retreated inside and closed the window. The sparrows abandoned their shelter and descended on the wet crumbs below.

Behind me the door slammed. It was Tom. The same smile, the same limp, he was even wearing the same brown jumper. And yet he looked different somehow.

Tom had been away from the age of fifteen, for the best part of three years, ever since Yossi was born. He had come to visit during the summer holidays, but those few weeks did not re-establish the closeness we once had. The family had moved on, had redefined its boundaries. Those boundaries did not exclude Tom, but they did not include him either. He had turned into a once-a-year visitor.

The weeks before his arrival Roza kept fussing: how will it work, the five of us again in a small flat? What will Tom do in Petrosani?

'He will work, study, then go back to Cluj and sit his exams,' Stefan said, 'Tom must gain a degree.'

So Tom was back. Our life was about to change, but his even more.

I knew little about what happened in the following months. My parents' conversations, my mother's monologues and the goings-on at home created a certain image of Tom in my mind, an image which did not include his feelings and struggles. It was incomplete and second-hand. His life was like a modern painting, a few brush strokes which can be interpreted in any way, its meaning the result of the onlooker's bias and mood, seemed comprehensive enough for me. Until he was sent away. But then I started to suspect that there was more to his story than I was aware of.

Now I was determined to find out what really happened when Tom returned home from university. I felt that the time was right, that Tom was ready to tell me, that he would not hold back this time. We were sitting in the kitchen on a single divan bed covered with a dark grey blanket. Above us a shelf of books and a reading light. Tom often sat there on cold winter afternoons with the gas stove on, the water in the kettle boiling on and off, as he read and cogitated. Some nights he even slept there because he did not want to waste gas to warm up the bedroom. It was a frugal life, but he would not have had it any other way.

Not long after he arrived home, across the border the most incredible thing happened – a revolution. A revolution in communist Hungary. Nobody could have predicted it. A collision with an asteroid would have been more likely. My father kept listening to Radio Free Europe and the speculations of Voice of America, wondering how it would all end. But outside, no one was brave enough to utter the word revolution. On the surface, life was going on as usual.

'Tom, what did you think about the revolution?'

He waved his hand dismissively.

'I couldn't have cared less about the revolution, I had more immediate worries.'

'Worries?'

'Yes, worries. Two days after my arrival, I was already working. My father made sure that I did not get the impression that I was back for a holiday,' he said, smiling. Tom often talked about his father with the indulgence of a father towards his wayward, but much loved son.

He had found me a job already. I was to be an assistant bookkeeper.

Bookkeeping. Remember those maths lessons? But as it turned out that should have been the least of my worries. I also had to keep attendance records of workers on a construction site. Those gadgets which stamped workers cards on arrival were in use in some places. But not there – there, I was it. Bookkeeping had not been automated. My maths was in demand.

Anyway, at seven o'clock every morning, I took my notebook and walked around the construction site, checking and recording who was there and who was not. Once finished, I returned to the office, copied my notes into a central file, carefully and as slowly as I could get away with. Why rush? But eventually I had to face my next chore.

I sat at my desk, calculating the cost of raw materials, the overtime costs or whatever the accountants asked from me. Suddenly Comrade Radu's deep voice descended from behind: 'Comrade, have you finished last month's overtime?'

'Just checking my figures,' I would say. Eventually I took the overtime book and handed it to him. Luckily, Comrade Radu did not believe in extra work and if the figures looked even remotely reasonable he signed on it. I could now sit back and relax.

From behind my small desk, I looked at the two accountants and I saw years and years of additions and subtractions, divisions and multiplications. How can they be so fast? How can they be so sure of their answers? I thought they were fast, you might not have. Maths always came easily for you.

Thinking back now, Comrade Cosma, the junior accountant, looked far more substantial than a collection of numbers.

Tom smiled mischievously.

She had a very womanly body. She was about my height, blonde, buxom, just short of fat. She was in her early thirties and had the voice of a twelve-year-old. If there were no immediate deadlines, she and Comrade Radu talked nonstop. They were a strange duo, she short and plump, he tall and skinny. Sometimes Comrade Cosma talked about what she cooked the previous evening. And whatever she cooked contained some form of hard-boiled eggs. Someone had told her that hard-boiled eggs make a man virile. Why on earth does a healthy-looking fellow like her husband need so many hard-boiled eggs, I wondered, while my mind was overstretched trying to understand how hard-boiled eggs make a man virile.

And while I clerked and fantasised, the construction outside acquired another floor. Checking on absentee workers was no simple task any longer. I had to climb a ladder every morning. I was not made to climb ladders. My left hand is strong, but my right is very weak. My left leg is reliable; the right is … well …

Tom shrugged his shoulders, meaning: what can I say?

Will I make it, I wondered, looking up the ladder every morning. I did, I managed it for a while. Then I didn't and I ended up a night guard until that too …

And Tom gave me a dismissive wave with his hand, a Tom's special, meaning, no point talking about it.

We sat in silence, Tom with his thoughts, me with my questions: how did he get up the ladder? He said he managed it for a while, then what happened? I tried my luck, not sure whether I should be pushing the topic further. 'Tom, how did you actually get up that ladder?'

He looked at me, unsure whether to tell me more.

How did I get up? I grabbed the side of the ladder with my left hand and held on like grim death. How else? I urged myself to take a step, then another, then I was committed. I kept on going. The right hand followed the left. Then the left foot climbed another step, the right one tagged along. Further up, my strong leg started shaking. By then I was just over the halfway point. I would look down, count the steps below me then look up; only five to go, the ground is even further. I continued climbing. Finally I reached the top floor. I took my notebook out from under my belt and proceeded to check who was there and who was not. Of course, some Comrades were not to be seen. 'He just went for a pee,' someone would shout. 'He was here a minute ago,' another one would say. I ticked the names of those in front of me. The other two? I'll think about them. I'll sort them out in the office. I had bigger worries, I had to get down that cursed ladder.

While Tom battled the ladder day after day, across the border in Hungary the Soviet tanks rolled in. But in Petrosani people kept going about their business quietly, vindicated for not having made waves. They had decided long ago that there was no point in fighting, that the system was invincible. It would prevail into eternity.

Winter arrived, but the construction did not stop. I kept doing the rounds, the mud half-frozen, the thin ice breaking as I walked. Some mornings the ladder looked wet and slippery, some rungs were covered with dark patches. Is it ice? I wondered. One day I just could not muster the courage. I did not go up, I ticked everybody off and returned to the office. And as I transferred my notes to the central file, Comrade Cosma and Comrade Radu kept chatting. Children, cooking, anything to pass the time.

Tom used to retell some of those stories at home, acting all the parts: the plump Comrade Cosma with the girlish voice and the nervy, slim and tall Comrade Radu with his deep voice. But Comrade Radu's parent-teacher night, when he was told that his son was not doing well, remained my favourite.

Tom set the scene, then slid into their roles while the rest of us looked on, smiling already.

"'How come he has such bad marks? I asked the teacher,'" and Tom, transfigured into Comrade Radu, paused to let the question sink in.

"'And what did he say?'" asked Tom, imitating Comrade Cosma. And on he went, replaying their conversation.

We all laughed, especially Roza. Stefan smiled a reticent smile. He would have preferred Tom to study more and spend less time telling stories.

These funny moments in Tom's work and his father's expectations kept him going, because the rest, the trips up and down the ladder and the excruciatingly boring work, day after day, with no escape in sight, must have been harsh misery. Tom picked up the story again.

> Then the real cold set in. The supervisor kept dropping in to check my record keeping. One day, two workers whom I'd ticked off as working on the upper floor were nowhere to be found. I had not checked the first floor that day. It was icy and I didn't dare to go up the ladder. The men most probably never turned up. 'Comrade, you did not check the top floor,' he said. He said it with such triumph in his voice you would have thought he'd discovered a new continent, not a poor soul who was too scared to go up an icy ladder one day. I tried to explain, it was icy, it was slippery. He was not interested. He wanted to sack me, but someone came up with a compromise: they would turn me into a nightwatchman on the construction site.
>
> Now my main worry was how to tell my father. But as it turned out, he knew already.

Tom rubbed his chin and stood up. 'That's how it was. Let's make a cup of coffee.'

While Tom was making coffee, I wandered away to look at his books. Among the history books on Romania was Ion Pacepa's *Red Horizons*. I had read it in Australia. It is an account of the Ceausescu regime, with stories of imprisonment, set-ups, murder, spying, conspiracies and scheming by Ceausescu and his wife. Pacepa had been the deputy chief of the Romanian foreign intelligence service. He wrote the book after defecting to the USA in 1987, two years before the Ceausescus met their fate.

I was no stranger to what the communist regime in Romania had been capable of, and yet I found the book extremely far-fetched. I wondered what Tom had to say. Were those stories true?

'Apparently it's all true,' Tom replied. 'But if only 50 per cent is true, it's still a shocking enough story.'

'And the story of the Jewish and German emigration?'

'That's true, all right. It's been confirmed.'

According to the book, the emigration of the Romanian Jews was a commercial transaction with Israel. Up to 1966, the Jews were exchanged for chicken farms, turkey, cattle, sheep and pig farms, and later for hard cash. It explained something I never understood when I lived here: why only Jews were allowed to emigrate. It was not a humanitarian deed as the Romanian government maintained, the reunification of the Jewish families whose relatives lived in Israel – it was to make money. As we waited for passports all those long years, there were rumours that we were being sold. We discounted them. We could not take every rumour as fact. Too many, too far-fetched. Some turned out to be true, but at times even truth was hard to believe. With time, the likelihood that Romania was making money from letting the Jews go became more and more plausible. But by the time we left, it had somehow turned into fact.

According to that book, when most Jews had left, Ceausescu set up a similar contract with West Germany, and the Romanian Germans were sold the same way.

As Tom was arranging the cups of coffee on the tray, my mind shifted back to his life in Petrosani and I asked the question which had been troubling me all through his story and would trouble me again during that visit, as I listened to his other struggles.

'Tom, why didn't you tell father about the ladder?'

'I thought the alternative they came up with was better, better than bookkeeping.'

I was not entirely convinced, but I let it go. We sat down again. And after some prodding Tom started to tell me what happened next.

> Reincarnated into a nightwatchman and rugged up to my ears, I walked around the site night after night, looking for thieves and hoping there weren't any. Checking for missing tools and materials. It was cold, it was spooky, but there was no bookkeeping. So it wasn't all bad. And from time to time I had some company. There was another watchman. He did the other parts of the site and shared the shed with me. He wasn't there a lot. He was with his woman. At times he brought her in and I had to make myself scarce. I went out for another round. I went around once, twice, three times. The snow glistened in the moonlight. It squeaked under my boots. The unfinished buildings cast long shadows on the ground.

Night, shadows. Was Tom afraid? Did he see thieves and ghosts and spirits lurking in the lengthy dark shadows? What could he have done with a thief, I wondered as my eye caught his right hand resting awkwardly on the arm of his chair.

> Other times, when I was on my own, I tried to study. At times the chief security man dropped in for a chat. He was a friendly guy; he broke the monotony of the long nights. Sometimes I fell asleep. Every now and then a strong gust of wind would shake the shed. It screeched and cried. I would wake up, check the door and look through the window. There was never anybody there but the dance of the blizzard. At times a faint wolf howl hung in the air for a moment then died.
>
> The other watchman returned to the shed from time to time to have a drink of his *tuica*. He always kept a bottle there. I get drunk easily, but at times I would take a few sips. One day I bought myself a bottle and from then on every night, after my rounds, I had a few celebratory sips. Sometimes more than a few sips. It warmed me up, it relaxed

me. I sat in my cosy sheepskin coat in the corner from where I could just see through the small window into the night. No one ever tried to steal anything and even if someone had, what could have I done? There was no phone, and if the other man was out, there wasn't anybody to help. Overcome by warmth, I would sit there dozing.

One night I heard a loud knock. I stumbled to the door and turned the key. In front of me stood a tall man I had not seen before. The new chief. 'Good evening,' he said and extended his hand.

'Good evening', I replied and extended mine.

The dud one, the one which can barely hold a hand, let alone shake it energetically. In a world where handshakes between men establish hierarchy and strength, it's not hard to imagine the chief's reaction.

And he comes in and spots the half-empty bottle in the corner and he is not impressed and I tell him that is only to keep me warm. 'The rules don't allow for such warm-ups,' he says, then opens the door and disappears into the night.

In the following weeks Tom continued to do his rounds among the shadows and the unseen. Back in the shed he took his warming sips of alcohol but made sure not to fall asleep. He smoked, studied and read books. The supervisor kept dropping in. In the morning he went home and headed straight to bed. And that's where all the problems started.

Tom slept during the day because he hardly slept at work anymore. But Roza only saw what was in front of her: Tom lying under the doona, day after day. Every now and then when Tom was out of earshot she would say to me, 'He should have passed his exams. He didn't even front up for all his exams. He didn't even try. Why?'

I hoped she asked the questions rhetorically, to unburden herself. So I remained silent. I had no idea why Tom did not pass his exams. I assumed that he did not work hard enough, but I wouldn't have said such a thing. I would not throw petrol on the fire of her resentment.

'He was in a big city, not in a coal-hole like this one. He had a big room, fine furniture, nice carpets. A beautifully furnished big room,' she repeated again and again.

In Roza's mind, Tom's real or imagined beautiful room in Cluj, which he gave up by coming home, had taken the place of our beautiful house in Kesdivasarhely, the house we were pushed out of by the authorities. Or maybe the one in Brasov which was nationalised soon after I was born. Tom abandoned willingly something she would have held onto with all her might. Tom was a layabout, a good-for-nothing.

'We sent him money regularly. We hardly had enough for food. And he had the audacity not to even front up for his exams.' I felt ill-at-ease listening to my mother. I had no answers to our situation.

'I spent my young years teaching him to walk. He was not like the other kids, he wore a brace on his leg. I put all my energy into it, my soul. When he started school, I sat with him day after day, patiently teaching him to read and write, to write with his left hand.'

And while she was telling me all this, Tom slept. He slept in the one and only bedroom in our flat, the bedroom where Yossi and I slept at night. Tom slept there until late morning, often till lunchtime. In the corner of the room there was a chest of drawers and a small wardrobe where the bed linen and the clothes were kept.

Day after day Roza walked past the doona-covered lump. She had to walk around him to clean, to put the freshly ironed clothes away, she would squat at the end of the bed to clean the stove and set the fire. Through all this Tom slept and slept, or maybe just hid under the doona, who knows. He would not have had the courage to lie there with open eyes and watch Roza. And Roza's resentment grew. 'How can he be such a nobody?' she would often ask. 'When other young men are studying or working, Tom is asleep. What will this lead to?'

In the morning, one or two hours after Tom had gone to bed, Roza would return home from her early morning queuing, sometimes lucky but most times not. On rare occasions she would announce: 'A whole kilo of meat!' and her face would be lit by a smile. A kilo of meat smile, because for four days she did not have to worry about food. The only way Roza could feed five people for four days from a kilo of meat was by extending the meat. She was good with extensions. She was good in making you think you ate rissoles – meat extended with bread – when in fact you ate bread extended with meat. For the stuffed cabbage, she extended rice with meat, when it should have been the other way around.

On cold winter mornings she would return half-frozen, put down her shopping and start setting the fire in the big brown-tiled stove in the lounge room. I can still see her squatting next to the open iron door of the stove, fire scrubber in her hand, her sleeves coated with a fine powder of grey ashes and black charcoal marks ...

She pulls the remnants of yesterday's fire onto a dustpan, then empties the dustpan into the bucket. One, two, three times. Ashes, cinders and unburned coal fall into the bucket. She repeats the scrubbing, gathering and emptying until the stove is ready for its next mission. She arranges the kindling on top of a scrunched newspaper and grabs the matches.

'Mummy! Mummy!' Yossi calls from his bed.

'He will have to wait, the fire is first,' Roza says to herself, but loud enough that I can hear.

Yossi is crying. Tom is asleep and I am getting ready for school.

Roza puts two scoops of coal onto the burning kindling. Will the fire take off? She is standing next to the stove ready to intervene. Yossi is calling again. I go to pacify him: 'Yossi, Mummy will be here soon. Shhh, Tom is asleep. And you don't want to disturb him, do you?' Yossi goes quiet for a few minutes. In the lounge room the fire is out.

'This useless stove! It's the same every morning,' Roza says, and squats next to the stove again. She pushes the coal to the side and starts to blow air into the remaining embers. The stove is full of smoke. The way out through the badly built chimney is difficult and the smoke decides to take a far easier exit, into the lounge room. Coughing, Roza runs to open the window. The smoke wanders out, the cold air rushes in. She returns to squatting and blowing. At last

168

the fire starts crackling again, but Roza is not about to budge. She keeps blowing. Head to one side, a deep breath, then back towards the fire, she blows and blows until her face turns red. 'Well, that's probably it.' She shuts the door of the stove and goes to wash her face and hands. Yossi is crying. He wants to get up but he knows he can't, not until the fire is on.

The lump under the doona does not move.

'It's beyond me how can he sleep through so much noise,' Roza says. She shuts the window and goes to get Yossi.

Yossi's face is covered with tears, tears of hunger; he does not cry otherwise. He is three years old already. He is beautiful, a joy to look at. He is much loved by everyone, but even more by his mother. She adores him. She did not expect to have another child at the age of thirty-six and Yossi is beautiful in a Pollak sort of way. He takes after her family and carries her father's name.

Roza plants a big kiss on his cheek and seats him at the table so she can go and prepare breakfast. Rugged up in a blanket, Yossi is watching me packing my school bag, not quite sure whether to cry or not. 'Here, just don't tear it.' I give him my history textbook because it has pictures and because I cannot stand children crying, and I can stand history even less.

Roza is back. Yossi gulps down the warm milk, takes a few bites of his bread with jam, his smile wider with every bite. And so are Roza's, who cannot take her eyes off him. She rearranges his blanket, ready to take him into the kitchen. 'I have to start on the soup and get the washing in. The wind from the mines is blowing our way again. The washing is frozen solid and covered with polka dots of soot. Sheets, shirts, towels, the lot. And I have to do another load today.' She washes everything by hand with water heated on the stove …

Around lunchtime Tom would get up, have a wash, have something to eat and try to study. But he must have found it difficult because he would soon put down his textbooks and start to read books. No one ever came to visit him. He knew no one in that town. He had spent his school years in Brasov and the previous year at university in Cluj. Yossi was his only company. I was at school or doing homework, or having fun with friends. My father was at work until nearly dinnertime.

Tom loved Yossi. He used to say, 'He looks like a pageboy.' He told him stories. Yossi loved listening to Tom's stories, but the story of the little girl worried him a bit, the little girl who wandered away from her mother into the forest and discovered a wooden house full of chocolate.

'A big fluffy cat guarded the house. The cat told her, "You greedy girl! If you eat much more you will turn into a boy." The little girl did not mind being a boy, so she kept eating.'

'It's okay to be a boy,' Yossi would say, looking worried.

'Of course it is. And she quite fancied the idea of trying it out. To see what it's like. So she ate and ate.

'Angry for not being obeyed, the cat used his special powers and turned her into a boy.

'The light was fading by the time the little boy left the magic house. He heard his father and mother calling out to the little girl. But she was now a boy, so how would she explain it?'

Sometimes Tom let the ending of the story hang, and when Yossi asked, 'What happened then?' the ending was always different. But it always ended well, whether the boy convinced his parents that he was the little girl by telling them things which only she could know, or whether they recognised him because he looked so much like their daughter. In the end the three of them went home happy.

———

A couple of months into his new job as a nightwatchman, Tom got the sack. He was found drunk at work. Roza was incensed: 'A *shicker* (drunk)! Only goys get drunk. We Jews have many faults but one thing we don't do, we don't drink ourselves to oblivion. A *shicker*! A *shicker* in my family!' she would repeat to me in the kitchen. 'What next? Poor Stefan, as if he does not have enough on his head. He did talk to Tom about it, about not drinking, about having a job. But did Tom listen? Poor, poor Stefan.'

Tom was home all day, the five-year plan was behind, my father kept going for long walks, to relieve the stress and clear his mind.

Another month passed …

It's early afternoon. I am sitting at the dining table doing my homework. Suddenly I hear my mother shouting: 'You can't go on like this, doing nothing all day –'

Tom is saying something, but I cannot hear.

'Can't you see? You're destroying your father.'

Oh no, not another argument. I have to make myself scarce, make sure that the war does not spread to me. I slip out quietly. But not fast enough.

'You will kill your father!' My mother screams between sobs.

Again I cannot hear Tom's reply. Tears are rolling down my cheeks. Tears of fear, of unhappiness. I am halfway down the stairs. There is a bang. And another one. How come the neighbours are not out yet? Dead silence. Was someone hit? Did someone fall? I stand there waiting. The stillness is frightening.

I run out into the street, past the next building and the one after. I cannot stand our life at home. I want to go and live at my friend Benny's place. He has a beautiful mother, she is always calm and relaxed, she is always smiling and loving. I run down the main street and turn into the little dark courtyard. I stop to get my breath and knock on the door. Benny is at home. I tell him that my mother is having a big argument with Tom, but I don't tell him the whole truth, just the bare minimum, because I am ashamed of our household, I am ashamed of having a mother like mine, I am ashamed that I hate her so much.

When I return my mother has red eyes. She is getting dressed to go out. Tom is smoking a cigarette. Soon my father will be home. Why is my mother getting dressed? Oh, to tell him what happened. They only have privacy on the street. A secret conversation after a big argument is a very bad sign indeed. It means my mother can give her side of the story, which is exactly that: her side of the story. I suspect that Tom's version is quite different.

My father is at the door. He puts his briefcase down and I hear my mother telling him that they'll have to go for a walk. The door shuts behind them and I am left with Tom and Yossi. Tom is not saying anything. I don't dare to ask what happened, but I know that something bad happened, possibly something awful.

Nobody says anything to me all evening. Tom comes and goes. The flat is silent and full of smoke. I look at my family. Their world is not my world. I am no longer the daughter or the sister. I am nothing but a witness.

The next day Tom is packing. Three days later my father and Tom are off to the station.

'I don't want to have anything to do with you until you become a decent human being,' his father says to him as they part …

Tom has not forgotten that morning. Or his father's words. It was a summer day, the sun shone in the misty sky. I remember it too. I barely slept the previous night. I wondered what happened between Tom and my mother. And what would Tom do in Cluj. Outside the window two dogs were fighting. One of them howled, long and sinister. It amplified the uneasiness and desperation I felt about Tom, about our family, about life.

'I never wanted to hurt him,' Tom said to me as we sat in his kitchen talking.

> I felt guilty. Then my father uttered those parting words which have stayed with me ever since. I felt guilty, but was I that guilty? True, I did not work hard enough and I ended up drinking. But let's face it, no hard work would have spared me from endless misunderstandings, from losing jobs I was not suited for. And the arguments with my irrational stepmother? Why didn't my father acknowledge that she was not always blameless? Whether she was irrational because of what happened to her family during the war, I don't know. I think she probably was, I think she needed therapy. But that's another issue.
>
> I would go to Cluj, I decided. I had no idea what I would

do when I got there, but I knew what I was leaving behind. I would get away from that God-forsaken place, Petrosani. Nothing had worked for me in that town. I had been sent away in the past and I managed. I would manage again. I would start all over. Nobody would ever tell me what to do. I was free.

That was all Tom was prepared to share with me. He did not tell me what actually happened between him and his stepmother. He acted as if nothing happened, but I know that whatever happened, he could not have forgotten. It ended up in him losing his family. But no matter how much I tried, Tom would not talk about it.

That parting took its toll on my father too. The following weeks he hardly said anything to us at home. He sat pensively in a corner and smoked, detached, a spectator of his own life. Every now and then he went for a long walk, and when he returned he sat in silence. Even little Yossi could rarely make him smile.

I tried to tell myself that Tom's leaving was just another event for our family, that he had been sent away before. But things felt different. Now, our family, a precious vase with lots of cracks, had taken another blow, a much bigger blow. I felt that we would never be the same again.

I was right. From that day our lives diverged like the branches of a tree. Tom ceased to be part of our lives, my mother's and mine, if not my father's. I suspect he never stopped hurting.

True to his word, my father did not have anything to do with his son for months. Then we applied for passports to go to Israel and he wrote to him to apply too. Tom wrote back that he was not going to.

We did not see him until we got our passports, nearly nine years later when my father and I went to say goodbye. Before we parted, my father asked me to leave him alone with Tom for a while. I don't know what they said to each other, or what they left unsaid. But they must have known that it could be their last encounter.

17

The autumn rain, which used to fall uninterrupted for days, forgot to arrive in 2002. The summer seemed unending. Looking at the tired sun and the sagging leaves on the trees, one could not help thinking that nature was in trouble, that all was not well on this earth. Nor was it in Cluj, or in that park where Tom and I were sitting watching the passers-by. The benches, all painted in the Romanian national colours – red, yellow and blue – ceased to be mere benches; they had become political statements, asserting a belonging.

Every now and then someone waved to Tom. He bowed his head and greeted them politely. He seemed to have many acquaintances. One of them, a slight man in his sixties who knew Tom from way back, joined us on the bench. The introductions over, Mr Szabo asked me, 'Well, what do you think about our latest craze? Tell me, dear Madam, which other country would place the national colours under the backside of its citizens?'

This was not a question I could answer. He told me that imbuing citizens with patriotism through their backside was a Cluj special, the idea of the chauvinist Romanian mayor, Gheorghe Funar. Within months of his election, commemorative plaques changed, Romanian flags appeared on every official building and national colours on every public surface, including every rubbish bin. He wanted to make sure that Transylvania would never be reclaimed by Hungarians. There was indignation in Mr Szabo's voice, a resigned indignation.

I have no doubt that the mayor's propaganda appealed to some.

There have always been Hungarians who dreamed of a greater Hungary, but others like Mr Szabo just wanted to get on with life. Many Hungarians had married Romanians and did not care about loyalty to either side. The thinking Romanians must have felt ashamed that such a chauvinist could become the mayor of a town, a university town of all places.

Having unburdened himself and enlightened me with the latest on Hungarian-Romanian coexistence, Mr Szabo stood up to go. 'In this country, dear Madam, we are all actors in the theatre of the absurd,' he said and departed.

Tom and I strolled to the café by the river, at the other end of the park. The café was nearly empty. An old Italian song played through the loudspeaker above the door. Tom ordered a coffee for himself and a mineral water for me. We sat silently and watched the ducks gliding on the river, their dark greens and indigos shimmering in the sun.

'By the way, Tom, how did you get to be this decent human being sitting in front of me?'

Tom laughed, then sat silently sipping his coffee.

'What happened when you came back to Cluj?'

He shrugged. 'I went back to work and study.'

'And then?'

'Then? Everything was fine for a while, then my life turned again.'

And in between cigarettes and silences he told me his story.

It was January 1959, a year and a half since Tom left Petrosani and our family for what turned out to be the last time, more than a year since that early Monday morning when his father had taken him to the station and said to him, 'I don't want to have anything to do with you until you become a decent human being.'

As Tom was getting ready for his evening shift, he wondered why the Government had suddenly announced a public holiday a few days before. The nation would celebrate one hundred years since the unification of Moldavia and Wallachia, the birth of Romania.

Did the Government just find out when the Romanian nation was born? He picked up his textbooks (he had two more exams to finish the first year of his Biology degree), put his warm overcoat on and walked out into the cold winter evening, in time for his night shift. Fifteen minutes walk away was the student dormitory where he had been a nightwatchman for more than a year. He walked past Piata Unirii (Unification Square) and soon after arrived at work.

Tom was not the only one wondering what was going on, why the late announcement. Possible unrest? Barely more than two years had passed since the 1956 Hungarian Revolution. Was there a whiff of threat in the air? Did they want to ensure that the troublemakers did not have enough time to get organised? Troublemakers? Tom was not aware of any.

The night passed uneventfully. In between recording who left the building and who came back, Tom tried to study. Early the next morning, the morning of the centenary, Tom finished his shift and went home. And while he slept peacefully in his bed, crowds of young people, many of them students, started gathering in Piata Unirii.

By lunchtime the celebrations were in full swing. Mingled in the crowd were the Securitate, some in khaki uniforms, others in civilian clothes: the Party's invisible eyes and ears, alert to every word and action.

This was not an orchestrated event. There was wholehearted singing and plenty of drinking. '*Multi ani traiasca!*' – 'Long should she live!' the crowd chanted.

'To the Birthday of the Nation!' shouted others. 'Happy Birthday, Romania!'

As the day progressed, the crowds got merrier and merrier, the songs more nationalistic. The *hora* went into full swing; all those who could move their feet were dancing. By evening all inhibitions were gone. Every now and then a call went through the crowd, not to the long life of the Party, but to the exiled King. The Party's eyes and ears kept walking around, listening and taking notes. Let the enemies of socialism show their true colours. The rest would follow later.

Tom was back at his night duties. The students were coming and going, mostly going out.

'On holidays I did not have to keep records of who went out and who came back,' Tom told me. 'But that night I didn't study, I sat and read H.G. Wells' *The Invisible Man*, which my colleague kept in our office. Brilliant book, don't you think? I kept pondering whether changing a person's refractive index to that of air makes him invisible and whether there is far more to this world than we can see.'

While Tom was immersed in reading, in Piata Unirii the students were having fun. But their fun was disrespectful to Matthias Corvinus, the fifteenth-century King of Hungary, born in that city and still sitting proudly on his horse in the middle of the Square five hundred years later. Some students joined him on his bronze horse. Matthias Corvinus was mocked, but so were the Romanian flags. Was the Hungarian king mocked by nationalist Romanians, or by nationalist Hungarians because he was half-Romanian by birth? Or was he mocked because many were under the influence, or were they just hooligans? But one thing was sure: the ears and eyes of the Party kept taking notes. They were not there to defend the image of an exploiting king but because crowd disobedience could not be allowed, not when two years beforehand, on the other side of the border in Hungary, disobedience had turned into a revolution.

A few days later, long before sunrise, the Securitate started knocking on doors. A few sons and daughters, husbands and fathers were taken away, under the watch of their family who could not hide their fear, mothers who swore that their offspring had done nothing wrong. In student dormitories names were called out. Some students were arrested. The others were frozen with terror.

> And then the Securitate wanted to see my records, they wanted to see the names of the students who went out that evening. I had no records. It was a public holiday, so I did not need to write down who went out. They became suspicious. My dossier did not help. My father was an ex-factory owner, my family had applied to leave the country. True, I hadn't,

but my parents had, and you know how that was. We all carried our dossiers like a camel carries his hump. I kept telling them that I did not know who went out and who didn't, I had paid no attention, I didn't have to. I said I was reading a book. And stupidly I cracked a few jokes.

Jokes? Cracking jokes and smiling at the Securitate? Only a fool would have done that. But maybe that was his salvation. Some people associate physical disability with mental deficiency. Maybe they thought that Tom was an idiot. But he was definitely no longer a trustworthy man. And what better way to resolve the conflict between nationalism, the rowdiness of students and the paranoia of the government with its unflinching determination to maintain the status quo, than to sack the nightwatchman? And so the unification of Moldavia and Walachia a century earlier, coupled with communist paranoia, colluded in Tom losing his job just as he was about to become that decent human being his father had ordered him to be. But some were even worse off, some were in prison. And Tom was grateful for his fate.

In the coming weeks I tried to get another job as a nightwatchman. I couldn't. I was running out of money. By mid-April I couldn't pay the rent any more. Luckily the winter was over.

He lit a cigarette and inhaled deeply. We sat in silence. Two young couples walked in and headed towards the table in the corner, the women carefully dressed.

'Tom, did you end up on the street?' I asked eventually.

'I just slept in the park for a while.'

'This park?'

He nodded.

'In April the nights can be freezing.'

He shrugged.

I dressed warm. I had blankets. The biggest problem was not the cold, although some nights were unpleasant. The drunks were more of a problem. They were unpredictable, sometimes downright nasty. I slept lightly, like a bird, part of my brain keeping watch.

He paused, dragged deeply on his cigarette, then exhaled slowly.

In the morning I got up with the sunlight. Anyway, I preferred to be away long before the students started streaming through on their way to the university.

Because the students would have recognised him. Many must have known him because of his limp, but also because he started conversations easily and probably had chatted to many.

One morning, I saw this middle-aged man sweeping a street, next to *Piata Unirii*. Suddenly I had this brilliant idea: surely even a man with bad social origins could get a street-sweeper's job. All of a sudden my day looked promising. I would ask him how he got his job and I crossed the Square. He told me to talk to his chief.

I was in luck. The chief had work for me, and I could start the next day. So next day, armed with a cart and one of those tall witch's brooms, one of those ending with a half-metre long head of fine twigs, I started on my street-sweeping career.

Tom laughed.

'Street sweeping? Wasn't it hard for you?'

He shrugged.

I did it bit by bit. Gradually. I set off from the bottom of the street. Sweeping, bending, was not a problem, but pushing the nearly full cart uphill was hard. But I was no longer cold. Drops of perspiration were rolling down my forehead. Remember how my father always insisted that we go for a walk, or play outside? Well, I was outside all right, and doing plenty of exercise.

At lunchtime, all the street sweepers gathered in the corner where one of the side streets joins the square and sweeping responsibilities converged. I got plenty of advice on how to cut corners. 'Just start from the top of the street. Believe me, it's much easier to go downhill with a full cart than uphill.'

When I finished work, I decided to visit Aunt Anna. Have a bath and ask for a loan. And later, if it was still light, to follow up on what the Gypsy man in the park had told me the previous day about a man with a hen house. The authorities were after him for keeping chickens illegally. He wanted to let it. A lodger would prove that it was not a hen house, at least not entirely. And it would be very cheap.

Aunt Anna was worried. Another blemish in my dossier. She advised me to disappear from Cluj. She promised to help, make some enquiries.

Next morning I was back at work. My mind was foggy. It would be easier among the chickens, I thought. No more procrastination, I would talk to the owner of the hen house as soon as I finished work and started sweeping from the top of the hill as advised by the experts.

Tom smiled mischievously.

The street had a small slope and I had to park the cart diagonally so it stayed in one spot. A female student I used to chat to in the library walked past. She looked at me, puzzled. One day in the library, another day sweeping streets? People did not lose their jobs in those days. It's my first week, I told her, but soon it would be summer and I'd get such a tan I'd be irresistible. She laughed and walked on.

There was hardly any traffic, only the odd bus. As I advanced, the slope got steeper and steeper and I was less and less able to park the cart. Now the problem was not pushing a heavy cart uphill, but holding it back. It had to be parked at the right angle, otherwise it kept trying to run away like a disobedient child. I had just decided that I had worked it all out, when suddenly the cart took off towards the opposite side of the street. I never thought I could be that agile. I dropped the broom as I ran and managed to grab the handles. Well, sort of ran.

Ran? More like leaped and jerked from one leg to the other, short leg, long leg, short leg, long leg.

I could not stop it. It was in charge; it pulled me across, hit the kerb and jumped back from the impact. And as it did, I lost my footing and fell into the cart. But that was not the end of it. The cart turned slightly, rolled down a metre or so, hit the kerb again, and landed on its side, rolling out the morning rubbish and me with it. Three men ran to help me. I didn't need help. I managed to steady myself with my left hand and leg, and picked myself up. The men stood up the empty cart.

And I have no doubt that Tom gathered the morning rubbish, smiling, then started to sweep again. Downhill he went, sweeping, gathering and parking his cart, all the way down the rest of the street.

This was as far as Tom's recollections about this period of his life went, the recollections he was willing to share with me. He did not want to talk about what happened next. It seems that around the time he rolled out with the rubbish onto the road, he didn't just hit the kerb, he hit rock bottom of his life. Did he finally lose his extraordinary optimism? The optimism which so impresses me, an optimism which seems to help him overcome all setbacks, all disasters, no matter how big and painful?

Tom stood up to go. I wanted to stay and have dinner.

'It's only six thirty, for goodness' sake.'

'How about one of those grilled chicken breast with –'

'Chips and salad,' he said and his face lit up. Tom could not resist chips.

I waved to the waiter.

The sun was about to set. *Non existe amour*, the old Italian song, came through the loudspeaker. Once it might have brought tears to my eyes, because I had not heard this song for thirty years, but on that day I felt only emptiness, as if my soul had been excised. I carried our family's guilt for not helping Tom when he needed us most. I was guilty, personally guilty, for not asking about Tom for years. And guilty for being part of a world which does not give the disabled a chance. I even felt guilty for having a biological mother who seemed to have displaced Hella from my father's affections. Or maybe she didn't. Maybe my father just couldn't cope with so many opposing forces in his life. Maybe he had to choose, maybe he gave up. Just like I did.

Back in Tom's flat we retreated to his cosy little room with the red Persian carpets, his mother's photographs behind me. I enquired about the hen house. How long was he there for? Tom refused point-blank to talk about it.

'Let's make a cup of tea,' he said.

He put the kettle on while I prepared the cups and the saucers, cut a couple of slices of lemon and placed a teabag into one of the cups.

'One teabag should be enough for at least two cups,' Tom reminded me every time I was about to use a new teabag. He lived in a very different world to mine, and yet he never thought himself poor or in need of anything. He barely had a carbon footprint. He hardly had any rubbish. If his bread went stale, he gave it to the school cleaners, who fed it to their hens and pigs. In exchange, every now and then, they gave him sausages and bacon. He gathered the breadcrumbs and put them on the windowsill to feed the pigeons. He lived frugally, not only because he could not afford a different life but because he could not see the point of living any other way.

As we were waiting for the kettle to boil, I tried again. 'Tom, what happened with the hen house?'

'I slept there too. I had chickens shitting on me at night.'

'For how long?'

'Not very long.' He paused. 'Long enough. No point in talking about that. Anyway, with all the changes in the school, who knows? I could end up on the street again.'

'It won't happen. I promise. I'll do everything I can to make sure that it does not happen.'

We returned to the small room with our cups of tea to watch the evening news. It was full of price increases and political in-fights. After twenty minutes Tom had had enough; he switched the TV off and told me the story of how he ended up in Nedelea.

While Tom was sweeping the streets, Aunt Anna was working on his future. She had an idea. She discovered a special school for the physically disabled, with courses in accounting or animal breeding. The choice was clear: animal breeding, of course. The school was in Nedelea, near Ploiesti. Tom would be away from Cluj for at least three years – who knows, maybe even longer. The emphasis was on being away. He would be out of sight and hopefully out of mind of all those who found him suspicious. With time, the 1959 student unrest would fade into the background.

It was raining, the sky a menacing dark grey when Tom got off the train in Ploiesti station in September 1959. In the distance the famous oil wells of Ploiesti, the oil wells which fuelled the German tanks during the Second World War and later pumped oil for the Russians, were nodding. It was a desolate sight.

A bus took him to Nedelea. He was not sure what to expect. A school for handicapped students, some young and some like Tom, in their twenties. He consoled himself that he would have a roof over his head, he would learn new things and he would end up with a professional qualification. Animal breeding? Well, so be it.

Nedelea was still being built when Tom arrived. There was no running water, the pipes were waiting in the mud to be laid.

> We washed in the river nearby, the Prahova which made its way down to the Danube, past the oilfields. The water stank of petrol. We got used to it. There were no toilets inside the building. At night the younger boys were too scared to go out. Nedelea was full of stray dogs. 'At night their bodies are taken over by ghosts,' the boys said, and just peed through the open window. One night a teacher passed under the window and got sprayed. The boy was nearly expelled. Nobody ever dared to pee out of the window again.
>
> Meanwhile the construction progressed, water pipes and internal toilets were installed within a few months, but the boys never stopped frightening themselves with ghost stories.

I looked at Tom. I could imagine him being terrified by the dogs driven around by ghosts. I had the impression that at times he was happy to switch off his judgement and shift into the supernatural, the mystical. Maybe it was related to meeting his mother again, of finding acceptance in a different life.

'I have enough people on the other side,' he told me one day. And seeing my puzzled look, he added, 'They'll look after me. Hope is my only religion.'

Tom did not complain about Nedelea, but an old colleague of his whom we met on the street said to me, 'I don't even want to think about that place, it was awful. I'd like to erase all memories of it.' She had no disability.

'Around ten per cent of the students had no disability,' Tom told me later.

> I guess she was one of the ten per cent. I don't know why she was there. But it was not all bad, she met her husband there. Half of his right arm was missing. Ninety per cent of students had some kind of disability. One had a short left leg, the other a short right leg, one had one arm, the other had one arm and a half. There were some really bright kids there.

Tom assured me that he did not mind Nedelea.

> The teachers were good. The best were there as a punishment for their social origins, or to be re-educated. Like the one who studied in France and later became a monk. By the time he got to Nedelea he was an ex-monk all right.

> I specialised in aviculture – chickens. Others did apiculture – bee-keeping. That wasn't for me, it needed more of a right hand than I had. I worked it out, people will always need chickens, I would always have a job. And with free eggs and free chickens, I would always have something to eat.

Tom tried to convince me that he did not mind being at a handicapped school, but he did not want to reminisce about it and went out for a smoke.

A strong smell of cigarette preceded Tom's return. He shuffled straight to the kitchen to make coffee and I settled down with one of his books. The book was about Gherla, the prison where political detainees were locked up by the communist regime. The prisoners were occupied making boxes of matches. Every box of matches in this country had printed on it 'Made in Gherla'. Everybody knew what Gherla meant and everybody used matches. It was a brilliant way to keep people under control.

'Tom, can we visit Gherla tomorrow?'

He was not enthused. 'My dear, the public transport is very poor on the weekend. Besides, it is not a riveting place. What about something more cheerful, you Westerner?'

'I'd like to see it.'

'Okay. Just don't say I didn't warn you.'

'Let's see what the weather is like tomorrow,' I proposed, not wanting to give in unless I really had to. 'Now tell me what happened when you graduated.'

And Tom recounted his time as a graduate from Nedelea, a fully-fledged aviculture technician.

'I landed a job in a *Gostat*, three kilometres outside Cluj. I was back.'

'Your past sins forgotten?'

'No doubt they were in my dossier. I was feeding chickens, cleaning shit, but I was no longer a threat to the system. I guess they could have blamed me for being a threat to the chickens.' He laughed. 'We cleaned lots of shit. Sorry, I should have said sheds. The *Gostat* had two thousand chickens. So we were not short of work.'

'*Gostat*? What's a *Gostat*?'

He shrugged his shoulder as if the name was self-explanatory. 'You should know what a *Gostat* is.'

'I don't.'

My *Gostat* was a chicken farm, a state chicken farm. We fed them, cleaned the sheds and kept statistics of how many were sick and how many died. Statistics were important, healthy chickens were important. Among other chores, I had to take chickens to the lab to be checked for diseases.

When I said that I might have been a threat to the chickens I meant it. One beautiful summer day, and luckily it was summer, I and another guy caught a dozen chickens, put them in boxes and loaded them onto a cart. This old cart was held together more by God's good will than the scores and scores of repairs and fixing by inept and uninterested people. The cart was drawn by an even older horse, which the *Gostat* got from the army because it was old and nearly blind and they could not use him any longer. The poor bugger was destined to be fed to chickens but no, the decision-makers detected some life in him and decided to work him a few more months. Why feed a perfectly working horse to chickens? Let him work for the honour.

We also loaded a few empty water containers which I would take to Cluj and have them filled with drinking water once I dropped the chickens at the laboratory. We had no potable water in the *Gostat*, it was too salty.

So after days of rain the sun was shining, not a cloud. My life is good, I thought; I had four eggs for breakfast. I have definitely chosen a good profession. As long as I can put up with the smell and the shit, I'll never die of hunger. So there I am, getting on the cart, the old horse waiting resignedly, the sun shining above. A perfect day. Just the right weather for a leisurely trip to Cluj, I muse, and give the horse a bit of a prod. The poor old sod starts out slowly, but then what can you expect from a blind old horse who is considered long past his best and destined to be fed to chickens in a few months? Finally we reach the river, the other side of which is the laboratory. A smallish river, a rivulet, which had filled up quite a bit after the latest rain. My horse puts his first foot in the river and I detect hesitation. Come on! I prod again. You'll be right.

He moves his second foot reluctantly into the water, then stops. I whip him slightly, enough to make him understand that he will have to keep moving, but he goes in faster than I expected, takes two paces, hits a small rock, loses his balance and falls on his side into the water, pulling with him the carriage, the chickens, the water containers – and me, of course.

I disentangle myself from the reins and manage to pull myself up somehow. The hens, those which have not drowned yet, are making a racket. Two workers are running to save the horse, but I think he prefers to be fodder to the chickens because he is coughing, convulsing, maybe drowning. By the time the boxes are lifted out of the water, the chickens are no longer a representative sample. I don't know if it was the good vet or just a miracle, but the horse did survive for a few more months.

The accident improved the statistics. That day the *Gostat* reported that there were no diseased chickens.

The *Gostat* was riddled with rats. To keep the statistics looking good we had to keep the rats away, we could not allow the chickens to die. We took turns with the chickens at night. But how do you keep hungry rats away from so much food just in front of them? I sat in the chicken shed and made as much noise as I could. I sang, I even sang the *Internationale* to them, but not even the threat of united workers could keep them away.

Tom was laughing.

After eight months of chickens and chicken shit, I decided to find a job in Cluj and get a permit to live in this town. I was still interested in animal breeding, but only in theory. I decided the practical side was not for me and my career as an aviculturalist was over. I do miss the fresh eggs, though.

'And what about the *Gostat*? Still farming chickens?'

'No. It does not. They could not control the rat population so they closed it down.'

'So you returned to Cluj. And then?'

I became a tutor in a construction school. I had to supervise the pupils in the afternoon while they were doing their lessons, help them with their homework, keep discipline. No, not Makarenko style. I'm joking of course, there was no physical punishment in those days.

I loved it. I love young people – they are clever and fresh. I even like their mischief as long as it does not go too far. But then you got the passports to go to Israel and they found out. I could not be trusted with young people any more. I could indoctrinate the kids with who knows what attitude, turn them into enemies of the state. Like me.

He smiled.

So after a couple of odd jobs, I became a gateman here in the school. I was twenty-seven years old. I have remained here ever since. Gateman, nightwatchman, street sweeper, but finally a permanent job, secure and with a roof over my head.

18

The Furious Doughnut did not sell doughnuts, not doughnuts as we know them in the West. It sold *langos*, a yeasty dough the size of a hand, fried in oil, with a savoury or sweet filling. At my suggestion, Tom and I joined the *langos* queue which extended nearly as far as the bus stop. At my suggestion, because I had not had a *langos* for decades, not since I had left the country. Nostalgia for old food, not because I liked it so much, but because it reminded me of my mother in the kitchen kneading the dough, her arms and eyelashes white with flour, the old dish sitting on the corner of the table covered with a clean cloth. And later, much later, my mother dropping squares of dough filled with cheese and onion in hot oil, just like they did in that shop.

The Furious Doughnut was a shop without a main street entrance. The queue came to a head at a small window where a nondescript woman with an apron and without a Western smile exchanged one's money for plain *langos*, *langos* with cheese, *langos* with cheese and onion, or sweet *langos* filled with jam, in a small piece of greaseproof paper if intended for immediate consumption or in a brown paper bag to be taken away.

We were about to reach the head of the queue when the woman fished out the last frying *langos* and placed it on a cooling rack. She topped up the oil and moved a tray of ready-to-cook *langos* close by. Her face was red from the heat, her apron covered with a fine dust of flour. One by one she picked up a *langos* and lowered it into the hot oil. Bad timing, I thought. We would have to wait until the new batch was cooked.

I stood and watched the *langos* sizzling, bubbling, jumping around as if furious about it all. After a while my patience wore thin and, shifting from foot to foot, I whispered in Tom's ear, 'I hate queuing.' He looked at me stunned.

'You hate queueing? My dear, we used to have much longer queues. It's where we socialised, made friends, met future wives. Forget about marriages made in heaven, in communism marriages were made in queues.' And turning to the smiling twenty-something-year-old standing next to him, he asked, 'See what you missed out on, Miss? You'd be engaged by the time you got to the head of the queue.' He shook his head from side to side. 'Bad luck to have missed out on communism.'

Miss, a plain-looking girl, went red between her pimples.

Soon our *langos* was cooling on the rack. The woman took the money, dropped the *langos* into a brown bag and we set off for Tom's flat – via a couple of bookshops, of course.

It was late afternoon. The sun was setting. A single star was shimmering in the sky and a pale crescent moon was looking at the town. The school was silent. Tom stayed downstairs to talk to someone. I went upstairs. I felt on edge, pent-up energy from sitting inside too much. I needed a break. I longed for the autumn hills and the lazy sunsets of the countryside. The fresh air, the long silent walks. I longed for a tired body, a blank mind, emotional detachment.

It was nearly dinner time so I made a salad and began setting the table. Since Tom's dishwashing was not up to my standard, setting the table started with me washing every piece of crockery and cutlery before use. The first time I took a 'clean' plate out of the cupboard and started to wash it, Tom shook his head in disbelief, then seeing my determination to wash off 'the unseen', shrugged his shoulders in resignation and left me to it. After a day or so he got used to it; he even expected it. 'You might as well go and wash it,' he said every time I took something out of the cupboard. No point in arguing with an obsessive.

The table was all set when Tom walked in. We sat down to eat, me facing the open window, he with his back to it. He did not like capsicum. 'It is Western and tasteless.' He liked the long pepper variety and brought one from the fridge to demonstrate. After I tasted both, I had to agree. Even the small tomatoes from the market seemed tastier than I had had for years. Perhaps they were fresher, or just less battered by chemicals.

Tom stopped talking to concentrate on eating. The cheese and the *taramasalata* (fish roe salad) deserved his whole attention. *Taramasalata*! He had never had such an expensive spread. We ate in silence. Through the open window I could see a crow gliding, circling in the sky. In the courtyard below a few youngsters were taking advantage of the last remaining light. I heard them kicking a ball and started to relax.

'Tom, did you meet Klara in a queue?'

'No, we met in the university library. She was finishing her philosophy degree and I was there looking for some book.'

'Was she pretty?'

He looked up from his plate, his gaze searching my face attentively, as if I had asked the wrong question, as if he never thought of her in those terms. But if I knew anything about Tom, I knew that he liked the company of beautiful women. The other day I saw him talking to the receptionist from my hotel, a tall slim young woman in tight slacks showing off her small waist. Her long dark hair shining in the afternoon sun, her beautiful brown eyes narrowed from laughter. Tom's face totally transformed, lit by the broadest of smiles. Tom has a strong aesthetic sense, an appreciation of beauty not many people have. Anything from art – to women, of course. He often joked about it. 'I want to reincarnate into a mobile phone, a mobile phone belonging to a beautiful woman who would hold and caress me all day long,' he said to me the other day and laughed himself into a smoker's cough. Women loved his company in short bursts. He listened to them patiently. Sometimes he was just company, sometimes a shoulder to cry on and to turn their troubles into laughter.

'Was Klara pretty?' I asked again.

'She was not ugly, but I wouldn't say she was pretty.' He stood up, rummaged in a drawer, pulled out a handful of photographs and handed one to me. Written in blue ink on the back: Klara.

So there she was, Tom's wife, a young woman with short wavy hair, big dark eyes, a pleasant face. No lipstick or makeup, but I was only guessing, because this was a black and white photograph. But something in Klara's look told me that she was quite indifferent to the impression she made. Maybe it was her functional nondescript grey coat, maybe it was the honest look. This is me, it said.

'She is nice,' I said and wondered about her sad eyes.

'She was intelligent and well read. We could talk about books, argue about philosophy, economics, all sorts.'

'Marxist philosophy?'

'And why not? I think that the Marxist theory of surplus value is interesting and right overall. Don't you?' But he did not wait for my opinion. 'The only way you can make a profit is by not paying people the value of their work. It's simple maths. The only way to get very rich, and I mean very, very rich, is by grotesque accumulation of thefts. I have an even better appreciation of Marxist political economy since the old regime collapsed. I can see the accumulation on one side, the poverty and struggle on the other. And not only factory workers, but the women serving in shops, teachers, nurses, university professors.'

'But Tom, in practice socialism didn't work, did it?'

'No, it didn't. In practice nothing works; theory is always better than its practice. But that wasn't the only problem.'

'So what was the problem?'

'Look, socialism had no time to develop. It had sixty years in Russia, even less here in Eastern Europe. The West did everything in its power to destroy it. Now let's just compare like with like. Put your mind back to early capitalism. The workers' conditions, child labour. It has progressed since then, but in the beginning it was hell. Capitalism had at least one hundred and fifty extra years to experiment, to improve.'

'That might be so, but we could hardly afford to wait another one hundred years.'

He laughed. 'We're talking about the big picture, my dearest.' He paused to consider the spread on the table, took another slice of bread, two slices of tomato and a sliver of cheese.

'You cannot blame what happened here only on the West,' I said.

'I don't. Socialism did not know how to use psychology. It tried to control it. Stupid dictators got into power, and true, they did not allow us basic freedoms. But with all its faults, socialism had many good things. That is even more apparent now, now that I see capitalism in action.' And he took another quarter of the *langos* and declared it his last.

'Once, I believed in free enterprise, but having seen how it works I'm leaning more and more to the left. I'll probably die a communist singing the *Internationale*, and he started humming: 'Workers unite …' then stumbled and laughed. 'No, I'm not joking. Uncontrolled capitalism is criminal. I get the impression that in the West, capitalism is even more fierce. And now, since communism fell, even wilder. There is no alternative, the alternative has been discredited. Now the major multinational companies can get away with anything. They don't need to curb greed any longer. It'll get worse, you'll see,' and he stood up to take the remaining *taramasalata* to the fridge. I followed with the plate of cheese.

'You know,' he said while we waited for the kettle to boil, 'I thought money is only the means for a fulfilling life. But in the West, making money has become the aim of people's lives.'

'For some.'

We were interrupted by a knock at the door. A young girl of around fifteen, a student at the school, wanted help with her work on the Enlightenment. Tom started talking about Kant.

'Yes, that's exactly what I need,' then turning to me, she asked if she could come back when Tom had more time, 'tomorrow afternoon maybe?'

'Yes, of course. If my sister is here I can give you some books, you can sit here, do your work and we can discuss it as you go.'

With our cups of tea ready, we settled in the easy chairs by the coffee table. Behind us was a wall unit full of books, from the classics, Dostoevsky, Dickens, Moliere, to Leon Uris; from Plato to animal husbandry; from *Das Kapital* to Ion Pacepa's book on Ceausescu. While Tom was sipping his tea, I returned to the story of his marriage.

'Did you love her?'

'Love?' Tom looked at me as if I was asking a ludicrous question. 'Love?' he whispered to himself. 'No. Of course not.'

'So why did you marry her?'

'Well, my dear, this is a long story.' He did not think it was a story worth telling, but I wanted to know more about the woman who became his wife. Tom remained silent.

'Tom, why did you marry her?' I asked again.

He shrugged. 'She finished her degree and went back to the Military Academy where her father's connections got her a job, teaching Marxism. Two months later she was back for a visit. She missed me. Me?' he said, pointing to himself in disbelief.

And why wouldn't she have missed you? This was not the Tom I remembered. Did life change him or had he inadvertently opened a window into insecurities which were always there? There, under protective layers of pretence, so well hidden that I had never caught a glimpse of them?

'And you? Did you miss her?'

'Sort of.'

'And then? What happened then?'

'She declared that she was so in love with me,' Tom said, incredulity stamped all over his face, 'that she couldn't live without me.'

One day Aunt Anna found out about her. 'What are you

waiting for? She is intelligent, educated and she loves you.'

Marriage to her would have meant giving up my permit to live here in Cluj, moving to Moldova. At the time, you could not live in Cluj without a permit, and getting a permit was a big exercise in perseverance against the bureaucracy. Months and months of forms and enquiries. I have tried to live in other parts of the country, but I end up coming back every time. I love living here. That permit meant a lot to me.

'A woman like that is in love with you and you don't want to leave Cluj? You don't want to give up the permit? Have you lost your mind?' Aunt Anna kept badgering me.'

Tom did not spell out what Aunt Anna's logic was based on, not because he didn't know – he did: a teacher, a woman of some status, is in love with Tom, a nightwatchman, a nobody, a man with a limp, and he dares to be choosy?

I was working here at the school. I was living in that small room, about twelve square metres. I did not have the flat you see now. I wrote to her: 'I have nothing, I am disabled, are you sure that you want to marry me?' She was adamant. She was ready to give up her job and move to Cluj. And Aunt Anna kept pressing. Eventually I decided to go ahead with it. We set a date for the wedding, but I still could not believe it. I told my aunt, 'She will not turn up, the wedding will never take place.'

Tom was saying something but my mind was stuck on what he had just said: 'She won't turn up.' Why wouldn't she turn up if she loved him? Was it self-defence? Was Tom trying to minimise a possible let-down, trying to hurt ahead of time so he would not have to feel the full blow all of a sudden? Did he still doubt that Klara, or any woman, might want to be his wife? Him, the man who people tried not to stare at but they did, because he was a limper, because one of his legs was shorter than the other, because his right foot pointed outwards more than the left? Had he finally taken on the identity society bestowed on him?

In my childhood Tom was not only my older brother; he was

the brother who knew a lot more than me, whom I trusted. He was confident enough to inspire confidence. But on that day, my brother sitting opposite me seemed small and insecure, a Tom I had never known. Did his story made me re-evaluate him? Stories can change perceptions. I was not going to let them.

While Tom was fretting whether Klara would turn up to marry him or whether his wedding would turn out to be just be another let-down in his life, I was at school. I cannot remember anybody talking about Tom's wedding, wishing for a long and happy marriage. Maybe my parents did. But how could I have I missed it? Where was my father on that day? Why wasn't he there to see his eldest son getting married? To meet the woman who would spend the rest of her life with him? To see Hella's son on his wedding day, to encourage him as he always encouraged me? Was he still angry at Tom? Surely not on his wedding day.

My father cared about Tom a great deal. I always suspected it, but he only openly acknowledged it many years later. He was obsessed that Tom should learn to be self-reliant, stand on his own two feet. I think he was more than obsessed; I think he was terrified that Tom would fail. He tried to be tough on him. Being tough on Tom must have been excruciatingly painful. At times it would have been much easier to feel sorry for Tom, to give in – easier for my father, but probably much worse for Tom in the long run. Not turning up at Tom's wedding was surely not part of imposed tough love. Not if he knew about it. But did he?

'What's wrong?' Tom interrupted.

Countless questions were about to blurt out of my mouth. Too many, too intrusive. The answers to most had probably been buried with my father.

'Nothing really.'

'But she did turn up. We did all the papers and the wedding took place in the registry office. Aunt Anna and her husband were our witnesses.'

I cannot stop the flood of images of that October day. The time is ticking, there is no sign of Klara. Tom is smoking, Tom is trying to make light of a difficult situation. Then the door opens and Klara walks in. Alone.

Yes I had doubts, doubts about her, about myself, about our marriage. I had nothing to offer, nothing except that small room with a bed, a cupboard, a chest of drawers and a small table. If she got a job we would manage, I thought. But I was the man, I felt I should earn more, contribute more.

After the wedding, Aunt Anna invited us for lunch. Klara seemed happy. Aunt Anna looked pleased. And I was a married man.

In the afternoon the newly married couple returned to Tom's place. Every hour the school bell rang. For ten minutes the school buzzed with noise and young energy, then the bell rang again, the noise died down for a whole fifty minutes before it started all over again.

A few days later I returned to work, to my nightwatch duties. In the morning I came back tired and went to bed. Klara kept busy. She made enquiries for a job, went to the library. When she got back she tried to read. There wasn't anything else to do inside this room; we didn't even have a kitchen. The school bell kept ringing on the hour. The noise was on and off again, some days till late evening.

She found a job in no time. Things should look up for us, I thought, but she could not take living here. She would come home after work and soon go out. She could not stand the noise. 'Just as I start relaxing,' she used to say, 'the bell rings again and the noise interrupts my thoughts. From there on there is no room for anything else in my head but noise.'

I took another look at Klara's photo. I couldn't help wondering if the sad look in her eyes was there before she married Tom. Or was she an unhappy soul who found Tom's company interesting and amusing? Was he her comedian, the man who cheered her up? Her father had a nervous breakdown after the war but he recovered not long after. Well, not quite, judging by the strong anti-Semitic opinions he did not even try to hide from his son-in-law.

Months passed. She realised what she had got herself into.
She started to drink. I begged her to stop. We had shouting
scenes. She cried, she sobbed, she said she loved me. I said it's
not you, it's the alcohol in you that loves me. But she couldn't
stop drinking. Barely a year passed and she decided she had
had enough. She returned to live with her father. Not long
after that she attempted suicide.

Tom paused. He looked troubled.

I did not know what to say. I felt painfully sorry for that woman.
What had she got herself into? Was she really in love, or was she
unbalanced? And I felt sorry for Tom, but I was also disappointed in
him. In him, in my father, in Aunt Anna, in us, his family. There was
not one blameless person in this story.

I never saw Klara again. But that did not mean that our marriage was over. Getting divorced was not easy in those days
and we continued to be linked by the marriage certificate for
years. It had no small implications.

One day, more than three years after we separated, I got
a visit from the social office. 'You have not paid a cent of
maintenance and the child is five months old already.' What
maintenance? It's three years since I saw my wife, I said,
thinking even an elephant has a shorter gestation period. I
now had a bureaucrat after me and he had nothing better to
do than try to get money out of me. It took forms and letters
to Klara, who to her credit acknowledged eventually that the
child was not mine. I never married again. I had a partner
for six years, I had other women, but I never wanted to get
married again.

'Have you kept up the contact?'

'No. We are wrong for each other. I heard that years ago, during
Ceausescu, she tried to escape to the West. She is an alcoholic now.
People have seen her drunk at a railway station.' And Tom signalled
that the story of his marriage was over.

I looked through the remaining pile of photographs. In two of them was Ilona, the pretty little blonde, Tom's partner of six years. I had seen this photograph in Israel. They used to write to us and my parents sent them parcels of clothes and shoes every year. 'She taught me to manage money and I'll be grateful for it forever,' he said.

Then there was another photo, Tom with another woman. She was leaning on his shoulder. She had an honest and happy face and Tom looked better than ever. They looked just right together.

'She wanted to get married. But I could not have taken her on with two teenagers. So she ended up marrying someone else.'

I thought that had been a mistake, but there was no point in saying it.

So Tom lived alone, his loneliness broken by short encounters with dubious women, as I was to find out later.

19

'See that man?' Tom pointed to a carefully attired elderly man, a couple of tables from us. He was scribbling something in a notebook, totally absorbed.

We were sitting in our favourite small café with wood-panelled walls where delicious tiny cakes were sold by weight and the coffee was always short and strong. No fancy coffee in this part of the world, just the original, primal variety.

'He was the chief librarian at the university.'

The man was wearing a grey suit which had seen its best times years ago, but the lapels sat flat as if just out of the tailor's shop. The white shirt beneath was impeccably pressed and the worn ensemble was finished off with a dark tie.

'He is a descendant of an aristocratic family.' And a few sips of coffee later, 'Recently he got back the family estate the communists expropriated after the war.' The man must have sensed that we were talking about him because he looked up absentmindedly. Then suddenly his face lit up with recognition. He closed his notebook and asked whether he could join us.

After a few pleasantries, Mr Munteanu told us that he had indeed got back the family estate. He was not the only lucky man to do so; another name was mentioned in the conversation I could not follow. Now he was a free man, he had no more financial worries. He had plenty of time to write poetry. And as he said that, Mr Munteanu reached for the notebook inside his jacket and asked if he could read us his latest poem, the one he was working on.

The poem was about love, about the love of books and knowledge. About a library, somewhere in the universe, a library with trillions of books. Books from earth and from everywhere else where intelligent beings exist. Computers did not get a mention, maybe because Mr Munteanu's working life dated back to a time when computers were still a luxury, or maybe his poem was intended to be about love only.

I told him how imaginative it was. I was not entirely honest, but I couldn't help but admire someone who was so passionate about his profession and about books. He stood up to go, kissed my hand – a habit I find difficult to accept graciously – and took his leave.

'I met him way back, more than two decades ago,' Tom said as the door shut behind him. 'I used to spend a lot of time in the library; the nightwatchman's duties were not exactly mentally stimulating. The only time I learnt something new in that job was when they sent me to a course.'

'A course? What sort of course?'

'Lectures on what is lawful and what is not. Courses at the police station on what should be done if there is trouble, whom to call.'

'But who would have dared to do anything unlawful in Romania? And in a school of all places?'

'Mostly drunks. There were nuisances at times. Eventually I became the best qualified nightwatchman. I had a high school certificate and had done lots of courses. Well, not lots, but quite a few. By the way, that cake was delicious, I might have another one.' He rubbed his chin and thought for a moment. 'Maybe a glazed coffee one.' But then he changed his mind. 'I'd better wait, let the first one settle.'

Anyway, they trained me for all eventualities. I even had instructions on how to sweep the pavement in front of the school. Of course there were street sweepers, but sweeping the front of the school was my duty. And there was a chief, of course. The chief street sweeper was an ex-office worker, some said engineer, sacked for being drunk on the job. His main duty was to prove that he was above us in every way.

He walked around, erect in his fake leather jacket like a party chief. He was taller than himself. He inspected, he instructed, he was of a different opinion. Was the street swept? Was the rubbish removed? Where was the rubbish disposed of? 'No, that's no good, you need to sweep this again. You should put the rubbish not in that bin, the rubbish from the front of the building goes in the bin behind the building.'

One day, he saw me sweeping and said, 'You should do it from right to left.' Right to left? Comrade, I can only do it from left to right, because of my hand. I liked disobeying him, and watched for his reaction. Of course you can. Just turn around!' he shouted. Did I care, left to right or right to left? I turned around and did it his way. He stood there watching me, cigarette in his mouth. He was the chief.

The truth is that nobody wanted to do any work. Early in the morning, as I was finishing my night shift, the street sweepers would get together in my office. You see, I was the nightwatchman, but since I had to sweep the street in front of the building I was part of the group. They had to negotiate rosters and I had a warm office. They discussed who was going to swap with whom and who owed work to whom. At times such a hullaballoo would break out that if you hadn't seen them you would have thought they were at each other's throats. Half an hour later, with nothing sorted, they would decide to have a cup of coffee first, instant of course, then resolve who would do which section. There was no hurry, the chief would still be in bed at that time, probably with a hangover from the day before.

Tom was always available for a chat, or for advice if needed. The other street sweepers respected him. He was a watchman in a high school, not just a street sweeper: an important distinction in the world he lived in. And Tom recounted the sort of advice he was called upon to give. By then communism had collapsed. Tom was still working.

One winter evening, a few years after the fall of Ceausescu, a man rings the bell on the front door of the school. I go to investigate who could be at the door at that late hour. One of my colleagues, the one who swept the street further up, is standing in front of me in the light, snowflakes melting on his face, his heavy jumper patterned with fluffy flakes.

'Domnu (Mr) Toma, would you mind giving me some advice?' We knew each other well so we were on first-name terms, sort of, the first name for familiarity and the title Domnu for a measure of respect.

'With pleasure, Domnu Sergiu,' and I invite him in. He shakes the snow off his hat and jumper, knocks the snow off his shoes and we go into my office. He looks half-frozen. I put some water in the newly acquired post-communist kettle, then prepare two mugs, a spoon of instant coffee and sugar in each.

'Nice and warm here, Domnu Toma. I didn't even take a coat, I didn't realise just how cold it is,' he says rubbing his hands. I pour the boiling water in the mugs and put a mug of coffee in front of my visitor.

'There it is; and now you'd better tell me what advice you need.'

'Domnu Toma, you know me, I'm no greedy man. But I am struggling a bit. With the new regime, with our freedom and whatnot, it's hard.'

'Yes it is.'

'And how to put it? I am not a greedy person, am I?'

'No you are not, Domnu Sergiu.'

'So if I am not greedy and if I suffered, I shouldn't feel bad about asking for justice, should I?'

'Of course you shouldn't feel bad about asking for justice. It's your right.'

'If Domnu Toma says so and Domnu Toma is a very educated man, then I reckon I should ask for justice.'

'So tell me more, Domnu Sergiu, how have you been wronged?"

'Well, under the communists, under those charlatans, I was locked up for two years. Surely you heard about this.'

'I can't say I did, but why were you locked up?'

'They said I had stolen from the state.'

'Did they?'

'Yes.'

'And was it true? Or did they just make it up?'

'I lived in that village you see, just outside Cluj. We were members of the collective. We had nothing, you know how it was. The collective sold everything we produced and the money – well, you know how it was. It went to the state. All of it, well, not quite, they gave us some crumbs. I had a family so I did take a few chickens, I took the odd duck.'

'Is that all?'

'A few tools, for my garden. To grow something to eat at home.'

'Well, it's not that bad.'

'To tell the truth, I took some money too, from the till.'

'That's not so good.'

'Look, Domnu Toma, I'm not saying I haven't stolen from the state, but I stole from the communist state. Didn't I? Surely this is not a crime. Not nowadays.'

'That's a hard one.'

'But the communists are the bad guys now, so if I stole from the bad guys I must have done something good. I should get compensation for having been locked up for two years for a good deed.'

'I sympathise with you, Domnu Sergiu. Your problem is not that you stole from the collective, lots of people did, your problem is that you were caught. It doesn't matter if you steal from the good guy or the bad guy. Stealing is punishable by law and I don't think you can make a case.'

'I still don't get it, Domnu Toma. They were the bad guys and I caused them damage, that must have been a good thing, so looking at this now, if I was locked up I should get compensation.'

'Look, I'm no lawyer. Maybe you're right. You should see a lawyer, Domnu Sergiu.'

'I might. They're a lot of money, though.' And he stands up and takes his hat ready to go. 'Anyway, many thanks for the coffee and the chat, Domnu Toma.'

'Wait a minute,' I say, 'it's cold out there and you don't have a coat. You can take this coat. And you can keep it. I don't wear it any more. It's nearly new, I've hardly worn it. It was too big and too warm for me.'

'Well I couldn't, could I?'

'You should, Domnu Sergiu, I have no need for it.' I took the coat from the hanger in the corner and handed it to him.

'Are you sure. Domnu Toma?'

'Hundred per cent.' So he took the coat and put it on, looked himself up and down and I could see that something was not right. Not comfortable? 'Too small perhaps?' I ask.

'No, it's perfect. But you are turning me into a baron, Domnu Toma.'

'That's okay. It's okay to be a baron nowadays, the barons are coming back.'

'No I couldn't, I am a street sweeper, not a baron. It wouldn't feel right.'

He took the coat off and carefully put it back on the coat hanger. But I think he appreciated that I saw nothing wrong in him looking like a baron.

And Tom smiled my father's smile. No, not quite. Tom's smiles were big and happy, whereas my father's were understated, somewhat reserved, but the enjoyment was there, internalised and savoured like a glass of vintage wine. But behind their smiles was the same sense of humour, the same way of looking at the world, and I wondered how it might have been if only they had spent time with each other during the later years of my father's life. That was not to be.

Part VI

In the Promised Land

20

Tom remained stuck behind the Iron Curtain while we metamorphosed into Israeli migrants, dislocated people who belonged to a different culture and a different language. And we were poor – not the Romanian way, the Israeli way. There was food on the table, but not much else. No phone, no washing machine, no hot water in the kitchen, and of course no air conditioner.

One night, two months after our arrival, gunfire erupted on the Qalqilyan border. The shots were eight hundred metres away, but they sounded as if they were just around the corner.

Back in Romania my father had warned us: 'The Middle East is a troubled region. Within twenty years there will be another war.' Within twenty years? The Six Day War erupted two years after our arrival.

I was studying in Haifa at the time. What did I understand about what was going on around me? The Hebrew I learned in the kibbutz equipped me with the words needed to work the land, pick fruit, milk cows, clean food halls and toilets. A year later my vocabulary had evolved; I had mastered street Hebrew and the basic terms for maths, chemistry and physics, but I was still unable to read and understand a newspaper.

In mid-May 1967 I overheard my colleagues talking about Egypt demanding the withdrawal of the United Nations peacekeeping forces. They were worried. But I was more worried about falling behind, so I kept studying. A week or so later, I heard people saying that Egypt had closed the Straits of Tiran. Straits of Tiran? In the south of course, but where exactly? I was too ashamed to ask. I had no atlas, television or radio. I lived in a student dormitory.

A few more days passed. The overheard snippets of conversation started to make sense. The narrow sea passage which separates the Gulf of Aqaba from the Red Sea had been closed to Israeli shipping and therefore to the oil which at the time came from Iran. Jordanian, Egyptian, Iraqi and Syrian soldiers were gathering on our borders. I heard war and war again, but I understood little of the commentary and the speculation.

War was imminent, even I understood that, but it did not sink in until my colleagues started to disappear from lectures, called up by the army. In the lecture theatre there were more empty seats every morning, until one day the empty seats outnumbered the students. The university closed down.

Men disappeared from the streets of Haifa. Women, children and the elderly sat on buses without uttering a word. Even the children were silent, silent like old men.

Egypt and Syria kept threatening to annihilate us, to wipe Israel from the map. On one side the Mediterranean, on the other hundreds of thousands of enemy soldiers. What next? I kept asking myself. I went home, terrified.

On our arrival in Israel, I was exempted from the army. The exemption was based on an IQ test. IQ test? I had never done or seen one. Since I could not speak or read Hebrew, my IQ had to be measured by a different method.

I had fronted up at the headquarters where my future was about to be decided. A young woman soldier led me to a small room, gave me a couple of pages of drawings and after a short explanation left me to it. I stared at the paper. What did she say? Something about matching, or breaking up diagrams. I kept looking at the paper. All of a sudden I saw a pattern. Of course, that's what they want! They want me to find patterns! My mind went into action. I had to find at least some, not because I wanted to become a soldier, I did not, I wanted to go to university.

I had always done well in tests. But now I was treading on shifting sands. Without the language and the knowledge of the unspoken rules, nothing was predictable anymore. But I had to prove to them and to myself that some worthwhile part of me was still there, that I had not become an idiot.

I was far from finishing when she reappeared and took my papers away. She returned in no time and took me to an office. They had decided to exempt me from army service, the uniformed man said, but in case of war, I would have to serve as a reserve.

Did they find an IQ? I still don't know.

When the war erupted, along with other young Romanian reserves who had never been in the army, I was called up. We gathered in the basement of the medical centre in Yoseftal, not quite knowing what for. Sitting on the concrete floor, on the opposite side of that big hall, was an older Israeli man, a sort of commandant, the man in charge of us. Evening fell ...

Outside the shelling is relentless. I have crawled under a small table and I am sitting holding my knees against my chin. Ridiculous, but that one square metre table top above me gives me a sense of security, protection against shells and bombs or whatever might fall on us. I am terrified. We are eight hundred metres from Jordan and less then twenty kilometres from the sea, the narrowest part of Israel. We are very vulnerable. The Jordanian troops will concentrate their forces here. To cut Israel in two.

The shelling is incessant. My friend Simone seems braver than me; she does not need a table top. She is sitting without a cover. Usually a chatterbox, she has not said a word. For hours.

No one in this shelter will survive. And what will happen to Kfar Saba where Yossi and my parents are?

The commandant is listening to a transistor radio. From time to time he seems to be saying something, I don't understand what. Maybe it's his fast Hebrew, maybe I can't hear the words clearly because he is sitting far from me. Or maybe it's the shelling. He has lit a candle. Another two candles are burning in other parts of this big room, but here in my corner under the table it is nearly pitch dark.

The shelling is getting louder. I am shivering. How long will it take the Jordanian soldiers to get to Yoseftal? How long will it take them to cover eight hundred metres with their tanks? Maybe they are coming from further away, maybe they have not massed themselves right on the border. But they can't be very far. My maths is good, but I cannot work out how long it will take. I cannot concentrate. Tanks move slowly. It won't take long. Bang! What's that? What happened?! The shelling is closer. They will be here any minute. They will burst into this basement. And then? Rape and killings. It will be a bloodbath. I break into a sweat, then start to shiver. Violently. More shelling. The commandant is saying something. I don't understand. I think there is a smile on his face. I think, because I can barely see his face. Whispers are coming my way. 'The Egyptian planes, around four hundred of them, have been bombed before they even took off,' someone says. Victory is imminent. Victory? The shelling is incessant. I do not move.

Another hour passes. The shelling is intermittent now, then less and less.

It is dawn. Outside, utter silence. I gather my courage, crawl out from under the table and join the others to investigate the outside world. The light is a rusty grey. I don't believe it. Simone next to me is rubbing her eyes too. Miracle of miracles. Yosephtal is intact.

'The Jordanians shelled Tel Aviv,' the commandant explains. 'They missed and the shells ended up in the sea. We were deafened by the artillery guns.'

I am no longer afraid, in fact I don't feel anything. I am totally detached because this is only a dream, an absurd nonsensical dream. Reason, logic do not belong here. Here in the rusty grey light the rules are different, the unexpected is the norm. And I am the onlooker.

The action on the Qalqilyan border seems to have died down completely. We stand watching the horizon, watching the sunrise.

I am worried about my family so I ask for permission to go and see them in Kfar Saba.

My father gives me the biggest hug and squeeze. He looks white. He lights a cigarette. His hand shakes as he smokes.

By lunchtime I am back in Yoseftal. There is a big hole in the road, close to the medical centre where we spent the night. There are pockmarks on the buildings next to it. A shell landed while I was away.

A few people are listening to the Cairo radio station, to the news in Hebrew: 'We are on the streets of Tel Aviv, killing women and children.' Above us two Israeli planes are flying into Jordan.

———

The war was nearly over for us. It continued in other parts in the country for another four days. Most Israelis survived unscathed, but not everybody was so lucky. One of my university tutors lay in hospital fighting for his life. A student lost a leg. Another colleague lost her fiancé. But the country, like a terminally ill man who has been given an unexpected clear bill of health, was rejoicing. We had survived.

Days later I was back studying and my father returned to his work and daily travels. Little did we know that the next war, the Yom Kippur War, was only six years away.

Within months, Israelis started to go shopping in the West Bank. Arabs came across to sell their produce. Qalqilya was no longer the enemy village on the hill where the lights twinkled at night. Jordanian donkeys pulling carts with fruit and vegetables paraded past our balcony in Yoseftal daily. Early every morning, buses of Arabs arrived in Israel to work on construction sites.

It looked like the barriers between Israelis and Jordanians were starting to break down. Still, at the time, the time before Sadat's visit to Jerusalem, before Israel made peace with Egypt and Jordan, we could not even imagine that Israelis and Arabs would one day sit in the same room, never mind negotiate peace. The Israeli Arabs were a different category. They lived separately; I knew nothing about them.

For some Israeli Jews, they did not exist. I was not the average Israeli, but they did not exist for me either. I had seen them on the way to Haifa as my bus stopped at an Arab village, I had seen them in Acre, in Jaffa, in Jerusalem. At times I bought a falafel from an Arab shop or a cold drink, but that was where our interaction ended. I never really got to know anybody. What did they think? What were their stories? Our paths never crossed – we lived in different worlds.

For years now my brother Yossi has worked with Arab doctors and nurses, but at the time, many Israelis did not have much contact with them, nor did they care about the lack of contact. The average native Jewish Israeli mind did not linger long on the newly arrived immigrants either, and I was one of those migrants. A migrant from Romania, an *Oleh Hadash* (new migrant), needed but not really wanted. In the minds of some who had been there for generations, I belonged to the group under the classification *Romanim ganavim* (Romanian thieves). I did not take this label seriously, but whichever way I looked at it, I felt it was not a compliment. I was young, I could cope with adversity. I was far better off than my parents.

21

My father put his heart and soul in his work, far more worried about completing it on time than his superiors were. He was in constant fear that his contract would not be extended. It was: years later he was engaged on other bus stations, first Rehovot, then Haifa, travelling just as far and slaving in the heat and the rain, past an age when anybody else would have abandoned it all. He was approaching seventy-one. He kept teaching himself Hebrew and fearing for Yossi, who would turn eighteen and be enlisted in the army.

The new job we all hoped for never eventuated. Not for him, and not for the other older Romanians. No longer in their prime, they were thankful to have any work. My father was grossly under-employed but others were even worse off, ending up in menial jobs. From early morning to late afternoon they cleaned cucumbers in the pickle factory close by, or worked in the small galvanising factory next to it, or in similar jobs in Tel Aviv. The women cleaned hospitals or schools.

They had no skills or energy to find other jobs. Having been teachers or clerks, they were now illiterate and most were barely able to put a few Hebrew words together in the wrong sequence.

Hebrew is a difficult language for a European. The writing is from right to left, the ancient characters unfamiliar to those who did not study the Jewish religious texts. The vowels are not spelled out, words are strings of consonants which can mean many things. The reader has to guess what it might represent by checking it against the rest of the sentence, against more strings of consonants, other guessed words. But how could anybody do this, not knowing the language? How could this vicious circle be broken? The younger people did, the middle-aged who went to intensive Hebrew courses got the basics and learnt it eventually, the older migrants did not. They could not afford the luxury of not earning an income for six months. So they kept working. The money they earned was just sufficient to buy furniture and a fridge on hire purchase. But they were Jews in a Jewish homeland, and that was enough for them.

The years rolled on. We were becoming Israelis, sort of. Life was work, sweat and little reflection. People lived from one news bulletin to the next. While the Holocaust was hardly ever mentioned in those days, there was an urgency to build a country, to be self-sufficient, because we did not trust the world to come to our rescue if needed. This lack of trust strengthened the community, the feeling that, come what may, we were in it together.

—◊—

One summer day four years after our arrival, I decided to visit my father at his work. Busy with studying and working, I had never seen where he worked and what he actually did.

It was nine o'clock in the morning by the time I left home to catch my first bus to Kfar Saba and the mercury had already reached thirty degrees. People had long left for work and the bus stop was crowded with shoppers. Yoseftal was still a dormitory suburb with few shops.

Some people shopped in Qalqilya, but most people shopped in Kfar Saba. Kfar Saba was clean, and Kfar Saba had everything. My mother never stopped marvelling that in Israel you could just go to a shop and buy food, that you did not have to queue for anything. 'Such a small country and there is no shortage of anything,' she would often say. She still did forty years later.

Two buses later, having covered the width of Israel, I arrived at the Tel Aviv central bus station, at that time an assembly of street bus stops sprinkled among burek, falafel and fruit stalls selling anything from oranges to pomegranates to strawberries, shoe shops, cheap stalls sporting T-shirts, singlets and underwear. People and more people. Among them Yemenites selling bagels, pretzels and fruit juices, all shouting, all advertising their wares. *Bagelah! Bagelah! Tapuzim, mitz tapuzim, eskoliot!* (Oranges, orange juice, grapefruit!) *Motek na bevakasah mitz tapuzim, mitz tivi.* (Sweety, please here it is, orange juice, natural juice.) Further up, *naalaim bzol!* (cheap shoes!) *Tahtonim eser lirot, hamisha tahtonim.* (underpants, ten lira for five underpants.) I loved it. Old, dirty, alive.

I caught the air-conditioned bus to Jerusalem and more than an hour later, having travelled this time the wider width of Israel in the south-east, I arrived at the new Jerusalem bus station built under my father's supervision and finished the year before. I had missed my next bus so I decided to go for a walk, to stretch my legs. In the distance shone the Golden Dome of Omar. Behind the old wall of the city, churches, crosses and crescents baked in the blazing sun. A call to prayer from one of the mosques fell over the bustle of the town: the shoppers, the Orthodox Jews dressed in black and the group of nuns who happened to be going my way. Two Eastern Orthodox priests with long white beards walked past. They spoke Romanian.

I loved Jerusalem, I loved it because of its people, all different yet all together, sharing the street and the sound of each other's religious rituals.

My last bus delivered me to the suburb where my father worked. It was midday, the temperature had reached the mid- to high-thirties. Unimpeded by trees, the heat of the sun, soaked up by the white stone buildings, oozed at passers-by. The new sunrays falling onto the stone bounced back in rejection.

And then I saw my father, in the middle of a big uneven construction site where a bus depot was being built under his supervision. He was saying something to a man and pointing to the edge of the site. They walked across to the other side and stopped. My father said something, showed him ten fingers and a few more. He hardly knew any Hebrew. He could buy a bus ticket, a drink, a newspaper. The rest was done by hands.

217

His face lit up when he saw me. He took me around. I said hello to a couple of Arab workers as we walked towards an old rusted windowless bus parked on the far side of the site. It was his office. There he sat to check the drawings, use his slide rule, eat his home-made sandwich, while the hot wind blew from the desert or on the breezeless days when, just like that day, the temperature soared towards the forties and the air was still. How did he do it? I still don't know.

Late afternoon or early evening he would return home, pale and exhausted, have a wash, eat something and lie down in the airless hot bedroom to read. Later he would move to the balcony and smoke and read the Hungarian or Romanian newspaper, sometimes write or calculate something in his notebook where every square milli-metre was used. After sunset he and my mother went out for a walk. Most people would be on the street at that time of the evening, some walking around and around the same twelve or so blocks of flats that were Yoseftal at the time, while others, old men and women, sat on the low cement retaining walls, gossiping and waiting for the temperature to drop.

The summer heat would last eight months, without a drop of refreshing rain. The rain would finally set in some time in December, and for the next three months our flat, with no internal doors, with its concrete floor and thin walls, would be cold, humid and downright nasty. In the evening, a two-bar electric heater glowed half-heartedly in the corner of our lounge room. Starting in mid-January, for about a month, heavy rain poured most days. It flooded the streets. The wall of my parents' small bedroom, which propped up their bed, became covered with patches of mould. Luckily it did not last for long; the summer was only a couple of months away. It would dry the mould to a powder within days.

Our relatives visited rarely. Some were working and could only travel on Saturday – but on Saturday there was no public transport. Travelling on Saturday was prohibited by the religious rules on which that largely secular country was based. If you were well-off you had a car. You could be secular, you could be free. But in those days most Israelis did not have a car, so religious or not, they had to obey the ancient rules.

My mother was not working and could have travelled during the week, but she wanted to be home when my father returned from work. Besides, she would think twice about spending money on such a visit, because it wouldn't have been only money for the bus. She was still in the Romanian habit of fronting up loaded with cakes and eggs and rissoles and who knows what else. And she felt that her sisters never quite reciprocated her generosity.

The clash of expectations was just another aspect of emigration that nobody had predicted: the expectations of the new arrivals, against what the relatives who had worked and sweated for decades were prepared to part with. They were far from well-off compared to other Israelis. Uncle Jacob was a nurse in a mental hospital; one of the sisters had a small convenience shop; another worked night shifts in a cloakroom in a club; and the other two were retired. But my mother saw what she saw. They were better off than us. She had helped some of them back in Romania after the war, when Stefan was still well-off. She expected the same generosity. They did get together a couple of times a year, and when they did they could not stop reminiscing, singing old Romanian songs and laughing until tears rolled down their cheeks.

Uncle Jacob did not live long enough to disappoint my mother. One day, two and a half years after our arrival, he was taken to the hospital. A 'perforated bowel', the doctor in the emergency room declared as my uncle writhed in pain. The doctor asked him to sign the consent form for an urgent operation. But my uncle would not sign. If God's will was for him to die, so be it. God's will or not, next day Uncle Jacob was dead. And our reason to live close to him, in Yoseftal, was no more.

There were religious people in Israel, but they were in the minority. Religion was omnipresent but it did not dominate politics. The settler movement was in its infancy. My father did not live to see the endless and inexcusable land grab under the various opportunistic governments which dominate Israeli politics nowadays. He would have hated it.

———∾———

Yoseftal, with its gathering of mismatched migrants, had a temporary feel about it. Was it the flimsy blocks of flats set out in a quadrangle in the middle of wasteland? Was it the lack of trees and vegetation? Or was it the nearly incompatible ways of life we brought with us that did not allow us to connect, to sprout roots? Apart from Romanians, there were migrants from Europe and Africa, India and Russia, Yemen and Morocco, educated and illiterate, religious and secular. We were the Yoseftali Tower of Babel.

We brought with us centuries of manners and habits which many could or would not abandon. While the locals wore shorts and sandals with no socks, our middle-aged Romanian neighbour, on the lookout for a wife, never abandoned his suit and tie. And never found a wife.

In time, people who could afford better housing moved away. New migrants moved in. Some mean, some generous, some believed in looking after the common property, but most did not. As time passed and the migrants churned through, almost no one cared. The block belonged to the state, so why should they pay for maintenance? Why should they pay for an electric bulb on the stairway? So they kept blundering up the stairs in the dark. And the council saw no need to impose regulations.

We shared our block entrance, the stray cats, the filth, the smells of cooking, appetising or nauseating, and willingly or unwillingly listened to each other's music because the walls were thin and the music always loud. My father, who could not stand noise and could stand Oriental music even less, suffered in silence. Despite all that, I liked Yoseftal. During the short university holidays when I did not work, I would still be in bed when the old man with the donkey passed under our window calling out in Yiddish, 'Old clothes, second-hand clothes!' It was a timeless and tired call, a sort of Middle Eastern

220

ghetto call, as if all those centuries of otherness had migrated with us and taken roots in the Promised Land. As if otherness was our destiny, and we would never escape it.

Later, I sat on the balcony having my breakfast and watching the old men returning from the synagogue. Among them was a religious Yemenite who lived next door, a tall thin man with a long white beard wearing an ankle-length white robe and clogs. A sort of Yoseftali Messiah. As he walked past, the bottle of Arak poking out from under his robe bounced against his thin, bony body. He had been to the synagogue, but took a little detour on the way home. Soon sad Oriental songs mingled with slurred Arabic words came through the thin wall. Sometimes he would fall quiet then suddenly loud, monotonous snores punctuated our conversation. At times he would wake up, tell his wife off then get angrier and angrier, shout and thump while she sobbed and cried.

The other neighbours were different. The Azulais, a Moroccan family with twelve children, occupied two adjacent flats below us. Monsieur Azulai was blind but was off to work every morning. Madame Azulai could see everything except the filth. Nor could she smell the stench in their flat. She sat motionless on the sofa all day, but she had a heart of gold. For years after my father passed away, she invited my mother often. By then I lived in Australia and every time I returned for a visit, I would bump into her on the stairway and she would tell me off for leaving my parents. Her words hurt, deeply, but I knew she meant well. She felt sorry for my mother.

But one visit I will never forget. It was in the year 2000. Downstairs the Azulais had just finished another set of improvements to their flat ...

'Roza, come in. Let's have a drink.' Madame Azulai invites us in. Like most native Arab speakers she speaks Hebrew well. My mother does not.

My mother is not inclined to receive hospitality from Madame Azulai, a problem of hygiene, but I put my arm around hers and lead her inside. While Madame is in the kitchen preparing the drinks, my mother tells me that she does not want anything to eat or drink.

'It's the hygiene, Madame's eye infection. Who knows? Anything is possible in this place,' she whispers to me in Hungarian.

Madame is back with the orange juice.

'Kitchen beautiful, very beautiful,' my mother remarks in her pidgin Hebrew.

Madame agrees. 'Beautiful, *Baruch Hashem* (thanks to God).'

'Children?' my mother asks.

'*Baruch Hashem*, good children. They help, pay for things.'

'Very good children,' my mother says and looks at me.

'*Baruch Hashem*.' Madame Azulai thanks God again.

She does not mention the son who, according to my mother, is or was in prison, or the drug addict, or the son who got in some other trouble with the law. Well, children are like shares, you never know how they will turn out. But it is true, hers is a close-knit and loving family. And as I contemplate the holes in Madame Azulai's story, my mother says something and I am blown over by whole paragraphs of masculines and infinitives at an incredible speed.

'He to come Saturday, every Saturday, to come, very good loves mother. He in you no trouble to ask husband to fix everything. Madame Azulai no to worry. He to pay for everything, cheap expensive.'

I watch her, not quite believing that she is my mother, the woman I know so well. I have never heard her speaking in Hebrew with such confidence, at such speed. She avoids speaking Hebrew if she can, but on the rare occasions when she cannot, she never says more than two words, always softly, half-swallowed, terrified of making a fool of herself. But now she speaks much faster than in her native language, faster than I could in any language. I try to look interested. No, I don't try, I am interested, because this is not normal; it is totally out of character. But there are signs that she is about to run out of steam. Thank heavens! Oh no, she explodes again. Faster and louder: 'To clothe, always. Never to go empty. Apple to cost ten shekels, potatoes five.' The words are pouring. As if all those words she kept in for thirty years cannot be kept inside any longer. As if all the shame and the humiliation she felt among native Hebrew speakers has to get out.

Despite being familiar with her way of speaking Hebrew, I do not understand what she is saying, but I am trying to look as if it makes sense, listening attentively, my eyes looking into hers. I can feel Madame Azulai's gaze on my cheek.

My head turns involuntarily. Madame Azulai's puzzled look begs for a translation.

My mother stops suddenly. Her face is flushed. I quickly fill the silent gap in the conversation and tell Madame that my mother is impressed by her good children.

'*Baruch Hashem*,' she says, 'why doesn't she go to Hebrew classes?'

I know that she did, years ago, and I remember the pages of hesitant *alefs* and *beits* (As and Bs), like those of a six-year-old. She was seventy by then. She had been in the country for more than twenty years. How could she explain that she still could not speak the language? There was struggle, there was sickness, there was death in those first twenty years.

I glance at my mother. Judging by her embarrassed face bordering on shock, she understood Madame's question. I don't know what to say. I just mutter: 'She did, they were not very good.'

'The ones I went to were excellent,' Madame replies. 'I can even read and write now. I couldn't back in Morocco.'

I look at my mother. She is gazing at her glass of orange juice. She looks up, in her eyes a painful and resigned look of surrender.

'Lets go,' I say.

We part from Madame and I promise to return to say goodbye before leaving ...

My mother hardly said anything that evening. She went into herself and I could see the pain in the hardened look under which she carried the quiet desperation, the sum total of her life, the life of an old migrant, a lonely soul laughed at, looked down on even by those she thought worthless. I knew that she would continue to live her life disconnected from the people around her, in an imaginary

223

world between the old and the new country, until her last gasp.

Emigration might not have turned out as she expected, but she loved Israel fiercely and she would not allow any criticism of it. Besides, in Israel she could celebrate the religious holidays, as she used to every year with her big family. That too gave her comfort.

And so we continued to live in Yoseftal for decades, wedged between the rising stink from Madame Azulai and the daily furniture rearrangements of the Moskotels, the Turkish family who lived above us. At six in the morning Mr and Mrs Moskotel pushed their furniture against the wall to allow space for the ample Mrs Moskotel's daily activities. At ten at night they rearranged the furniture for the night layout. Beds, tables and who knows what else were pulled around on the cement floor until it screeched with pain.

The other neighbours had a different solution for the lack of space. They knocked down internal walls. The kitchen, the lounge room and the balcony became one big room. Years later, Mr and Mrs Moskotel did the same. My mother fretted: the building would collapse, Mr and Mrs Moskotel would one day land on us, furniture and all. But they were the best neighbours we could wish for, always there when we needed help.

My mother spoke Hungarian or Romanian with us, French with the Moskotels, bad Hebrew with the Azulais, and Yiddish with the old Russian couple next door. I tried my school Russian on them. We drove each other mad at times, but if someone was in trouble people rushed to help. We gave each other cakes on High Holidays. My mother had a special charity run two or three times a year: she gave flour, oil, sugar and rice to a sad old Iranian widow who lived on her own in the next entrance.

I spent most Saturdays in Yoseftal, studying. On Sunday morning, the beginning of the Israeli week, I would return to Haifa, to university. I would catch the early morning bus along with other Sunday morning commuters, many of them soldiers returning to base. As the bus approached Haifa I felt a sense of loss, even dread, like a school kid on his first day at school. It wasn't because I could not part with my family; it was because in the Technion – the technical university – which was getting closer and closer, I felt very much an outsider. I had made a few friends among my colleagues, Romanians of course, but I never made it into the student community. The native Israelis were loud and confident, sure of themselves and their opinions. They had friends, girlfriends and boyfriends, many dating back to their school or army days. The badly dressed Romanian who wore her brother's shoes, whose Hebrew was pathetic, was of no interest to them. On the very rare occasions when I did join them, I often missed the meaning and understood even less the jokes and the nuances of their conversation. I tried to be part of the group in the only way I could – smile when everybody smiled, laugh when everybody laughed. Eventually I would give up imitating and stand there, embarrassed like an intruder who stumbles on a secret party of his friends, unable to leave but sensing that nobody wants him around.

Even a few years later, when my Hebrew improved, when I no longer wore Yossi's shoes and I was quite well dressed, among the native Israeli students I remained a Romanian, a migrant from a strange communist country. But I no longer felt Romanian, and I did not quite feel Israeli. Loneliness was creeping up on me.

In Yoseftal I belonged, I was there with the rest of them, strange and warm-hearted, clean and dirty, educated and illiterate, the *Olim Hadashim* (new migrants) who, in spite of their dedication to the country, never quite made it into Israeli society. Non-belongers, who belonged with each other. Sort of.

———

A few years passed. My father continued to catch the 5:30 morning bus to go to the same construction site and the rusty windowless bus which baked in the heat of the pitiless sun. On Saturdays, his only weekend day, he sat designing cheap air conditioners. He even built a prototype and experimented with it in the bedroom on the small coffee table, where there was hardly enough space to get to bed. The cheap air conditioner did not materialise.

He had been immersed in the desalinisation of sea water for some years. 'The greatest future challenge of mankind,' he kept telling me in the late sixties, trying to get me interested. But I had no time and he did not have the knowledge to make any inroads. He persevered, reading chemistry, doing engineering calculations.

On Saturdays when I had time, which was not often, we went for long walks. Ever since I can remember, I used to go for walks with my father. We have very few photographs from Romania, but one is of my father with Tom on one side and me on the other, my father looking at me, smiling and explaining something. I must have been around four years old. In Israel, on Saturdays, we walked in the late afternoons around the new orange plantations next to the border with Qalqilya. He kept encouraging me to persevere with my university studies: 'Just remember, knowledge is your only possession and nobody can take it away from you.' That's how he survived twenty years of communism and the years in Israel. From the fruits of his knowledge.

On one of those walks, he said to me that the best thing in his life were his three offspring. He had three only children: his only eldest son Tom, his only daughter and his only youngest son, Yossi. And I realised how much Tom was still on his mind.

There was regular correspondence between my father and Tom, three or four letters a year. My parents sent him a big parcel every year, shoes, shirts, singlets, the odd jumper. At the time we assumed that he would join us soon. After the Six Day War my father wrote to Tom not to apply for a visa, not yet. We had just been through a war and a very frightening time. Financially we were barely coping; we had been in the country for two years only. Judging from Tom's letters he was reasonably happy, so there was no point in turning his life upside down. Israel was not the land of milk and honey; it was the land of hard work and relentless heat. 'What could Tom do here,' my parents kept asking, 'without a profession? Let's establish ourselves first.' Tom had a partner, Ilona, a petite young blonde

Hungarian woman. They sent us photographs. My parents sent her blouses, lipstick and scarfs. We could not believe how pretty she was. She looked a bit girly, naïve. She was wearing a small tiara. Tiara? She must have dressed up for the photograph. I had never seen anybody wearing a tiara except in the movies. Tom had a partner, the rest did not count. She always wrote a few lines at the end of Tom's letter. We were happy for him.

Bit by bit, we realised that Tom might never join us. Looking at it from the heat and the sweat of Israel, Tom's situation did not seem dire; it looked quite good.

What did my father think when he realised that he would not see his eldest son again? I don't know. I don't remember it being discussed. But then I had no time to worry about Tom. I was stretched to the limit, having had to wrestle with two foreign languages, Hebrew and English, and an academic standard much higher than Romania prepared me for.

I was about to finish my second degree in science when one day my uncle from Sydney arrived on a visit. He told us how wonderful Australia was and offered to buy me a one-way ticket. My family encouraged me, especially my father. He wanted both Yossi and me to emigrate to a peaceful country.

'And you?' I asked.

'We are getting old, for us it does not matter.' His words broke my heart.

I was no longer the new migrant; I had become more confident but my life in Israel was not shaping up as expected.

I wanted to travel. I wanted to be as free as the swallows which used to fly above my head in Romania every autumn, on their way south. Maybe I would go to Australia for a few years, I thought. I will perfect my English, work, save money and go back.

But I remained in Australia. My life had changed too much and going back is never simple. It is another migration.

I missed my parents and Yossi enormously, for years. Sometimes, as I walked down the street, I saw someone who reminded me of my father and tears would roll down my face. At times, I saw families sitting in a café and suddenly the image switched. There they were, my mother, my father and Yossi, and I fantasised how it would have been if they could have joined me. That was not to be.

Ten years after our arrival in Israel and barely four years after I left, my father became very sick. When he felt better he read, he kept working on the desalinisation of sea water and wrote letters. He seemed content. But those times were interrupted by nasty chemotherapy sessions. On those days he would catch a couple of buses to the hospital, have his treatment and catch the buses back. The treatment took a few hours and he returned exhausted and went straight to bed. At times he said to my mother, 'Can you imagine, young people and even kids have to undergo the same therapy.' He felt very sorry for them.

Sometimes Yossi dropped in, or went to talk to the doctor, since my parents could not speak Hebrew. At times he helped with the hospitalisation, but mostly my parents were on their own. Without air conditioning, or even a phone to call a doctor, my mother nursed him for the rest of his four years of life. I was on the other side of the world in Australia, trying to start a new life.

My father passed away a couple of hours after I arrived back in Israel.

Next day, wrapped in a prayer shawl he never wore, and to the sounds of a Hebrew prayer he would not have understood, his body was lowered into his final resting place. A man who was a Jew but not Jewish enough, an Israeli but not quite, a Hungarian Jew among Romanians and a Jew among Hungarians. Finally he left this world with its divisive nationalisms, ideologies and religions which had marred most of his life. He was just another man on whom history inflicted its painful and murderous pursuits: Nazism, the Second World War, the communist dictatorship, the Arab-Israeli conflict and Israeli religiosity. History had match-made him, history had controlled his life. It was over. He joined the infinite Universe.

Recently I re-read a couple of his letters, letters he wrote a year before he died. One of them ends with: 'Outside it is cold and raining, but here in the lounge room the heater is on and we are warm. We sit inside reading, listening to the radio and of course talking about you. I embrace and kiss you a thousand times. Father.'

———

I did tell Tom about my father's life in Israel, not everything of course – I did not want to upset him.

'Eight hours work and five hours travelling daily at seventy years of age?' Tom asked. He looked embarrassed. 'I didn't know.'

'Of course you didn't. How could you?'

'You should have stayed! You should not have left!'

'Who knows what would have happened to him in Romania during Ceausescu? Mother is content, sort of. After the Second World War she could not help but feel that most people were anti-Semitic and her home was in Israel.'

'Yoseftal is a big suburb now. A big suburb shaded by tall trees. It has two small parks and lots of solid new blocks of flats. With our help, Yossi's and mine, mother lives with a carer and more comfortably than she did for decades. She still lives in the same flat, the flat we got on that first day, the day of our arrival when the hamsin raged, the cold water in the tap was warm, the nights were suffocating and the cries of the jackals curdled the blood.

'Yossi is an Israeli, he grew up there. He worked excruciatingly hard to put himself through university while helping my parents with their problems. He is a spine surgeon and a big success. And I moved on.'

Part VII

And now

22

'She said she wants to meet you.'

The story of Tom's relationship with that woman was emerging like drips from a tap gathering into a murky puddle. 'I told her if my sister is still here after 10 p.m. you can meet her.'

Ten? By ten I would be on my way back to the hotel. Now I was determined to leave even earlier.

'She was beautiful once. A beautiful Gypsy woman, with dark olive skin, grey eyes, black wavy hair,' Tom said, then fell silent as if savouring her beauty a bit longer, as if not wanting to let go. Curiosity had deserted me. Something about Tom, or just a feeling that I would not like what I was going to hear. Was that a relationship between two people at the fringe of society? I felt as if I had inadvertently crossed the border into a foreign country, into unfamiliar, daunting territory, and the only way to escape was for Tom to keep silent. But he kept talking. I told myself off for being too precious, too squeamish, that I had to face up to other worlds, Tom's world, a world of much greater compromises than my own. I told myself that if I wanted to find out more about my brother, I had to find out more about his life, his real life, not just the changes in the country we both grew up in. I knew about his sad marriage, I knew about his partner and his other longer-term relationships of years ago. But what about his later life? Was there a woman who knew the real Tom, who saw more in him than his disability, his poverty, his insecurity? Did he love, was he hurt more than most of us? And what about his life now?

'I want to remember her as she was. I don't want to be with her now.'

And I hoped that was the end of his story.

The sun had set. In front of the window pink puffs of clouds were drifting across the sky. Tom took a mouthful of cheese and red pepper and reminded me again that the latter is so much better than the red capsicum, the Western variety. This remark was only an introduction to what was to follow, because the slim red Romanian pepper had become associated with Eastern Europe and it was so much tastier than the big fat capsicum which he said was Western and tasteless. In Eastern Europe the food tasted better, people were friendlier, families closer. That's what people who returned from the West told him, teachers who spent years washing dishes in West Germany and others who went to England or Ireland and ended up in menial jobs.

For the middle-aged and the old, the change had come too late. They couldn't even go abroad to wash dishes. Their future was uncertain, even scary. Tom too had his worries. The Unitarians, who owned the Brassai School where he lived, had been very charitable. 'They live by their word, they are decent people,' he said to me a few times during my stay. But the school was expanding, taking more and more students. They needed more dormitories for students from the country. Would they want his flat for some other use one day?

'The school needs space and there is no guarantee how long any-one can be charitable in a world run by market forces.'

The American Unitarians had been helping. They donated sig-nificant sums of money to the school. The latest American donation was for a lift. 'A lift for teachers and visitors only,' Tom was quick to clarify.

'And you?'

'Only if I take up American citizenship, but judging by the woman who came to visit, I need to be a hundred kilos heavier to qualify.'

'You can't have a segregated lift.'

'The lift is for them only. But I wouldn't worry, they dug out the shaft and ran out of money. It could be another decade before a lift runs up and down that hole.'

It was past nine already and I wanted to go. Tom started to look for his keys. He always walked me back to the hotel.

Along the dark school corridors he kept switching lights on so we could see the stairs, then off again to save electricity. While he was performing his green duties my eye caught the picture of last year's graduates. On the bottom was the motto: 'Don't question why you were born, don't question why you will die, but question everything in between.' It was so right; it was one more reason why I liked that school. Tom did too. He loved living there. He loved being surrounded by young people, the bell ringing every hour, the friendly cleaners and gatekeepers always ready for a chat, the teachers who dropped in every now and then to discuss politics, the physics teacher who talked to him about CERN, the particle accelerator which might unravel many questions about the origins of the universe. These people had been part of his life for more than three decades. This was his family. He loved the old-fashioned high ceilings, the long corridors, the freezing winters and the sunny summer mornings. And he was going to keep climbing the one hundred and seven stairs while his legs would carry him.

After switching the last light on and off again, we emerged into the street. It had been another long day. The late evening air was cool and refreshing. I craved a long walk, but I resigned myself to the short stroll back to the hotel. We walked in silence. Every now and then Tom stopped to flick off his cigarette ash. He seemed anxious. I suggested we walk another couple of blocks. The street was unusually empty. A few people were waiting at the bus station. A homeless person shuffled by.

Tom stopped to rest his leg.

'I was in my early forties, she was in her late twenties. It was years since I had split up with my latest partner, nearly two decades since my marriage. Nothing had worked for me: marriage, relationships, nothing.' He looked at me. 'So I changed. At first it was sex for money. Come on, don't be so prudish!'

'Okay, go on.'

Bit by bit Tom gave up the world of so-called respectable women for the world of prostitutes. He felt comfortable there. Among the outlawed, among the looked down on. He expected sex and they expected money. It was an honest transaction, unlike his relationships with women who claimed they loved him. He could not be deceived, he expected no emotional return.

'It was money for herself, money for her older brother. Her brother was everything to her, he was the only family she had. She never knew her father, her mother had passed away.'

The murky puddle was getting murkier – her brother was a petty criminal, small jobs, pickpocketing, the odd theft from tourists, her pimp. He got her an endless supply of clients. Prostitution was outlawed in Romania, so she had to be careful.

It seemed that she did not mind being a comfort woman – that's what Tom called her. It was good money, better than she could have made in a dirty factory. A daily job? Regimented working for a tiny income, an income she could make in a day instead of a week? No. Quick money and freedom. Then there was tricking, cheating and pickpocketing. An art, even fun at times. That's how they saw it, she and her brother.

Some Gypsies have jobs, some are rich with big houses, but many are at the bottom of society. It looked like the two siblings lived up to the Romanian Gypsy stereotype. They lived outside mainstream society with other non-belongers, they compared notes and learnt from each other. They lived in a world of rusty cars, of cheating and tricking, of wheeling and dealing. Were they worse than others? If the party bigwigs had special privileges, if the state could rob people of their possessions, why couldn't a Gypsy pickpocket the odd tourist? And why couldn't his sister sell her affections, her physical services?

Still, Tom's story had transported me into a world I had only read about, a world as far from my experience as the world of Dickens.

I was totally unprepared to find my brother acquainted with that world.

'Prostitution serves a purpose,' he said, and I had to remind myself again that I had no right to judge.

'Anyway, she came to me one evening and kept coming back. She poured out her troubles, about her brother, the problems with her boyfriend. And I listened.' She lived in a world where so many things Tom could not even come close to understanding were quite acceptable.

Tom listened and felt sorry for her, because her beauty would fade with the years. He felt sorry for the old woman who would no longer be of use to her brother. What would happen then, who would look after her? He listened, he paid, he advised. And she kept coming back to him.

But he also felt sorry for her because she was vulnerable. Not in the same way as he was, but she was vulnerable all the same and Tom knew how that felt. He would have liked to help her out of her way of life, to protect her. Although he did not admit it, I had the impression that he loved her, that he loved her because she was beautiful, because she was in a weak bargaining position with life.

'Her brother introduced her to the trade. He still uses her, he still takes all her money and she is past middle age.' He wanted to protect her, to help her leave her circumstances, turn straight. 'The time will come when she will not be able to continue with that way of life. She will be too old. Her brother will rob her of her earnings and she will be left with nothing. There is not much time left.'

It looked like this ageing woman who had no other relations apart from her brother the crook, still found some comfort in being with Tom. She turned up every now and then; sometimes she stayed for a couple of weeks before she disappeared again.

Tom glanced at his watch.

'And now? Why did she come back?'

'Because her hot water is on the blink. She said she'll come to have a bath. At least she'll fish me out of the bath if I need it.'

'What if she arrives before you're back?'

'She'll break in.'

'Break in?'

'To look around and take what she can.'

I thought that I was prepared for anything, I thought nothing would surprise me. She would betray the man who gave her shelter for weeks, the man who cared about her, who wanted to save her while it was still possible! She would betray my brother.

'But she'll get into trouble.'

'She'll say that she thought I am not well.'

At least Tom was realistic about it, I tried to console myself. Maybe she could not really hurt him.

'Does she think I gave you money?'

'She did ask. I said you didn't,' he paused. 'No, of course not.' Tom looked at his watch again.

'Let's turn back,' I suggested, 'I'm tired.'

Back in the hotel I was relieved to have some quiet time, but I could not get Tom's relationship with that woman out of my mind. I wondered if I should have advised him against it. No, I have no right. We all need intimacy. One has to settle for what one can get.

I recalled asking Tom which woman he loved most. He looked at me. 'I have never loved any of them. We got on, we did things together, we laughed, we talked. But love? No, I never loved anybody.'

I did not believe him. I am sure he did love that woman once.

The hotel carpet stank of cigarette smoke. I longed for the mountains, for the fresh air. As I stepped into the bathtub and turned the shower on I remembered Tom's words: 'At least she'll be there to fish me out if I slip.' I tightened my grip on the handrail.

Later, refreshed, I lay down and stared at the ceiling.

23

'*Kezit csokolom!* (I kiss your hand)' Tom said loudly in the direction of a slight middle-aged woman typing on a computer. 'The secretary,' he whispered in my direction and went to join her. The sun was streaming through the tall window. Below, in the courtyard, a few pots of green bushes softened the walls.

The offices of the Jewish Community had an old Viennese atmosphere. The high ceilings, the chandelier, the Persian carpet, all conveyed a quiet spaciousness and grace. The furniture looked worn, the carpet was fraying at the edges, but the parquet floor was as shiny as if it had been polished yesterday.

From the opposite corner, without pausing in their chat about a burst pipe, the overdue plumber and the cost of it all, two women acknowledged Tom's greeting with a wave. A deep, loud voice was talking on the phone in the next room. This was a busy place.

'Nowadays,' Tom recounted the latest joke to Magda, the Hungarian secretary, 'to live is an art, to get sick is luxury, to die is total lack of consideration towards your relatives who will have to spend a fortune to bury you.'

They both laughed. I laughed too and not only at the joke. I laughed because Tom looked totally at home. I had not realised just how much Tom's situation had been weighing on me.

Magda had not been to customer service training: no fake jollity, no fake interest in my wellbeing. A breath of fresh air. She did want to know where I had been, what I had seen. 'But what about the operetta at the Hungarian Opera?' she asked, 'or *Rigoletto* at the

Romanian Opera?' Could she arrange anything for me, help in any way?

But Tom did not want to talk about the Opera. He was in a rush and urged me to go and meet the professor, also the president of the community and the owner of the loud voice, as it turned out. At Tom's greeting he looked up from his papers and struggled to his feet with the effort of an unwell man.

'Your sister?' he asked. 'Very happy to finally make your acquaintance,' and shook my hand. He was in his early seventies, small build, heavy glasses. He was wearing a worn suit, collar and tie. He told me that he was still teaching at the university, teaching mathematics. He was not healthy and neither was his wife, and presiding over the community, over its six hundred members, took it out of him at times.

I was curious why they stayed behind, why they didn't emigrate.

'Some of us were too old, some had no children, some married Romanians, some believed in communism. I beg your pardon – maybe they did not believe in communism, at least not the sort we lived under, but they did not want to live in a capitalist country.'

'And where do you fit, Professor?'

'I have no children. There was no point in leaving. This is my native land, my language. I belong here.'

His words lingered. 'My native land, my language.' For most people, the sound of Hungarian is awkward; for me it is poetry and delight. When I say 'flower' in English I refer to a plant with petals and colours. But the word in Hungarian, *virág*, sounds to me melodious and joyful. Yes, you can learn to speak a language, you can even learn to think in a language but will you feel the same joy and sadness at the sound of those words? Feel the black desperation or be uplifted by hope? Will the word *love* evoke the same tenderness and ardour? I don't think so.

The professor stole a look at his papers. A man put his head around the door and called for Tom.

'I like your brother,' said the professor, when Tom was out of earshot. 'He knows so much. I can talk to him about anything.'

I tried to steer the discussion to his future.

'Don't worry. We'll look after him. For the foreseeable future he is all right living where he does. Then we will see. Unitarians are decent people.'

The phone rang. It was the professor's wife. He had to go.

I joined Tom in the next room and as we chatted to Magda, the door opened and three people walked in. Three Americans, two men and a woman. They had come by taxi from Vienna the night before. They came to visit the grave of the older man's mother. They had been to her grave that morning, and now they wanted to talk to a gravestone maker to renew the writing.

'How much will it cost?' the younger man asked.

'A dollar per letter,' Magda replied, and judging by her quick response I got the impression that these sorts of requests from visiting westerners were not rare.

At the time, a dollar was no small change in Romania, and I could nearly hear the people in the room calculating the kilos of apples and potatoes for each letter on Mrs Frenkel's grave, the dear mother of one, the much-loved grandmother of the other, the woman for whom her dear descendants had come all the way from Vienna to pay their respects and reflect on her life for a whole fifteen minutes. Fifteen minutes, that was how much time they spent at the grave that morning. They were in a hurry. They wanted to pay and return to Vienna straight away. They were flying back to the States the next morning with the first plane.

The older man pulled out a piece of paper with the lettering on Mrs Frenkel's gravestone and handed it to Magda. They counted the letters, he paid out and with Mrs Frenkel's memorial sorted, the Americans departed.

In the corner, the two women had organised a plumber. One of them was writing something in a notebook, the second was looking over her shoulder. Tom interrupted to ask for the phone number of the taxi driver who did jobs for the Community.

'You know who, the taxi driver, the engineer,' Tom explained.

'You want an engineer?' the woman with glasses asked, her voice a little louder than necessary.

'No, a taxi driver, but the one who used to be an engineer.'

'If you don't want an engineer but a taxi driver, why don't you say so?'

'Because I want a particular taxi driver and everybody knows that he used to be an engineer.'

'So who cares what he was? He is a taxi driver now. Who cares what anybody was once?'

'You mean Moshe's son, David?' the other woman asked.

'That's the one,' Tom replied, looking relieved.

'So why don't you say so?' the first woman asked as she grabbed a school notebook and started leafing through. 'Now Moshe, now David – that's the one,' and she wrote down a number. We were in business.

So those were the people who had become Tom's family, the warm and caring men and women, the mentally agile with whom he could have interesting arguments, the few senile whom he comforted and even the very religious men and women for whom Tom was not Jewish enough. I was glad that I had met them.

We started on our walk back to Tom's place. The street followed the Small Somes river. Why Small? I pondered as torrents of water rushed noisily past. Small Somes, big Somes, my mother, Jidovitza, my mind played word associations again. But I did not want to linger on any of those, I needed to concentrate. We had turned into a narrow street; cars parked everywhere, on the side of the road and over the footpath. As we walked along the narrow strip in the middle of the road, the only space big enough for Tom to walk comfortably, a small car came around the corner. We retreated to the safety of the footpath, between two adjacent parked cars. Just as we walked back to the middle strip again, another car appeared.

'Once you could walk here at your leisure,' and Tom cursed the cars, capitalism and hooligans, because only hooligans would drive like that. I kept laughing at his cause and effect interpretation and his colourful language, while quietly wishing they would drive that slowly in the centre of Sydney.

Tom was wearing a jeans outfit, a dark grey cotton shirt and vest, and a lighter shade trousers. He looked very comfortable. Most days he was quite well dressed, but that outfit looked as if it had been made for him. Of course it wasn't. It was from the Jewish Community, second-hand clothes sent by the American Jews to help the ageing Eastern Europeans. Tom was grateful to the Community. 'What would I do without them?' he said to me a number of times during that visit.

What indeed? The Community provided subsidised food, affordable with the pension. Every day except Saturday, Tom had lunch with the other members in the communal room, variations on beef and vegetables. They had been eating beef for years because they didn't have a kosher chicken plucker. No kosher chicken plucker meant no chicken on the menu. Not all members were religious, but the ancient rules had to be respected, for the sake of the religious members and to keep the American money coming. Like most Western Jews, those who run the JOINT – The American Jewish Joint Distribution Committee – don't seem to understand secular Eastern European Jews; they don't understand that you can be Jewish culturally, acknowledge religious practices, but have absolutely no interest in following them. They don't understand that most of these people's families lived through or were killed in the Holocaust, whether the chicken on their plate was kosher or not. Later they lived through the unofficial communist anti-Semitism. These experiences formed their Jewish identity far more than a rabbi's unintelligible Hebrew mutterings and the kosher chickens would. But these old Jews would not argue. They needed the money to survive so they had to put up with the thousands-years-old rules even if it meant beef every day for the rest of their lives. And as I contemplated a daily beef diet, the goulash, the rissoles and the much hated boiled beef (forget roast beef; in that part of the world there is no such thing), my stomach started to feel heavy.

'Why not have vegetarian a couple of times a week?' I asked.

'Vegetarian? We were vegetarians for nearly fifty years.'

He was right, of course.

Once a month each member got a big parcel of food: a dozen eggs, sugar, coffee, tea, flour, and whatever was cheap and not perishable. 'It's a heavy parcel,' Tom said, 'and there are one hundred and seven stairs, but I manage. It covers some of my dinners.'

At other times he reverted to his favourite food: bacon, red onions and black bread.

After the fall of the Soviet Union, the Jewish Community in Cluj had its funds reduced. The money had to extend to the Jews left in Russia. The entrance of Romania to the European Union was an added worry for Tom. 'The prices will go up and the pension will not keep up the pace,' he said to me a few times. But Tom trusted the Community. 'They'll manage somehow.' They would be there, one way or another; he would not be allowed to starve.

The Unitarians gave him shelter, the Jews the rest. Inadvertently, or through mere personality, Tom had brought together the Jews and the Christians. Thousands of people engaged in interfaith committees all over the world are trying to do that, without much success. I told him so. He laughed.

He would have preferred not to have to rely on help; he would have preferred to manage on his pension. 'I worked for forty-five years, and what do I get? Sixty dollars per month. That's my pension. Americans spend twice as much on their pet dog. I must be worth half a dog,' he said, his smile shaded by a hint of bitterness.

I was grateful to the Community for the financial help, but even more for the sense of belonging they gave Tom. He worked there as a librarian once a week, and made up the numbers for the communal prayer, the *minyan* which according to Orthodox rules requires a quorum of ten adult males. According to those rules, Tom is not a

Jew because his mother was a Christian. But according to the Christians who classify people by their father's religion, he is a Jew. So for most of his life Tom was a Christian among Jews and a Jew among Christians.

Thankfully, the Cluj Jewish Community had taken him in. Each Friday night, or during religious holidays and funerals, Tom sat among the ten old men. He listened as the rabbi or the cantor recited the blessing: '*Baruch ata* ...' The words connected him to the other nine men in that small room, not because he believed in what was being said – he did not understand a word – but because it was a tradition which had defined Jews for centuries as it defines many Jews in the world to this day, whether they are religious or not. And Tom continued to sit and listen through the entire service. Some words were vaguely familiar; he even came to understand a handful, but most were strange and foreign. Someone stood up, and the other nine men followed, Tom among them. They murmured in unison until the old Hebrew letters of the prayer ran out. Then the man who was first to stand up, the man who understood the text, was the first to sit down. Everybody followed.

The Yom Kippur service was unending. Every now and then Tom understood why he stood up and why he could sit down. One of the men, Marton, used to whisper a translation of most prayers. At times someone would say, 'Shush!'; at times someone got annoyed, but the prayer followed its destination to the end. Marton passed away. But Tom still found a willing whisperer and the old Hebrew text came alive, sometimes in Romanian and sometimes in Hungarian.

'I help preserve an ancient tradition,' he said to me. 'Besides, I'm interested in comparative religion.'

Our upbringing did not prepare him for Jewish prayers. I do not know what my father believed in. If he did believe in anything he kept it very private; he never talked about it. But I know what he did not believe in: he did not believe in gods invented by men, or the stories of the old religious texts.

'The Ten Commandments were the work of a genius,' I remember him telling me, 'more than likely invented by Moses to turn the unruly Israelites into civilised people. He disappeared up the mountain. Days later he returned with the tablets on which were inscribed the Ten Commandments. He proclaimed that they were given to him by God. And of course the Israelites accepted God's laws.'

That was the extent of the religious training our father gave us, which was probably further reinforced by the communist regime's diagnosis: 'Religion is the opiate of the masses'.

—⁓—

Back at the school, Tom took me in through the students' gate, a small door at the back of the building. The big door at the front, where he worked in the later years, was for teachers and visitors. It turned out that Tom spent many years manning the students' gate. He had never mentioned that before.

That day the gatekeeper was Imre, a rotund middle-aged man. He was there to check who came in and who went out. His grubby office, a two-by-three-metre room, was full of cigarette smoke.

Imre was in a chatting mood. He enquired about my holiday, but what he really wanted to talk about was life in Romania, how difficult it was to make ends meet, even for him who doubled as an after-hours electrician and plumber – actually, any trade in demand. I admire tradesmen; a good tradesman has a solution for every problem. He was definitely one of them. He built the toilet in Tom's flat and was very proud of the way he solved the lack of space.

We were interrupted by a loud commotion outside Imre's office. He jumped up and stormed out. A couple of minutes later he was back with a student. He asked the student to leave his bag in the office. The student refused politely.

'May a dog fuck you to exhaustion!' and other unusual curses rolled out of Imre's uninhibited mouth. Faced with such a dark choice, the student put his bag in the corner and departed.

Tom walked out and I was left with Imre.

'So with all the extra work you must be managing okay,' I said.

'Well enough for me. Not as well as your brother. He gets help from the Jews.'

My heart sank. I didn't like the tone of his voice. I didn't like the way he said 'the Jews'. Why? Maybe because it had resonances with the nursery rhyme my six-year-old friend had recited to me, or the occasional exclamation of the derogatory Romanian word *Jidan*, much more common, which I recalled from our later years in Romania. Maybe those hurts had inserted themselves somewhere inside me, the way some viruses insert themselves in one's DNA, only to be triggered at times by an odd event.

Am I oversensitive, or does the word Jew in my mother tongue trigger feelings different from its translation in English? Does that word have different connotations in Europe than in Australia? In Europe, where sixty years after the Holocaust most synagogues – maybe not in Cluj, but I have never seen a synagogue here – have to be manned by security guards? Is it because I am in the poisonous Europe where Jews are history?

Curiously, I keep coming back, because in some ways Europe is my home, because that land with its mountains, its cool air, its forests and birdsong, its misty hills, its haystacks, is part of me. I return to that land to see the same scenery, to breathe the same air, to hear the same sounds. But when I lived here, there were still Jews in Europe. Nowadays synagogues are historical buildings where local guides offer tours and make money out of that curious lot, the Jews and their sad history. All over Europe, tourists come to take photos of buildings devoid of Jews, silent buildings which know how to keep secrets, photos to take home and show their friends. Photos don't show the fear of those who have been taken away, or the feeling of otherness and distrust of those who survived. Only people who know the history can imagine some of what went on in these parts of the world, between the times when these buildings were in use and alive, and years later when their gates were shut for service. For most visitors these are buildings where strange people practised a bizarre worship.

'He gets help from the Jews.' The words resounded in my head again. Only someone who lived in Europe would detect the complexity of what he meant.

'You probably help him too,' he said, examining my face.

He thought that I was loaded. Isn't everybody in the West rich? And if Tom's sister is rich, so must he be.

'No, I can't. I have to help my mum.'

'Still, he's better off,' Imre added.

Imagined or not, I sensed envy in his voice. I remembered my mother's paranoia when we lived there, not to stand out, not to give the impression that we were in any way better off than the *goyim*. Nausea welled up in me.

Tom was back. He ushered me out. As we walked up to Tom's flat, I kept thinking of the conversation with Imre. What if Tom was considered well-off? I panicked. Was that why he seemed reluctant to take me to the Jewish Community? He was justified to be worried. If they decided that he is well-off, they could decide that he did not need their help, that there were more needy people than him.

I felt like someone who had committed an unlawful act. I had not been caught, but I was guilty. Guilty of insisting on meeting the people from the Jewish Community, guilty of socialising with people at the school, guilty of disturbing Tom's peace of mind.

A couple of days later I asked Tom whether he had any issues with Imre. Was he an anti-Semite? Tom was adamant: 'He is not.'

Maybe I read too much into his reluctance to take me to the Jewish Community. I hoped I did, because I enjoyed my visit there. I enjoyed meeting the warm people, Tom's family. And I will forever be grateful to them.

24

It was a beautiful morning. In the dining room a faint gauzy sunlight illuminated the breakfast smorgasbord: neck ham, black bread, tomato quarters, slices of cucumber and a plate of cheese, arranged unpretentiously by the beautiful teacher turned hotel receptionist.

The coffee seemed a long time in coming.

'He gets help from the Jews,' the gatekeeper's words kept echoing in my mind. Perturbed by his real or imagined resentment of the Jews, or by my oversensitive reaction, my peace of mind suddenly vanished. And whether it was a word association, or just an association with the history of that land, my mind jumped to Jidovitza.

Once my younger brother, Yossi, had said that he would like to visit that village, my mother's birthplace. I did not reply. For me, Jidovitza was like the last page of a book, the blank page after the story has ended. There was nothing left to say. But its name, 'the village of the Jew', filled me with curiosity and left me vaguely uneasy. Perhaps I had spent too long outside Israel and a village of religious Jews in Eastern Europe brought connotations of otherness. Maybe somewhere else, where the word Jew was not so loaded, the name would have been acceptable, but in Eastern Europe? In Eastern Europe in the 1900s? Why would people let themselves be identified so easily?

Yossi kept telling me that it must be a really nice place, but I could not work up an interest. I was more interested in Comandau where my father had spent his childhood. A fairytale place, deep in the Carpathians where the sun's rays barely filtered through the dense forests, squirrels ran up the trees and vanished, rivers streamed down the mountains, birds sang and on occasion a mother bear and her cubs would shamble down to the river. Those were the stories my father told us, and when he did, I smelled the pines and felt the breeze on my face, worrying that the mother bear might decide that I was a danger to her cubs. But the woodcutters were near and their sawing reassured me. I saw a squirrel high in the tree and feared for his life; I saw starlings in their nest and was anxious for their chicks. In the autumn, I would rustle my feet among the dry leaves, kick the pine cones on the path which led to the river and look to see if the swallows were still around. It was sad when they left. I felt like a child who is left behind by someone dear, who would never come back. I have yearned for Comandau ever since I remember, but my father never took us there. People did not travel in those days; they had no money for such luxuries.

Judging by the German video on the internet, the Comandau of the 1920s has long disappeared. Logging has taken its toll. Most of today's Comandau is deforested and desolate. A couple of old photographs of well-dressed people surrounded by dense wild forests capture how the place looked once upon a time.

Unlike my father's stories where people hardly figured, my mother's were dotted with names of people: brothers, sisters, cousins, friends and neighbours.

After the war, my mother swore never to see Jidovitza again. Maybe she did not trust herself; maybe she did not think she could face reality, the proof that all the people she once knew had disappeared, to see their houses occupied by strangers, people carrying on with their lives, bringing up children, cooking, laughing as if the killings and pillaging never happened. She said she would never go back and she kept her word. And I? I had no interest in the place. I did not connect. Perhaps for most of my life I did not want to connect. It was something awful and it was remote enough to keep it that way. But now here I was in Cluj, two hours' drive from Jidovitza. Ideal for a day trip. Ideal but … I did not understand my own reluctance. I was not ready yet. Not for that. Perhaps some other time, perhaps never.

But we had to go somewhere, out of that town, away from Tom's flat and our reminiscences.

'Here's the coffee.' The beautiful receptionist interrupted my thoughts.

As I sipped the coffee my mind stumbled on the obvious. We could go to the painted monasteries up in the hills of Bucovina. I recalled seeing the Voronet Monastery on television back in Australia. The Sistine Chapel of the East, they said, its walls painted with frescos in vivid colours. Scientists still don't know the makeup of those paints and the secrets of their six hundred years' longevity.

I was amazed that monasteries had survived communism, survived Ceausescu who bulldozed so many beautiful old buildings. Perhaps even communism had holes and anomalies I was not aware of, or perhaps deep down Ceausescu was religious and buying his place in heaven.

A few years after communism fell, the monasteries were declared a UNESCO World Heritage treasure, so perhaps they are now safe from politics, safe from demolition. This was my chance, I thought, and if I don't make it during this trip who knows when, if ever.

I would talk it over with Tom. Maybe we could convince David, the mechanical engineer turned taxi driver come tourist guide, to take us to the monasteries.

A feeling of peace descended on me as I contemplated a beautiful day in the mountains.

—◊◊◊—

We were in luck. David was happy to take us.

'To the monasteries?' I asked.

'No problem.'

'How far are they?'

'Depends which way we go. Through Bistritza ...'

My heart skipped a beat. 'Would you have to go through Bistritza?'

'It's the shortest way.'

'Wait a minute. Can you take us to Jidovitza? Jidovitza is in the Bistritza region.'

'I've never heard of Jidovitza, but I'll find out where it is. It shouldn't be too difficult.'

From Jidovitza he would drive us to the painted monasteries of Bucovina. A two-day trip. I was now committed.

A day later my phone rang. It was David.

'It's not on the map. I don't know where it is. I rang the Jewish Community, but they have never heard of Jidovitza. I'm not sure if I can find it.'

'If we can't, we'll just continue to the monasteries.' I tried to defuse the worry in his voice. Anyhow, I was more interested in the monasteries than in Jidovitza.

'I'll pick you up at eight.'

Intrigued that no one had heard about the place, I headed straight to the internet café on the corner of the street. Google understood the name and came up with some confusing coordinates. It was not clear if the place still existed, or if it was a historical place, or where it was in relation to Bistritza, the regional big town, or Nasaud, a somewhat smaller but nevertheless significant town in the same region to which Jidovitza once belonged.

Next morning, at eight o'clock sharp, David was waiting in the lobby. He and his son the lawyer had been up till midnight trying to find Jidovitza and he was none the wiser. I conceded that there was not much hope. The place seemed to have been razed from the face of the earth.

'I have some idea where it might be,' David added, 'on the out-skirts of Nasaud, but I can't promise anything.'

I got in the car ready for any eventuality, but I was not going to let Jidovitza and its history vanish so easily. I now had to find out more.

A one-lane road led to Bistritza, roadworks all along. The road was being repaired and widened with money from the EU. Sprinkled on the sides of the road were new two-storey houses, the likes of which I had never seen in Romania, outside big towns. The hills rolled past us like a dream, a slow movie slightly out of focus: peasants plough-ing the earth as they have done for centuries, horses with colourful pompoms pulling a cart full of hay, slowly.

On a narrow lane we found ourselves stuck behind a cart piled high with hay. The man sat behind the horse, whip in his hand, more out of habit than for any specific purpose. The woman sat at the back, high up on top of the hay, facing us, her big floral skirt spread widely, her gaze far into the distance, past us, past the village, perhaps into another world. She looked as if nothing would shake her out of her languid and resigned mood. The sun shone lazily through the thick mist. The horse paced leisurely. Man, woman, hay and horse progressed as if in dreamtime. The church bells chimed. A woman stood at a window gossiping with a neighbour; others were working the fields.

From time to time David pulled me out of this old world with a comment: 'In the next two or three years the carts will disappear from the main road.' And when he saw my baffled look, he added, 'Just another condition for Romania joining the EU.' He did not think it was a good idea. He had travelled through Western Europe, taxiing tourists around. Western Europe was all right for Western Europeans and driving was easy, 'But why take what's Romanian out of Romania? The horses, the slow carts and peasants make Romania what it is, and I love it.'

A road sign pointed to Nasaud; more houses appeared on the hills. We were approaching an industrial site. David stopped the car. 'I'll just ask the fellow over there.' He pointed to a young man.

After a short discussion and lots of finger pointing, David was back. We travelled for another kilometre or so and slowed down behind a bent old woman pulling something which looked a cross between a shopping bag and a wheelbarrow.

'Jidovitza is over the bridge,' she said. 'I'll take you there.'

David parked the car and we joined the old woman. The bridge was only thirty or so steps away. Past the bridge, on the right, stood a big two-storey house, with a small shop on the left. Four or five houses on each side of the street, the main street of Jidovitza. Two young Gypsy women dressed in jeans and T-shirts, one holding a baby, were chatting in the middle of the road. To my left, along the

Somes River, there was an even shorter street with a yellow house on the river side and a few small houses opposite.

'She lives there.' The bent old woman pointed towards a small house, next to the shop.

'The oldest woman in the village,' David explained.

We walked across to the house of the oldest woman in the village. David knocked on the gate. Eventually, a woman in her fifties appeared. She can't possibly be the oldest woman in the village, I thought, but then life expectancy in Romania is less than in the West so perhaps she is.

She did not know anything about the Jewish families who lived in the village before the war. 'Never heard of them. I moved here twenty years ago. There were no Jewish families here then.'

'Do you know who might?'

She shook her head, she didn't. I looked at David. He signalled patience.

'I just returned from the hospital. I had a gallbladder operation,' the woman said unexpectedly.

I felt for her. From what I had heard, Romanian hospitals were not places to be pampered. Besides, I got the impression that she lived on her own. But she had a good healthy colour so I decided she was not in real trouble and my mind returned to the reason I was in that drab village. I asked her who was the oldest person in the village.

'My next-door neighbour,' and she pointed to a blue door three metres further up.

We knocked, but there was no answer.

'She should be back soon. She often goes out at this time of the day,' said the woman who turned out not to be the oldest in the village, and disappeared.

We hung around waiting. Worried about David's schedule, I wondered aloud how long we would have to wait. I had no idea how long it would take to the monasteries, or where we would sleep that night.

'Don't worry,' David said, 'just take your time.'

254

I walked back across to the bridge. Reality and my childhood picture of the place, a vision I had formed from my mother's stories, did not match. The river bed, nearly all pebbles, was three times the width of the water. A man was fishing in one of the side pools under a bush. I wondered if they had had a major drought, because in my mother's stories this was a big river, just as in the song she used to sing:

> The deep waters of the Somes are flowing quietly.
> Lean on my shoulder my sweetheart.
> I will not lean on it my dear,
> Because I am to be married on Thursday.

My mother had a beautiful voice. Her dream was to be sent to a music school for voice training, but there was no money – no money, just religion. The song filled our house with melancholia. Why was that love so helpless, I wondered at the time.

And where is that big Somes River? I asked myself as I looked at the pebbles in the river bed. The climate had changed, it snowed less and there had been some dry summers in Romania, but I started to think that my mother's nostalgia might have magnified the river. And who knows what else?

Yet the Somes is a major river, they taught us in school. What is a major river in Romania? Is my memory all right, or am I mixed up? If the river in Cluj is the Small Somes, shouldn't this be the big, the real Somes? I felt let down. By the Somes, by my mother.

The old woman who would tell us all was not back yet. I decided to ring my mother in Israel. Within seconds I was talking to her.

'Guess where I am?'

She knew that I was in Romania. But where in Romania she did not.

'Jidovitza,' I said.

The line went quiet. The old childhood helplessness encroached on me again. What am I going to say? What can I say? I still didn't know. So I waited. She gasped, 'Jidovitza?'

My heart pounded. 'Listen, I need you to tell me where your

house was. Nobody seems to know. I am standing on the bridge facing the village.'

'On the right side as you cross the bridge.'

On the right side was the two-storey house and I had never heard her talking about a two-storey house.

'Was that a one- or two-storey house?'

'One,' she said, 'only one.' She paused. 'Just a minute, Mali told me that they built another storey on the old house. The people to whom my brother sold the house.'

The brother who was captured by the Germans and forced to pick mines all the way to Russia and back, then thrown into a concentration camp. He survived it all, but lost his wife and young daughter. After the war he returned to Jidovitza, sold the house and emigrated to Australia.

'I didn't know Mali came to visit.'

Mali was my mother's childhood friend. She survived the war and immigrated to Israel. She passed away a few years ago.

'She did visit. Once.'

'Tell me again how many families lived here in Jidovitza?'

'Can't tell you exactly.' She paused. 'Around thirty. Can you see the street opposite?'

'Which one?'

'The one opposite, the one which runs along the riverbank?'

'Of course. It's the only side street in Jidovitza.'

'There was a flour mill there, on the left side as you face the village, on the bank of the Somes.'

It all started to make sense. The building on the left, the only building on the bank of the Somes, was a flour mill.

'Tell me …'

'What?'

'I thought the Somes is a big river. There is very little water in it.'

'They redirected the water, Mali said. Industry, or irrigation, I'm not sure.'

'If it was such a big river and the riverbed was full, you must have had floods … it must have been quite a difficult place to live in, especially in the spring.'

'There were floods sometimes. Once we had to go and stay in the school because it was too dangerous to be at home.'

There were no discrepancies in that story. The past, the present, and everything which happened in between were a seamless continuum.

'Listen, I will call you if I find someone who lived here at that time.' We both knew what *that time* meant. 'It does not look promising though. Anyway, I'd better go.'

'Just one thing,' she said. 'There was a rivulet in front of the house. Behind the gate, not far from it. Can you see it?'

I walked to the gate, my mobile to my ear. A couple of metres behind the gate was a three-foot bridge.

'You're right. It's still here. There's no water, but there is a small bridge. What a memory!' I said to part on a positive note, but also because it was true. My mother had a brilliant memory.

'I'll talk to you soon.'

I went back to the big bridge and looked at the house again. The biggest house in the village, now a rich man's house, clearly not what it used to be. The trees in the garden were loaded with pears and I suddenly understood why my mother loved pears so much, pears which for a long time she could not afford in Israel because they were imported and expensive.

I looked towards the village again. Hardly a village, just a handful of houses. Decades ago that was Jidovitza, the village of the Jews. Around this time of the year it would be Rosh Hashanah, the beginning of the New Year. A week and a half later Yom Kippur, the Day of Atonement, the day when one fasts to be forgiven for the sins of the past year. Nobody would eat until sunset, children and the sick excepted. In the synagogue, men draped in their prayer shawls would pray all day. Women would sit at the back, the older mourning relatives who had passed on, the younger keeping an eye on their husbands or other young men. It would be a difficult day. Eventually the first evening star would rise high in the sky and people would return home. Cleansed of their sins, families would congregate around a table to eat, talk, kiss their children and be thankful to God.

As I looked up the street my mother's stories converged. I saw two barefooted young girls playing hopscotch, a boy climbing a tree. I saw a couple of adolescent girls swimming in the Somes, while young men eyed them from afar. I saw my mother and her favourite sister Dora eating plums and pears.

Autumn arrived. Weeks of rain followed. One of those days my mother left. She left with the swallows. She was twenty-three. She set off for Romania, not knowing if she would get there or what was waiting for her. Abstract Romania was concrete enough for her. What would happen when she got there was not a problem; getting to a 'safe' country was. The family she left behind would soon follow.

That was long ago. Time moved on, no point in bringing it back, I told myself. My mother moved on, but some things stayed. They stayed with her, and in some ways, lurking somewhere under layers of helplessness and inability to deal with my mother's tragedy, they stayed with me. But what about Tom, how did all this affect him?

He was calling. A woman was walking towards him and David. I hurried back. She was the neighbour, the oldest woman in town. She did not look more than sixty, but it turned out that she was in her mid-seventies. She must have been a teenager during the war. She had blue eyes and a long ponytail, something between blonde and grey. I quickly came to the point. I told her that my mother used to live there. 'Not sure about the house.' I didn't want to give her too much information; I didn't want to influence her answers. 'The Pollaks.'

'Don't know. Never heard of them.'

'Do you remember anybody who used to live here before the war?'

'No, I don't. I was young. People moved out, others moved in. They demolished the old houses, they built new ones.'

'Yes, it was a long time ago. Do you know anybody else here in their eighties, or at least late seventies?'

'No, there is no one that old in this village.'

'Pity. I would have liked to talk to someone who knew my grand-parents.'

She stared at me with piercing blue eyes: 'I don't know anybody.' I looked at Tom and David, about to give up. Suddenly she blurted: 'Don't you think I suffered? I am German, but don't you think I suffered enough? I was in a concentration camp. A Soviet one.' Then she turned her back at us, opened her gate and disappeared.

I was stunned. Life can throw up the most unexpected surprises. Maybe she had been in a Soviet camp, but I was sure that she knew more than she let on. There was something more to that place than these people were prepared to tell me. I walked back to the corner shop and turned right towards the flour mill. Energised.

Behind a tall fence, I heard people talking. The wall of the house which rose above the fence was covered with flowers. A wall of colours, the only colours inside that grey, dull village. Just as I decided to go and talk to whoever was behind the fence, a woman appeared. I explained why I was there and asked her if she knew someone old, someone in their eighties. She called back to a shortish woman with a floral scarf, a dark-brown long peasant skirt and a cardigan. The woman greeted me with the smile and clear eyes of a much younger person. I told her that I was a relative of people who lived there once. She invited us in but I declined, not wanting to impose. I told her that I would like to know if anybody knew my grandparents, the Pollaks, who lived there before and during the war.

'The family who lived over there?' She pointed towards the big stone house. 'Of course I do. They had a daughter Roza, a tall girl with beautiful long wavy hair.'

'But she is my mother ... Please tell me more. What else can you remember?'

'Her mother sold *tuica*, clandestine.'

'And soup?' I added but she did not confirm it.

'It was a big family. Their house was demolished. This is a new house.'

'Was it a big house?'

'Not big, not small, just right for the family. But why didn't Roza come with you?'

'She is not well. She cannot travel. How many families lived here?'

'About thirty-five.'

'And how many Jewish?'

'Most of them. Only about four or five were not. And over there was the flour mill.' She pointed towards the lonely house by the river. My skin was covered with goose bumps. My mother had been right all along.

'After the war they turned it into a power generator.'

'And now?'

'Now it's defunct.'

'And what happened, tell me what happened with the Pollaks?'

'Once something awful happened there, but I never found out what. Later they came and took them. They took them to the marketplace on the hill.'

'What do you mean?'

'They took all the Jews. The same day. The poor people could only take a few things with them.'

'Where did they take them?'

'As I said, to the marketplace on the hill,' and pointed her finger towards the road leading to Bistritza. 'And you know what?'

'What?'

'The next day, seeing that they were not back, my mother made two big loaves of bread. She was going to take them and give them to our neighbours. They were taken there too. Our families used to be good friends. I always sat next to their son in school. One day he turned up with a yellow star. They all had to wear a yellow star to school, the kids I mean.' She paused and looked at me with her clear eyes. 'My mother took the loaves to them, but they didn't let her in.'

Tom limped past. 'They all say that,' he whispered to me in Hungarian. He wanted to go. But I needed to find out more.

'They told my mother to take the loaves and go home. And you know what?'

'What?'

'A few days later hooligans broke into the Jewish houses and took what they could. A week or two later, the rest were taken to a hall in Nasaud, I think by the authorities.'

She looked at me, checking for my reaction, maybe just checking if I was strong enough to take it. Of course I was, I had heard such stories many times. I didn't feel anything except gratitude. I was grateful to her that she acknowledged what had happened there, she acknowledged that those people lived there once, she confirmed my mother's stories. I was enormously grateful.

'I never saw them again. The Pollak family, or the other families. I only saw two sisters from another family a few years ago. They came to reclaim their house. But the others? What happened to the others?' She looked at me with her intelligent eyes. 'Is it true that many were burnt?'

I nodded.

'My dear God!' And after a long pause she added, 'Roza should come. I will tell her the whole story.'

'Maybe next time.'

I had so many questions, but I felt I was imposing on David and Tom. She wanted to tell me about herself. She lived alone. Both her husband and daughter had passed away.

'Life is hard here,' I said.

'Probably everywhere. But I have only a half-pension.'

She had to make do with about thirty dollars a month. I tried to find out more about her so I could tell my mother. Her maiden name, Moldovan, should ring a bell with my mother. But how much should I tell my mother?

I thanked her for everything and gave her some money. Too little for what she did for me. She did not want to take it. 'But we just had a chat.'

'You don't know how grateful I am.'

Three women were coming to talk to us. I asked them if there were any Jewish families living around Jidovitza.

'Only in Bistritza, an old woman,' one said. 'I bought the house from her. She sold it and moved to Bistritza. We all bought our houses here. Every one of us.'

I was not sure if they did. The families who lived in our house in Brasov did not buy their flats. They lived in far better conditions than Tom in Cluj, or my mother in Israel. But I had no energy to fight Romanian bureaucracy.

We said goodbye to them. As the taxi left what was once Jidovitza, I thought about the huge metamorphosis the young Roza had to undergo when she met Stefan. I never quite appreciated the great contrast between the life she left behind and where she ended up. Between the poverty of that village and the wealth she found in my father's house, the close-knit warm community she had to abandon and the snooty, cold, irreligious family she ended up in. In her new surroundings she couldn't have been more of a misfit. The war didn't just kill a large part of her family, it destroyed her sense of belonging. She never again felt the warmth of a community, she never again belonged.

'That was some trip.' David broke the silence. 'I've taken other people to similar places, but that's the first time that I've found someone like this last woman. Someone who knew the people who lived here.'

The taxi started climbing the green hills and I wondered whether the hill on our left was the market where my grandparents, aunts and cousins were gathered sixty years ago to begin their death journey.

The sun was chasing the mist from the hills. Here and there pastureland alternated with pine forests and a house or two. We were approaching Bistritza.

It was early afternoon, and we were overdue for lunch. As we sat talking about Jidovitza, it occurred to me that David was also a Transylvanian.

'David, was your family in Transylvania during the war?' I asked reluctantly.

He nodded.

'And how did they manage to survive?'

'My mother was sixteen and a half when she was deported. She said she was eighteen so they sent her to work. At sixteen she would have been considered a child and the Nazis would have killed her within days.'

'Where was she from?'

'Nasaud.'

Nasaud was a few streets from Jidovitza. I was ashamed that I did not ask sooner.

In that part of the world, all Jews had a story. But I resolved to close that chapter, and started looking forward to the trip to the painted monasteries. We still didn't know how long it would take or where we would sleep that night.

———

The headlights pierced the darkness. The roads were nearly empty. David had been driving for hours. Tom, who had never sat in a car for long, was complaining, 'I've developed calluses on my backside.'

We reached Vatra Dornei, a small town which made its living from mineral springs, bottled mineral water and tourism. The hotel we settled on had big clean rooms and a pleasant modern décor, and was very cheap. Not many Westerners adventured that far.

David was happy to share with Tom, but I decided to get a room for each. David needed a good rest after the long drive.

Tom looked at his room in disbelief. I showed him how to use the remote; his own television was still of the knob-turning generation. He went to the queen-size bed and turned the bedspread back halfway. I told him that the bed was his, the whole bed. They'd change the linen anyway the next day.

'But I don't need the whole bed,' he argued.

'It's not about need, it is about comfort, about spoiling yourself.'

He looked at me. Spoiling oneself? It made no sense to him. He would sleep in half the bed and would not disturb the rest.

I showed him the bathroom. It had a shower, a basin and a toilet, all new. But you had to lift your foot and step over a fifteen-centimetre tiled wall to get into the shower.

'I'll probably fall down,' Tom said.

He was right, there was nothing to hold on to and the shiny tiles on the floor looked as slippery as an ice rink.

Next morning Tom and David emerged refreshed and happy. They slept well. I did not. My bed was broken and lumpy.

'Do you realise what a treat you have given him?' David asked me when Tom was out of earshot.

'Treat?'

'He has never been to a hotel in his life.'

I was sure that he meant well, but I felt my face burning with shame. Later Tom too acknowledged that this was his first hotel experience. I think he realised that this was the type of hotel I used when I travelled. I tried to console myself that I work like a robot most of the time. But nothing helped my guilty feelings.

It was a glorious sunny day, the air was crystal clear. We were approaching the first painted monastery. Tom was not keen on religious buildings and monuments, but after some convincing he decided to join us.

As we stood in the middle of the big rose garden, admiring the six-hundred-year-old painted frescos – the Last Judgement, Noah's Ark, apostles and martyrs, angels and devils in vivid blues and reds – I sensed peace descending on us all, a serenity I had not felt for a long, long time. Perhaps it was not the monastery but the clean air and the smell of the roses which amplified my feelings, my happiness at being with Tom, at having met David, one of the gentlemen of this world, at seeing the mountains opposite and the nuns busying themselves in the gardens. For a few moments Jidovitza and its orchard displaced the rose garden. My happiness was now mixed with a faint pain, the pain familiar to all Jews who once lived in Eastern Europe and cannot escape the memory of the past. I refocused my mind. I was in the mountains, the sun was shining and on that day more than any on any other, life felt a great privilege.

25

The phone rang. It was the receptionist. 'A man is here to see you.'

It was Addy, my friend who had been expelled from university, condemned to physical work and had disappeared.

After decades of wondering if he had survived communism, I had tracked him down one evening through the internet. Was it him or someone else with the same name? I fretted.

I wanted to find out what happened to him since I saw him last, walking towards me on the other side of the narrow street, the Securitate man behind him. I had walked past him as if I did not know him. I often thought about that moment; I thought about cowardliness and courage, about how some people are more daring than others, about how much one is prepared to pay to stand up for what is right. And where did I fit?

I had thought of Addy on and off for years. I hoped that his life had worked out somehow, but feared that it had not. In 1989 Ceausescu was shot, communism collapsed and I thought of Addy. I did not know where he lived or even if he was still alive. But I hoped that one day I would find him, one day I would be able to thank him for what he did for me. I owed him more than two decades of freedom, because if he had told them that I knew about his plans I would never have left Romania, I would probably have ended up in prison.

The phone number on the internet showed the right name, but his is a common Romanian name. Whoever it was, Addy or someone else, lived in Deva not far from Petrosani. Could it be him? I wondered.

One hot summer night in Sydney, I sat on the edge of the bed, picked up the phone and dialled the number. My heart pounded, thumping filled my ears. What will I say? It's me, remember? It's me, your friend, it's the young woman you trusted with your plans three decades ago, probably the only person who knew about them.

Why? Why did you trust me? Was it because I was such a trustworthy friend? Or was it more than friendship? Trustworthy I was, but love I did not deserve. I had a boyfriend already. It did not work out, but in the end it did not matter, because the one thing which mattered to me at the time, the one thing I yearned for all my waking hours, was freedom. Everything else came second.

The phone kept ringing, my thoughts jumping around. I could not think of the right words to say. None of the openings were right. I started wishing that no one would pick it up, that the phone number was out of date, that Addy had moved on. Suddenly I heard a click, then a woman's voice: 'Hello.'

I composed myself. 'I'm ringing from Australia. I am trying to track down a school friend of mine, Addy ...'

'My husband,' she interrupted. 'Please wait a moment. Addy!' she called and my heart started climbing the hill again.

Within seconds there he was, surprised, somewhat overwhelmed, but probably less than me. Suddenly I had too much to say, but my thoughts did not translate into words. Suddenly my Romanian was not good enough, I could only say 'Hi.'

He asked me how I had found him. He had tried to find me a number of times and could not, so he gave up. He was now married, had one son and was about to become a grandfather.

I recovered. 'What about the communist times?' I asked. 'What happened after they expelled you from the university?'

'I spent two and a half years in prison, doing physical work. In a labour camp.'

'A labour camp?'

266

So that's what the official meant when he said, 'He will only be allowed to do physical work.' Now it seemed obvious, but it was not obvious to me then. I assumed he would work in a factory or on the land somewhere in the country.

'Labour camp? Was it awful?'

'Remember Jean Valjean?'

Jean Valjean, the main character in *Les Misérables*, Victor Hugo's novel, imprisoned in the infamous Bagne of Toulon prison for stealing a loaf of bread. Addy and I read that book as teenagers, and in my mind's eye I saw the two of us sitting in the lounge room in Petrosani discussing it.

'It was forced labour, long hours, breaking and carrying rocks. Day after day.'

'You're a strong man.'

'You had to be. But then I got lucky. There was an armistice and they let me out. So after two and a half years I was a free man again.'

'And what happened then?'

'Well, you know how it was. I was a marked man. I was an ex-political prisoner, I could not go to university. I did a surveying course. I met my wife, then my son was born.'

He was still surveying the mountains, summer and winter. 'The summer is fine, but some winters can be bitter cold.' He was away a lot but he loved the mountains, his co-workers were warm and friendly, so the hard life had its compensations.

Our conversation was coming to an end. I promised to ring him soon.

I put the phone down and sat on the edge of the bed for a long time. Relieved, happy, exhausted. The missing piece of the puzzle, the one which had nagged me for years, was found; the question which needed an answer had finally been answered and could be put to rest. Nearly. But not quite. I wanted to see him.

—⁓—

I rang him again from Australia just before I left. We arranged to meet. And now he was waiting in the lobby.

From the top of the stairs I saw a man pacing impatiently. Is it him? I wondered. There was no one else in the lobby. Heavens above! Did I expect the nineteen-year-old I used to know? I did expect a man with some grey hair, tanned, skin aged from years of working in the sun and rain in the mountains, but I did not expect the stout man waiting at the bottom of the stairs. Maybe it's the padded wind jacket, or the brown beret which finishes him, sort of unexpectedly. So far and no further. Heavens above, I too must be unrecognisable.

At the bottom of the stairs a vaguely familiar face looked at me as if I was not what he expected. As our gazes searched each other for the long-ago friend I realised that it was not the lines on Addy's face, but the look in his eyes and the lack of the old sureness, perhaps a timidity, which stood in the way of my recollections.

We embraced because the occasion demanded it. We embraced in memory of our friendship, of beautiful trips to the mountains, of heated discussions about Russian and French literature, of all the things we said to each other and all the things we did not dare to say.

He reached inside the plastic bag in his hand. 'I brought you a present,' he said and handed me a miniature old-fashioned Romanian village well. It evoked the mountains and the villages we both loved.

It was 9:30 in the morning and I suggested we go to a coffee shop. I wanted good old-fashioned Romanian coffee, but the locals preferred the Western style shop around the corner which served orange juice and flavoured coffee. Flavoured coffee was new in Romania and since everything Western meant progress, it was to be preferred. Addy steered me towards it.

The waitress came to take our orders.

'Coffee please,' I asked and looked at Addy.

'A small whisky for me.'

'Sorry, we don't serve whisky in the morning. Coffee or juice?'

Addy opted for coffee. I asked about his wife.

'She is not working.'

We sat in silence. He took a few sips of coffee. 'She keeps herself busy.'

As soon as we finished the coffee Addy wanted to go. We walked towards the city centre. At the base of Matthias Corvinus' statue there were new archaeological diggings. I looked at the maze of the ancient walls below and wondered what was the ulterior motive behind those diggings. Were they digging to prove that Romanians descended from the Romans? Or was there a more important message to unearth? An uneasy feeling was rising in me. Not the boredom I felt in the history lessons in that country, but resentment. In my experience, history never strives for truth: it supports the rulers, the politics of the time. If facts do exist, they are twisted and spun until they emerge as if reflected by one of those Luna Park mirrors, taller, slimmer, grotesque. That was the case when I lived there. But I was sure that in the West it was different. So when I saw Second World War documentaries made in English-speaking countries, my astonishment could not have been greater. They were all about the D-Day landings and other major battles of the Allies, the British and the Americans. The Russians were barely mentioned. No one will deny that those were big battles where too many young men died, too many sons and fathers perished, too many soldiers and families were maimed, but not to include the battles fought by the Russians, who died in much greater numbers, who fought all the way back to Berlin, was a breathtaking omission.

History, especially modern history, is not an unbiased analysis of facts but a collection of biases and stories for a political system or a nation's self-aggrandisement, to prove its greatness. So I do not trust history; but before I asked Addy who built those walls below us and what had been discovered so far, I saw him reach inside his wind jacket and out came a small metal bottle, like those used by soldiers and mountain climbers. He took a sip and I smelt alcohol.

He explained to me how the diggings were done, the machinery used. Then he told me about diggings in other parts of Romania and their history. I could barely follow the names, the dates – he knew so much. Then he reached for his bottle again. No! I wanted to stop him, take his bottle and throw it at the half-dug-out Dacian or Roman walls.

He kept talking but I was no longer listening.

We passed a bar. He proposed that we sit there. It was barely eleven, but the waitress was happy to serve him whisky.

My dear one-time friend who needed to drink whisky in the morning and sip alcohol every half an hour began to worry me. The conversation turned to his son who lived in Belgium.

'We used to see him often. Used to,' he repeated and fell silent.

'Your wife must be missing him. How does she manage with you being away so much?'

'She has lots of relatives, they visit. She's okay.'

'I'd like to meet your wife. She must be a pretty strong woman to have taken you on at the time. A lot of baggage.'

'Maybe next time,' he said and I sensed that he was not enthused by the prospect.

He wanted to talk about our colleagues, about those who had made it in a big way. Among them a woman, the dimmest of all my colleagues, became the director of a research organisation. There are miracles in this world and there are political appointments. Some, who made it big during the previous regime, were making it big under the new one. An amazing list of surprises of who had become who. The most talented young man committed suicide, the most dim-witted became a director of research. A young doctor who drank himself to death, the maths teacher who set me up for a life in science and was blamed for collaboration with the communist party. My head was spinning. Others just got on with life quietly.

'We, the ex-political detainees of the communists, have organised ourselves,' Addy said, and showed me a membership card of the Former Political Prisoners Association of Romania. 'Some communists penetrated the new government; they occupy top jobs. You know how it is. Scum floats to the surface. They're again the bigwigs. But we will hunt them down. We won't let them live in peace.'

There was passion in Addy's voice. And I caught a glimmer of my old friend.

—ᴡᴡ—

Tom had a different take on my gratitude to Addy. 'He shouldn't have asked you to join him. He could have destroyed your life.'

We were meeting him for lunch. Every time we passed a restaurant Addy checked the menu. He seemed to be interested only in restaurants which served alcohol.

At the agreed time of 12:30, Tom was walking towards us. He was wearing a pair of grey trousers which I knew he found uncomfortable, and a jacket. He looked very good. I knew Tom, he wanted to make a good impression. He wanted Addy to look up to me. The two had never met.

The restaurant Addy had chosen was empty. We sat by a window covered with vine leaves. It barely let the sunshine through, but broke the unfriendliness of the empty long hall with its two long rows of vacant tables. In no time Tom and Addy were chatting about politics, about history. If they had been other people, I would have felt an outsider, but since I loved them both, I didn't mind that the names were foreign to me, the events unheard of and that I was a fish out of water.

The food was less than average for that town, but this did not worry either of them. Addy kept drinking, Tom kept smoking and laughing, his baritone voice resounding in the big empty room.

After lunch Tom said goodbye.

'He is great company,' Addy said as we walked to the train station. He was going to catch the next train.

There were hardly any people at the station. We kept walking around. Addy was searching for something. Suddenly his face lit up; he had spotted a small window and steered me towards it. He handed his army bottle to the man behind the window to fill it with plum brandy. I had never seen that sort of business anywhere else in the world.

The train pulled into the station. Addy kissed me on the cheek and boarded the train. There was a whistle and I waved the last to my friend.

Back in the hotel room I rang a common friend in Israel. The three

271

of us had known each other since primary school. He had met Addy a few months previously. Does he drink a lot? I asked. He resented my question. He was adamant. He had never seen him drinking.

What if I misjudged him? What if he was just overwhelmed by our encounter? I felt ashamed.

'Have you met his wife?'

'No, she's been in a wheelchair for years. They had a car accident. Addy was driving.'

I remembered Addy boarding the train. His stout figure, the beret, the wind jacket to keep him warm and to hide the bottle of alcohol. The tragedy of the accident, his son's estrangement, the Jean Valjean memories, the freezing days surveying the Carpathians would have turned most men to alcohol. One way or another, I had no right to judge.

I consoled myself that he had forged new friendships with men made of much stronger stuff than I, men who broke and carried rocks for years in Romanian prisons and men who surveyed the mountains come summer and winter. I was comforted by the thought that he would never again be as lonely as he was on that day when he stood in front of a hall full of people to be condemned to years in a labour camp, or on that day when I passed him on the street without acknowledging his existence.

26

It was my last evening with Tom.

Through the open window I could see the dark sky, the flickering bright stars, perhaps eternity. In the distance where the horizon met the earth was a barely visible star, and as I contemplated its faint light I wondered if it was still alive, or was I looking at light emitted at the beginning of time.

Isn't our past like the image of an extinguished star, still with us although it ceased to exist a long time ago?

The years I spent in that land came alive in Tom's stories, at the sight of the autumn leaves quivering in the breeze, in the mannerisms and attitudes of older people, at the sound of familiar melodies which spilled out through the open doors of cafés onto the street. Tomorrow I would leave all these behind. The old world would fade again, but its dim light would carry Tom's mischiefs and struggles, the look in my father's all-knowing eyes, his warmth and his reticent smile, my mother's emotional outbursts and her ready laughter. Their life stories will linger with me for as long as I live.

Tom would not come to the airport. He did not like partings. He asked tentatively, 'When will you come again?'

'Two or three years,' I said, not wanting to raise his expectations. He seemed pleased. He asked me to wish all the best to the rest of the family.

We finished dinner and there was not much to say. We took refuge in the neutral ground of politics and price increases. Suddenly Tom stood up and disappeared into the little room. As I waited for his return, I thought of Tom tomorrow, tomorrow when I would no longer be there. He had got used to having company; he would have to get used to being on his own again. And I? I was facing another difficult parting.

Outside the dark sky hung constant, eternal, a perfect contrast to my unsettled self.

Tom walked back in. 'I want you to have this,' he said, holding up a ring.

In front of me was the ring I fell in love with at the age of nine, back in Timisoara, the ring my mother kept in the aluminium box along with the other jewellery, the ring for which she beat me when the fear of the Securitate got the better of her, when she thought I told the militia woman that we had valuable jewellery. Maybe because of the memory of that beating, or because I loved that ring so much, or because Tom wanted me to have it, or because it was our last day together and I was leaving my ageing brother in Romania with nobody to look after him if he was sick, I broke down and sobbed. He asked why but I could not explain. Eventually I told him that I was overcome, that I was worried about him being left on his own.

'Don't worry. The building is full of kids, I can always call on someone.'

We both knew it was not that simple, but what could either of us say? I wiped my tears with the back of my hand and hugged him as a thank you. That ring meant a great deal to me.

While Tom went to get his jacket and keys, I took one last look around the flat, tears still rolling down my cheeks.

By the time we left the building I was nearly recovered. I had slammed the gate on my emotions. As we walked back to the hotel, my elbow touching his arm, I tried to think of something to say. To talk about trivia would have been dishonest, to say something meaningful would have been too painful. So neither of us dared to utter a word. In front of my hotel I said my goodbyes and climbed the stairs. At the top I looked back and caught Tom looking back too. I waved. He waved back, then limped away.

Next morning David, the taxi driver, was waiting in the lobby to take me to the airport. The sun's rays were breaking through the lifting fog as he drove past the run-down suburban houses and blocks of flats of Cluj.

We were early. David insisted on waiting with me until the check-in opened. We talked about Tom.

'Flight number … to Vienna is ready for boarding.' My visit had come to an end.

—⁓—

Back in Sydney I slid into routine again. From time to time I wore the ring Tom gave me. It troubled me that the sparkle was gone, that there was grit between the stones. I knew those stones could sparkle. I wanted that ring to twinkle as it did once in my mother's hand. Outside was full daylight, but she pulled the curtains and we sat on the edge of the bed sharing the secret. The sparkle of a real ring under the light of a bedside lamp. I wanted to see its once-upon-a-time marvels.

A few weeks after my return, as I walked past an antique jeweller in Sydney, I decided to take a detour. I went in, showed him the ring and asked if he could clean it.

'Of course,' he said and promised to restore it to its previous glory.

A week later, expectations high, I went to pick up the ring. The jeweller remembered me, rummaged in one of the drawers, picked up a small box and lifted out my ring. It looked much better, the grit between the stones was gone, but the ring was not what it once was. The sparkle was not quite as I remembered.

'I take it that dullness cannot be entirely removed,' I said. 'It still does not quite look like it used to.'

'It could be restored but I would have to remove all the stones, clean and mount them again. It would be a major undertaking. This is an antique, about one hundred and thirty years old. In those days they did not mount diamonds like we do now.'

'One hundred and thirty years old?' My maths stepped in. 'It must have been made in the late 1870s.'

'I think so.'

One hundred and thirty years old! I had expected it to be no more than seventy at most. As I walked out of the shop it hit me that the ring I was wearing must have belonged once to Tom's Austrian great-grandmother. It must have been made for her when she was in her twenties. It was on her daughter's finger, Tom's grandmother, when the Archduke Franz Ferdinand of Austria was shot and the First World War started. It was on Hella's finger as the Nazis rose to power and Hitler became Germany's Chancellor. And I know it was on my mother's finger from time to time during the Second World War while her parents and four of her siblings were killed in the Holocaust. Hidden in the aluminium box, hidden just like the unutterable thoughts of people, this ring had witnessed the rise of communism and the Stalinist terror. It witnessed the Ceausescu era, the fall of communism and the return of capitalism. That ring had survived the tragedies of the twentieth century, not to mention our family tragedies. And it occurred to me again, as it does every time I visit Europe, that inanimate objects are the real witnesses of history. Maybe that's why they cannot communicate. They have seen too much. If we were constantly reminded of all the wars and horrors human beings inflict on each other, life would be unbearable. So, in their wisdom, they keep quiet.

I looked at the ring again. Shiny or dull, I felt privileged.

I wondered what Hella's great-grandmother would say if she could see the ring on my finger. Would she approve? And what would Hella say? Would she approve of me telling the story?

27

It is New Year's Eve. I have been back in Australia for more than a year now. On a day like this I miss my overseas family. And I miss Tom. It is six in the afternoon and the sun is still unforgivingly hot. It has been a very hot summer. I think of the cool air in the Romanian hills, the slow pace of life, the peasants in the misty fields.

I often ring Tom on New Year's Eve, not only because I like talking to him, but because I worry that on a day like this he must feel very lonely. Ringing Tom is no simple matter. He does not have a phone. I have to call the gatekeeper's room and arrange a time for Tom to be in the Principal's office. The phone at the gate can only be used for three minutes, but on weekends and public holidays, when the school is closed, the caretaker opens the Principal's office so Tom can talk uninterrupted. It takes a few calls to organise the times, but a day later everything is lined up. We don't talk often, but when we do the conversation goes on for a couple of hours. So I ring. Not without trepidation. I never know what to expect, after all Tom is not a young man. But he is there and I sigh with relief. He is happy, but then he always is. Soon it turns out the Gypsy woman is there too.

'She is busying herself, she's been cooking all evening. Not quite sure what.' He laughs. 'How much can you cook for the two of us?'

I sense his contentment. I picture them in the little flat, the smell of cooking, Tom sitting on the sofa pontificating, his mother's photograph on the left wall and the woman whose name I never found out cooking in the tiny kitchen. I don't want to speculate, I don't want to know whether she is only there tonight or if she will be there for weeks or months. I don't even want to know whether he is careful, whether she might be tempted to steal from him. The only thing I am prepared to acknowledge is that this New Year's night he is not alone. He is happy and contented.

Next morning, on New Year's Day, I play one of our tapes again. Tom is talking. And here across oceans and continents I laugh with him again. I laugh with him and with a young credulous girl, the girl of half a century ago. A girl I hardly recognise, someone who listens to his every word. And as I listen to the tapes I understand why I like being with him, why I keep going back.

Tom laughs wholeheartedly as only Tom can; he laughs until his cigarette cough cuts in. Then I stop laughing too, and wait for him to recover.

'Every couple of months we had a meeting at work. The usual propaganda, socialist productivity, the five-year plan. The man in charge would often start by saying that today is *o cotitura* (a turning point), from now on we'll do things differently. One day this quiet fellow put his hand up: "Comrade. Comrade, every time we have a meeting you tell us that today is *o cotitura*. I don't understand, Comrade, but in my view if one keeps turning one stays in the same place." The chief went red, as red as that carpet over there. And us? We stopped breathing. The man added: "Comrade Ceausescu told us that we are on the road to great progress, you are telling us that we are turning." And we breathed with relief.'

'What happened then?' I hear myself asking.

'Well, the chief mumbled something, something like you can take a few turns on the way to progress, and we relaxed back into our chairs.'

'Was he brilliant or stupid, or brilliantly stupid?'

'I don't know. I did not know him personally. I think he was a bloody genius. We have been turning. We had capitalism, then we had socialism and now we have capitalism again. *Cotim, cotim.*' And he laughs with gusto.

Acknowledgements

I wish to thank Anna Blay, Managing Editor at Hybrid Publishers, for turning my manuscript into a book. Her professionalism and flexibility made my first experience of the publishing world a very positive one.

I am indebted to Dr Margaret Johnson for her appraisal of the initial manuscript and for copy editing the final version.

My special thanks to Diana Giese especially for her structural edits and her invaluable advice and support through all stages of the production of this book.

The gratitude I owe to my husband Alex cannot be expressed in words. I thank him for sacrificing countless weekends to read my revisions. And I thank him for the hours and hours of discussions, for his advice, his questions and misunderstandings, which all contributed to the final shape of this story.

Gabrielle Gouch was born in Transylvania, Romania. At the age of twenty she and her family emigrated to Israel. Seven years later she emigrated again, this time to Australia.

Trained in science, she worked as a Research Scientist in universities, major companies and most recently in the Public Service.

She has a daughter and lives with her husband in Sydney. This is her first book.

DEC 0 2 2021

CPSIA information can be obtained
at www.ICGtesting.com
Printed in the USA
FSOW02n1942260916
25447FS

9 781921 665998